DRAWING A BLANK

Improving Comprehension for Autistic Readers

EMILY ILAND, MA

DRAWING A BLANK
Improving Comprehension for Autistic Readers

All marketing and publishing rights guaranteed to and reserved by:

FUTURE HORIZONS

(817) 277-0727
www.fhautism.com

ISBN: 978-1-963367-40-9

DEDICATION

This book is dedicated to readers with autism and the parents and professionals who want to help them. I dedicate it to my cousins who are facing the same struggles that my son Tom and I did nearly two decades ago. *Drawing a Blank* is also dedicated to Tom. I appreciate the insights you've shared about how you think and learn. I'm grateful that with a great support team, you were able to unlock meaning and create the life you want for yourself.

ACKNOWLEDGMENTS

Thank you to my mentors at California State University, Northridge for encouraging and supporting my independent study of this topic.

Thanks to Karen South and the Future Horizons team for your efforts to make this second edition happen!

I'm grateful to my sister Barbara T. Doyle for excellent suggestions and edits of the manuscript, and unwavering positivity and support.

Thanks to Dr. Timothy Shanahan, professor emeritus at the University of Chicago, for an interesting dialogue on this topic.

Thanks to my friend Libby Pridmore, a fifth-grade teacher, for many interesting conversations about teaching and learning in 2025.

Finally, I appreciate the encouragement of my husband Steve, and my family, friends and colleagues—thanks for your faith in me to update this book and your patience in waiting for it to be ready!

E. I.

TABLE OF CONTENTS

INTRODUCTION

Why Update *Drawing a Blank*?

For more than 35 years, I've been keenly interested in the dramatic differences in skills among readers with autism, particularly those with excellent decoding skills but poor comprehension. I've gone from being an unsuspecting parent, to a concerned parent, to a professional in the field of special education, actively seeking information and answers.

Because understanding what is read is crucial to the success and lifelong outcomes of those we teach and/or love, I studied the reasons behind the comprehension problem in autism, read the research about it, and searched for effective interventions. The first edition of *Drawing a Blank: Improving Reading Comprehension for Individuals with Autism Spectrum Disorder* (DaB) was the outcome of that process.

I started writing DaB in 2006, nearly two decades ago; it was published in 2011. As is customary, writers typically rely on research from the previous ten years. Most of the information I consulted was written between 1996 and 2010. As I'm getting closer to retirement, I knew I had to explore this topic again and discover what has been learned since then to add to the body of knowledge.

My cousin "B," a senior in high school, and his mother also inspired me to update this book. I was discouraged to learn that families and educators are still struggling to identify and address the comprehension issues of good decoders with autism. Like many other autistic students, B is a good decoder who can recognize words automatically and read fluently. In contrast, he does not necessarily understand the meaning of the words, sentences, paragraphs or passages that he reads. I call this an "uneven" reading profile, when a reader's decoding skills and comprehension skills are not equally developed.

I thought the link between autism and comprehension breakdown would be generally well-understood by now, nearly two decades since I started the first draft of this book. Unfortunately, "B" is just one of the many autistic readers whose potential is being blocked by a lack of awareness and action on this issue. I could not retire a decade or so from now without updating *Drawing a Blank* for him and everyone else who needs it!

In truth, I was hoping that many researchers and educators would be actively pursuing this topic, making DaB obsolete. Instead, (foreshadowing here), I was disappointed to discover that in the past fifteen years or so, there have been **no large-scale experimental studies about effective interventions to help readers with autism and comprehension issues.**

To make up somewhat for this setback, I was happy to find more than six recent meta-analyses or literature reviews about smaller studies on this topic. That is when I realized that it is *still* important to update DaB. We need to learn everything possible about **high-impact, effective interventions** for autistic readers, even if the studies are small-scale! The ultimate goal is to provide you, the reader, with the information and tools *you* need to help your children, students, and/or clients unlock meaning and benefit from whatever they read.

I read and compared the literature reviews, looking for common findings, and I summarized highlights from the approximately 10-15 small studies that were reviewed in *each* literature review. The largest two studies had 45 and 29 participants. The majority of the studies had just three participants each, but the information can still be helpful.

Next, I integrated the information into my book chapters to be as user-friendly as possible, highlighting new proven and promising interventions. I've tried to weave together as much relevant information as possible to help you develop a deep level of understanding of reading comprehension issues and autism, the causes and effects of the difficulties, and how you can help. I hope you'll feel like an expert on the topic when you read and refer to this version of *Drawing a Blank* to help you in teaching and advocating for the needs of readers with autism.

Happily, I've also discovered that much of the information and foundational material cited in the first edition of DaB is still valid, so I've kept it in this version (even if the studies would otherwise be considered "old)." Many newer references cite the same thought leaders that I do because their ideas are still relevant.

I've also added lots of current information and references. Several promising strategies from the first edition of DaB have since been endorsed by recent studies and are presented with their "effective" status.

The Purpose of This Book

Most readers of this book want to know something specific: **What can I do to help autistic readers understand what they read?** Comprehension difficulties in readers with autism can be subtle, qualitative, and difficult to tease out. As a result, their substantial level of risk for reading comprehension problems is often overlooked or unaddressed. This book offers as many teaching strategies and tools for improving comprehension as possible, because addressing the problem effectively is key for these individuals, no matter their age. Of course, the comprehension strategies and suggestions may also be helpful for readers with autism who struggle with *both* decoding and comprehension.

The literacy needs of every child deserve attention. As is often the case, teaching methods that help learners with autism can often benefit *most* learners. The reverse is *not* true: things that benefit most learners do *not* necessarily benefit learners with autism! The reasons for this reality are explored in depth in Chapters 2 and 3.

You, the Reader

The material in the book is intended for a variety of adults. For simplicity, I use the terms *professionals* and *parents*. No matter what your role is in the life of a struggling reader, his book is designed to help you understand and identify the needs of autistic students who are good decoders but have reading comprehension difficulties, and then use this understanding to find effective ways to help them.

In many of the chapters, I refer to *students* because of the need to reach the substantial number of learners with autism who are still in school. The individuals of interest to you may be children or adults, in public school, non-public school, private school, or being homeschooled. When you see the word *student*, think "client," "son," or "daughter," or whatever relationship that is most appropriate. Also, please note that I use **s/he** as a global pronoun in my writing. It's my way of simplifying *he* or *she*.

Many students with autism struggle in silence in general education classrooms. Many general education teachers do not know what to do when they realize that a student on the spectrum is having problems understanding. Professionals, including reading specialists, speech pathologists, and resource teachers, are ideally involved in remediation for students with autism and comprehension issues.

Very capable educational professionals in general education *and* special education settings welcome ways to expand their competencies, especially if they have limited training and experience helping readers with autism. One of the most important first steps for them and for all readers of this book is becoming well-informed about the features of autism and the many ways autism affects learning and literacy. The developmental issues underlying autism have a direct relationship to appropriate, effective intervention. This topic is explored extensively throughout this book.

This book is also intended for educational therapists who wish to better serve clients with autism in individualized therapeutic sessions. Until I entered the field of special education and chose a specialization in educational therapy (ET), I did not even know what ET was! Educational therapists (ETs) work with individuals of any age, even adults who left school and need assistance in learning *how* to learn. (If you are not familiar with the field of educational therapy, please visit www.AETonline.org.)

During my graduate program, and while teaching a master's-level course on autism at my alma mater, I recognized the need for educational therapists to become more familiar with autism to help struggling readers on the spectrum. Ed therapy has typically focused on intervention for learning disabilities. Methods for intervening with students with learning disabilities are not necessarily effective for readers with autism and comprehension issues. It is encouraging to see ETs expanding their practices to serve this population.

Role of Parents

Parents often realize that their child has difficulty long before it is verified by an outside expert (inference: parents are experts on their child). Therefore, parents play an important role in identifying and addressing their child's comprehension challenges. Parents (and those in parenting roles) want to help their children read and understand, and they want to know *how* to do it. The community of homeschool parents is also actively seeking information and strategies to be effective in their role of parents-as-teachers.

As a mother, I realize that parents of children with autism (or related diagnoses) need to educate themselves quickly in areas they never expected to know about. Parents want to become partners in the literacy process to meet the needs of their children, particularly because of what is at stake. For this reason, I try to write in a clear manner so that the material about autism, literacy, and intervention is helpful to readers with different backgrounds and needs.

As a grandmother, I'm delighted to sit my two little granddaughters on my lap and read together. The enjoyment almost masks the fact that by reading with them I'm actively participating in the literacy development of the young preschooler and the kindergartener. With heightened awareness, I'm witnessing how social connection, language, and curiosity intertwine and contribute to their interest in books and their excitement for learning. The experience also helps me look back and recognize when and where that process did not occur as expected in my eldest son, in the children of my friends and relatives, and for the hundreds of other children for whom I've advocated in the past.

Working Together

Parents and professionals can achieve the best possible outcomes for autistic readers by understanding the same essential concepts, working together to identify needs, and collaborating on interventions for home and school. It's logical to learn as much as possible about autism, and identify certain features or characteristics of the "group." Learners with autism are truly unique compared to learners with other cognitive profiles.

At the same time, each person with autism is unique. Information should be **adapted to the unique characteristics, personality, preferences, temperament, strengths and needs of each individual.** This approach is consistent with the mantra of educational therapy and educational ethics.

The information in this book may also be useful to *prevent* comprehension problems. For students with autism, it is important to **monitor comprehension from the start** and address gaps in understanding. The National Early Literacy Panel report (2008) urges teachers to emphasize comprehension in the early grades, rather than waiting until students have mastered "the basics" of reading.

- Conscious efforts to build comprehension from the earliest stages of reading, what I consider a kind of "early intervention," have the potential to prevent or mitigate future difficulties.
- This perspective is being verified by researchers such as Newman and colleagues (2007), Macdonald, Luk, and Quintin (2022), Whalon and Hart (2011), and Whalon and colleagues (2015).

In fact, MacDonald, Luk and Quintin developed a tablet-based intervention for preschoolers with ASD who were early readers, to be used with their parents (2022).

- The goal was to improve oral *and* reading comprehension at the word, phrase, and sentence level.
- The intervention resulted in a **significant increase in reading comprehension scores**, compared to typically developing children who received the same intervention.

Lastly, individuals with autism can become involved in understanding and addressing their own comprehension issues. Readers on the spectrum are likely to need support to *demystify* their difficulties, understand their challenges, and learn to manage their reading. Demystification (or self-understanding) can be a huge relief, reducing feelings of shame, stigma, self-blame, and anger. Demystification can also lead to significant growth in self-awareness, self-advocacy, the use of strategies, and access to accommodations in higher education and the workplace.

A Note About Word Choices

From the beginning of the social inclusion movement for individuals with disabilities around the late 1980's, person-first language was promoted as a way to refer to a person first and then to a disability they have. Examples are "student with autism" or "child on the spectrum." This wording was intended to help people see what they have in common before focusing on differences. Educators in teacher training and support service staff have been taught to use person-first language since that time.

In contrast, some adults with autism are expressing their preference for "identity first" language. They see their autism as their identity and want to own it. They refer to themselves and others as "autistics." To respect both choices, I will use both options.

There's also been a shift away from labels such as "high-functioning" and "low-functioning." These terms are considered *ableist*, a type of discrimination that devalues people who are deemed "less capable." I'm onboard with this social equity movement. At the same time, research is full of functioning labels (especially older research that is otherwise still valid). That is the sole context where functioning labels are used in DaB.

When I first wrote *Drawing a Blank*, the criteria for "autistic disorder" were defined in the DSM-IV or *Diagnostic and Statistical Manual of Mental Disorders*, 4th Edition (2000). Separate but related diagnoses listed under the umbrella of pervasive developmental disorder (PDD) included autistic disorder, Asperger syndrome, pervasive developmental disorder not otherwise specified (PDD-NOS), Rett syndrome, and childhood disintegrative disorder (CDD). These conditions were often referred to as autism spectrum disorders, or ASDs. Many of the references in DaB use the term autism spectrum disorders, or ASDs.

The DSM-V (*Diagnostic and Statistical Manual of Mental Disorders*, 5th Edition, 2013) consolidated the separate PDD diagnoses to autism spectrum disorder, or ASD. You will find "autism" used throughout the book for ease of writing and reading! In 2022 the DSM-5-TR (text revision) was issued to clarify specific aspects of the criteria for ASD; this will be highlighted in Chapters 2 and 3.

Some people object to the "medical model" of autism, particularly because the diagnostic criteria focus on deficits and "inabilities," rather than what the person can do and/or has learned to do. People think and learn differently. The term *neurodiversity* and neurodivergent are sometimes used instead (including by me) to take away the stigma of autism as a disorder and celebrate the abilities of autistic individuals. Autistics are telling the world that they are not broken and don't need to be fixed. Autism is a natural part of human diversity.

Please don't be offended by references to information based on medical models using words like "deficits." This information is useful to help unmask difficulties and reveal the person's needs, which otherwise could be minimized and ignored. The ultimate goal is to help these learners realize their potential, succeed more, struggle less, and achieve the goals they want for themselves. If these are also the goals you have in mind, please read on!

PROLOGUE
A Personal Perspective on a Pressing Problem

It may be helpful to begin with a brief version of my own family's experiences, to which many families and professionals can relate. When I tell our story at conferences, parents tell me, "That's my child!" Teachers and interventionists tell me, "That is what I have been wanting to know!" This is a story waiting to be told on behalf of all those who are trying to make sense of and address the struggles of "uneven" readers with autism, a group that is growing as the population of individuals with autism continues to grow and grow up.

My first exposure to the issues of reading and autism was as the astounded mother of a toddler, who, while still in diapers, revealed that he could read *and* spell. I came into the kitchen one morning when my son, Tom, was around three years old and found the magnetic letters on the refrigerator arranged to read "don't walk," "one way," "cerrado," and "agua." When I asked my husband, Steve, about it, he said that he had not arranged the letters and that he thought I had done it. That only left our little boy as the one who had faithfully reproduced six of the *Sesame Street* sight words on our fridge, leaving just a few letters unused.

More than thirty-five years later, I have not forgotten that moment. It was especially shocking because Tom had spent several silent months after his second birthday. He had been saying over one hundred single words but had gone down to using only six. I wrote all of his words in four columns on a sheet of loose-leaf paper and took the list to our pediatrician. Alarmed, I asked, "Why is he only using six words?" The doctor answered, "I don't know, but don't worry. He'll talk again."

So when Tom did start talking again, just before he turned three, and could also suddenly read and spell, my husband and I, and even the pediatrician, decided that Tom had experienced a "pregnant pause." He stopped talking so he could listen. This was followed by an amazing explosion of speech, reading, and spelling. We noticed that a lot of Tom's talking was repeating lines from TV programs or even from entire videos that he watched repeatedly. His amazing memory and the big words he was saying were impressive. The "pregnant pause" theory made sense to us, so we were relieved.

Many other examples of Tom's remarkable untaught ability to read emerged over the next few years. On the first day of preschool, when he was three, Tom spent most of the day putting his hands on every word on the classroom walls and reading aloud as he moved around the perimeter of the room. When I picked him up, the teacher asked, "Did you know that Tom can read?" Unfazed, I said, "Yes." As a new mother, I did not know that other three-year-olds typically don't know how to read. I didn't realize that the teacher was surprised that Tom could read.

Around Tom's fourth birthday, we went to Ireland to visit his granddad. We have a photo of Granddad and Tom on the floor that shows Tom reading the words of every rhyme in the new book Granddad had given him. Granddad looked up at me and Steve and said, "He can't be reading; he must have memorized this!" We replied, "You just gave him the book five minutes ago. How can it be memory?" We all agreed that whatever it was, it was amazing!

A few months later, we visited Tom's grandmother. Tom had been fascinated by the *Wheel of Fortune* TV show since he was an infant and watched with rapt attention every day. That day, my mother and I looked on in utter disbelief as Tom stood in her living room and solved the bonus round puzzle, "Spring Break," before the contestant did.

Tom's precocious reading skills continued to develop. He was fascinated by letters and numbers. He preferred reading, alphabet, and book activities to everything else. He seemed to decode automatically, not stopping to sound out words. He read rapidly and with good fluency, often echoing the accents, intonation, and phrasing he had heard on his books on tape or TV.

He read signs in the environment, read books to his baby sister, and began to write. One day when he saw a road sign that read, "Signal Ahead," he said, "Sign-al ahead." I did not correct him or try to explain; his pronunciation was more logical than English!

When getting together some materials for a scrapbook, I looked at the artwork that I had marked "First day of preschool, age 4." It was a picture of a squirrel. Tom had colored it in a very organized way, with a single stripe from each crayon in the box going from top to bottom.

I turned the picture over to find that Tom had written *"In cannis corpore transmuto."* The Latin phrase means "I change (transmute) into a dog's body." It's from the 1959 Disney movie *The Shaggy Dog*. Wilby, the hero of the story, chanted the inscription found inside a magic ring. Then he was turned into a shaggy dog.

Tom was an avid fan of the film. He watched the video often and rewound his favorite parts, but I had not realized that he was spontaneously writing in Latin at age four! Figure 1 is a copy of that preschool page. This image may also include the ring and the dog; it's hard to say (Tom's fine-motor skills were less developed than his spelling).

Figure 1. In cannis corpore transmuto

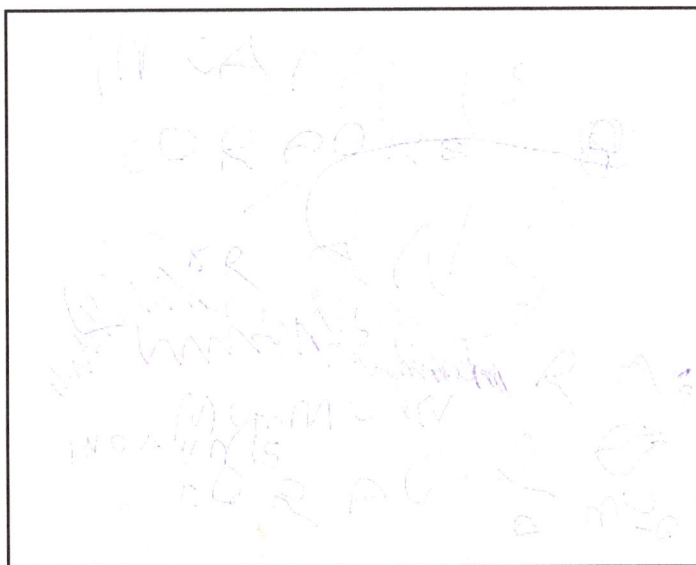

Tom's passion for reading became the focus of his time and attention. We praised and encouraged him and followed his lead. He had obvious literacy skills and a photographic memory. We were amazed and proud of him and his "super ability."

At the same time, his "reading talent" also became an explanation for other things that were happening (or not happening). When Tom did not answer when we called him, we assumed he was too engrossed in his reading. Tom did not interact much with other children or play imaginatively, which led our neighbor to observe, "My kids may not know how to read, but they *do* know how to play." I was taken aback by the comment and thought my friend was jealous of our son's ability.

When Tom wanted to read a certain set of books again and again, I did not worry. After all, they were years above his age level. More importantly, I never questioned whether he understood what he read. How could he *not* if he read with such great inflection and fluency?

In my mind Tom's reading talent explained everything else. I did not recognize that another pattern of differences in his development was revealing itself. When my sister Barbara T. Doyle, an autism expert, told me. "Tom has hyperlexia," I answered proudly, "Yes, isn't it great!" I did not realize that she was suggesting that hyperlexia was not only a gift, but an explanation for the social and language deficits associated with it.

I was only focused on the gift. I looked at the American Hyperlexia Association website when Tom was in the primary grades. There was mention of social difficulties associated with hyperlexia, but no direct association was made with hyperlexia being any kind of problem. Therefore, it didn't raise any alarms in my mind.

Barbara *was* alarmed. She was trying to warn me about *something* when she said, "When Tom gets to school, the other kids will learn to read, and they will catch up to him. Then it won't matter if he learned to read early." I felt that she was pouring water on our fire of enthusiasm, but in reality she was trying to encourage us to focus on building Tom's underdeveloped play, social, and communication skills. I was far from the point of recognizing the close link between autism and early untaught reading, but I eventually came to understand that reality and its implications.

Fast-forward from age four to grade four, and to a changed mother with the same child. By now, Barbara's prediction had come true—Tom's ability to read was no longer exceptional. That otherwise positive gap had closed. Tom's ability to decode had remained constant, but I was becoming more and more aware of his comprehension difficulty.

I was alarmed by his increasing academic struggles and saw a new, problematic gap opening. Fourth grade seems to be a turning point for good decoders with poor comprehension, for multiple reasons. Looking back, Tom changed from a happy boy who had an easy time at school into an anxious and struggling student (who ironically still looked good on paper!).

Since then, I've discussed the "fourth-grade turning point" with many parents and professionals. The issues and factors that contribute to the timing of the comprehension difficulties will be expanded upon in different chapters of the book. Suffice it to say here that fourth grade was when we, as a family, hit the wall. It was at that point that I resolved to get help for my son.

Unfortunately, this time, *everyone else* seemed to think that Tom was "fine," "doing well," and "at grade level." Tom's teachers and the school staff did not understand what I was worried about. This was the "masking and minimizing" phase of our journey. As frustrated as Tom was with his schoolwork, I was equally frustrated because I was getting the "nothing is wrong" response even as I knew that something *really important* was wrong.

My only option was to manage the situation on my own, which involved hours of daily one-on-one time, re-teaching his school lessons so that Tom could complete his homework. Once I was so surprised about how little of a lesson he had grasped, I asked, "Did you *go* to school today?" It really seemed as if he hadn't been there.

The situation deteriorated so greatly that by the end of sixth grade, besides being a full-time homework tutor, I decided to research the problems and find someone who could delve deeper into the situation. My sister Barbara, who never stopped looking for answers, phoned one day in 1994 and said, "I think I found an answer. Wait 'til you hear about Asperger syndrome!" We turned to a famous professor at a Los Angeles university to begin the diagnostic process.

At that time, Asperger's and autism were thought to be separate but related diagnoses. Although he was capable in many areas and appeared to have no language difficulty, Tom received a diagnosis of autism due to his language regression and other features seen in his first three years. Because he was bright and articulate, Tom's autism was considered "mild" by the diagnostician who saw him. That was a hopeful statement for us, but at the same time, the effects of his autism and the circumstances we were in did not feel mild to Tom or to our family.

A team of school district specialists assessed Tom to identify his needs when he was thirteen. Tom's reading comprehension was at a fourth-grade level. His mathematics skills were at a grade sixteen level. Not only was he four years behind in reading comprehension, but Tom also had a twelve-year gap between his ability to do math and his ability to understand what he read.

Believe it or not, the math and reading results were averaged together. As a result, we were told that Tom's overall academic performance was in the average range and that, therefore, no help was necessary. This was a devastating roadblock.

We asked the school team to reconsider the validity of averaging scores in this case and instead focus on the one area of need which they did. As a result, the district agreed to provide resource services. This was a step in the right direction, although we later discovered that more intensive remediation was needed.

Around the time of his diagnosis, Tom described his difficulty understanding, which was affecting all the schoolwork he was being asked to do. He told me, **"Mom, if it hasn't**

happened to me, my mind is a blank page." Imagine not being able to imagine the world created by the words on a page, but instead having a concrete, literal understanding based only on personal experience. That was a fabulous insight and led to the title of this book!

Reading comprehension is the foundation for all literacy skills, including learning from textbooks, writing, listening, speaking, following directions, and critical thinking. We had a lot of work to do so Tom could be successful in high school, college, and life. Becoming eligible for special education and receiving resource support in eighth grade was the first door that opened for Tom.

Goals and services expanded during high school to address multiple areas of need, including speech and language, social skills, and intensive help with reading and writing. Tom also spent two years in a specialized high school for students with autism, where he thrived. Although he made great gains from the interventions, there was not enough time to catch Tom up on vocabulary, comprehension, and writing skills before high school graduation. He had **not** met his IEP (individualized education program) goals in these areas at graduation, although he met the other academic requirements.

Addressing the comprehension issue is critical so that competent, capable people can fully realize their potential. For us, the crucial issue was whether Tom had the skills required to pass English 101 at the community-college level. If he did, his career plan to become an accountant would move forward. If he did not, his post-high school academic career could completely derail.

When he was in twelfth grade, we set up an appointment for Tom to take the free, computerized placement tests in English and math at the local community college. Math was fine, but Tom tested into the most remedial English class. I had my answer. He was not ready to take English 101. Now I needed to be sure he received the services and supports that he needed.

I'm convinced that the key to Tom's success was the continued work on his unmet comprehension and writing goals through an individualized transition plan implemented by the school district at a community college. Tom needed more time and more assistance to develop these skills. Had he been exited from special education with a diploma at eighteen because he met graduation requirements, he would not have received the support he needed to be successful at community college. With extra time and instruction, Tom successfully graduated with an associate's degree, with honors, from our local community college.

Moving on to college to pursue an accounting degree, Tom realized that sometimes the meaning of a single word he did not know in a test question (like *conservative*) prevented him from solving a problem, even though he understood the mathematical procedures involved. To explore this further, Tom took a standardized reading test and came out a few years below grade level in both vocabulary and comprehension. This continued delay in vocabulary raised concern about reading comprehension for taking the certified public accountant (CPA) exam that he needed to pass for his career.

For this reason, *Tom* documented his vocabulary problem and applied for an accommodation for the exam. The Board of Examiners granted the accommodation of using an electronic dictionary. (What a great idea! Don't wait until college to start using this accommodation or another technological equivalent!).

The rest of the story is history, as they say. Tom is now 42. He earned his BS in accounting, passed the CPA examination, and spent nearly a decade working as an accountant. He decided that accounting was not the right career for him and chose a new path in life. He is realizing his potential and his new dreams, including getting married.

I also moved on, from learning what I needed to know to help my own son, to becoming very active in the autism community. I worked as a professional advocate for a decade, serving nearly two hundred families. I worked with parents and school teams to focus particular attention on students' "hidden" comprehension issues.

In 2007 I completed a master's degree in special education with an emphasis in educational therapy (ET). I enrolled in the course hoping to find answers to the two big questions about reading comprehension problems in autism: (1) What exactly is the problem? and (2) What works to improve comprehension?

While graduate school and my post master's certificate studies were wonderful, this topic was not being discussed in any of my classes! I didn't find the answers I was looking for, but I didn't give up. I did an independent study of reading comprehension and autism and wrote the manuscript for *Drawing a Blank.*

I enjoyed three years as an adjunct professor at my alma mater, teaching a master's-level autism course for in-service teachers. In addition to the usual curriculum, I made sure that everyone in the class was aware of the ways that the features of autism affect comprehension. (This information is covered in depth in Chapters 2 and 3, but is still not covered in typical teacher training, even special education teacher training at the master's level!)

Presently, I consult and collaborate on projects; write curricula, books, and articles; provide training and education; and speak at conferences on many topics related to autism and neurodivergence. I intentionally incorporate comprehension strategies into all the work I do, including this book, to help all readers, autistic or not, understand better!

A Growing Concern, a Lasting Concern

Tom was one of ten thousand people with autism when he was diagnosed in 1994. A dramatic and alarming increase in the incidence and diagnosis of autism has been documented in the past two decades. As of 2025, the Centers for Disease Control reports that about one in thirty-one children has been identified with autism spectrum disorder (CDC 2025).

At a minimum, that means that 3.2 % of the child population has autism, affecting all racial, ethnic, and socio-economic groups.

- Black, Asian, and Hispanic children are finally being identified at rates similar to White children. This is not by chance, but due to concerted efforts to promote access and equity to diagnostic services and healthcare.
- Girls and women are still under-identified, so the true incidence is probably even greater.

As the number of children with autism continues to grow, and children with autism grow up, more and more autistic students will be enrolled in the public school system and in higher education. In the 2022–2023 school year 980,000 students ages three through twenty-one were classified as having autism and being served in public special education programs nationally. The number just one year earlier was 882,000 (Korhonen 2024). Compare this to 211,610 students with autism served in 2006 and 22,664 students served in 1994 (CDC 2008).

These shocking numbers affect more people on a personal level than ever before. There are also clear and far-reaching repercussions in the education and service systems. **There are significant differences in the learning profile of a student with autism compared to learners with other exceptional needs.** It is critical to connect the developmental features of autism with the resulting challenges, including academic, social, cognitive, etc.

More students than ever will need help with reading comprehension and related skills, such as writing. Developing comprehension is essential for students with autism; unfortunately, this need is often overlooked. Readers with autism of any age and grade level may need support to develop comprehension skills if their skill gaps were not identified and addressed early on. It is never too late to identify comprehension issues, even for adults, because they will continue to affect and interfere with understanding until addressed.

Further, educational professionals will be called upon to respond to the unique needs of the ever-growing population of readers, and more parents will want to identify and get help with the literacy needs of their children with autism. My hope is that the insights in this book will provide direction to meet the needs of these students *and* the adults who are trying to help them.

The good news is that each individual can be helped to develop in his or her areas of need. With appropriate education, therapies, and supports, people on the spectrum can learn and improve. The strengths and abilities of autistic individuals, along with awareness and skill on the part of interventionists, can pave the path to success in reading comprehension. Because readers with autism and comprehension issues often have many strong reading skills (such as decoding and fluency), it is possible to focus on the crucial reading skill that is missing: **comprehension**.

How This Book Is Organized

I hope to support each reader's comprehension of this fascinating topic by being a good author: organizing the material logically, using visuals like charts and color coding to guide interpretation of the material, highlighting key points, and summarizing main ideas. You may also notice I repeat key points in various places. This is intentional! Besides knowing that readers may choose to jump around in the book, research shows that readers retain more information if they have repeated exposure. Understanding new, unfamiliar information can be challenging; repeated exposure helps build familiarity with new ideas.

To these ends, the content of the book is organized into four major themes:
1. Definition of the comprehension problem.
2. In-depth explanation of how features of autism can affect comprehension at the word, sentence, and text level.
3. Methods to identify comprehension issues in "good readers" with autism.
4. Evidence-based, effective, and promising practices to improve comprehension, matched to the needs and learning style of individuals on the autism spectrum.

The Appendices offer specialized information on particular topics.

I hope that all readers will take advantage of the information in the chapters and appendices to understand the reasons behind the comprehension difficulties that are specific to autism. This foundational knowledge helps create a holistic view of a person's needs. Understanding the precise nature of hyperlexia and autism can help in selecting curricula, materials, and activities for remediation. The suggested interventions and research on the topic will make even more sense when connected to the evidence and rationale behind them.

While some ideas are original to this text, other ideas may simply be considered part of good teaching. Once the problem is clearly defined and understood, educational professionals will find that they already have many tools in their toolboxes that can be effective in helping readers with autism. Remediation may be a matter of assessing needs and *selectively* applying good teaching methods in a different way than expected.

I hope that all of this information contributes to the continuing discussion on this topic and progress in the field of special education for this population. I will leave it to each reader to analyze, synthesize, internalize, elaborate, gain meaning, and apply the information as you see fit ... because that's what good readers do!

CHAPTER 1

Autism & the Task of Reading

This chapter offers foundational information about the process of reading and discusses:

- How young children learn to read
- The building blocks of reading
- Important definitions of reading, from simple to complex
- An updated definition of hyperlexia
- Specific skills needed to comprehend text
- Five different types of reading comprehension
- The nature and extent of comprehension difficulties in autistic readers
- The vulnerability of readers with poor comprehension
- Reasons to prevent reading comprehension failure

The Paradoxical Reader

For most children, learning to read is an easy and enjoyable part of childhood. It's a shock when a child who learned to read words easily suddenly struggles to understand what s/he has read. Yet, this pattern is becoming more common, especially as the number of children diagnosed with an autism continues to rise.

- Current statistics show that about 3% of children, one in thirty-one, have an autism diagnosis (CDC 2025).
- Many of these children, even those who seem to read well, will have reading comprehension issues. The first question to ask is, "Why?"

How Do Young Children Learn to Read?

Reading readiness begins at an early age, through the development of language, which is one of the foundations of literacy (Vukelich, Enz, Roskos & Christie, 2020; Hamilton & Hayiou-Thomas, 2022). For example, children start to develop **receptive language**, or understanding of language, when they hear other people speaking, reading, and singing.

- Children learn by observing. They develop **expressive language**, the ability to express themselves, by copying the things that the people around them say.
- Young children engage in imitative play, pretending to do chores and activities like they see adults doing at home. They are actually learning and practicing real-life roles *and* the vocabulary and conversations that go along with them.

Stimulation from people and things in the environment supports the cognitive development of young children. Growth in thinking and learning contributes to the natural development of language. Children listen and learn the meaning of spoken words and are encouraged to express themselves.

- Children begin to link the words they know to the written words they see in print (Armbruster, Lehr, & Osborn 2003).
- One of the first indicators of this print awareness is when young children start to recognize signs in the environment, like their favorite place to eat french fries or their name on a cubby at preschool.

The link between development, language, and literacy is illustrated in Figure 1.1. These related, interactive processes comprise the bioecological model of child development (Hamilton & Hayiou-Thomas, 2022).

- Problems with the expected stages of language development often affect literacy skills such as reading, writing, and speaking.
- Because autism is a developmental disorder, it can interfere with multiple aspects of the typical process in ways that will become clear as we explore them.

Figure 1.1. The Development, Language, and Literacy Link

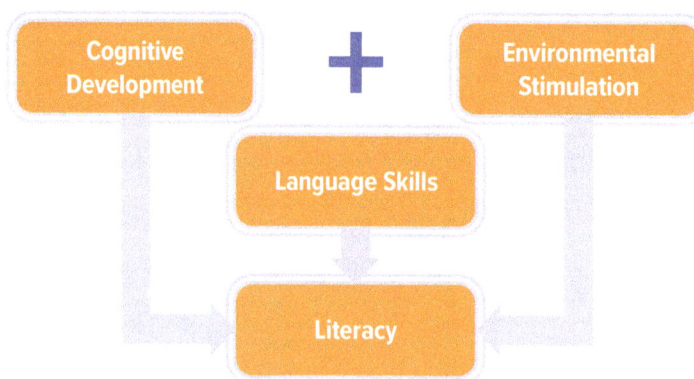

Typical literacy development is an interactive, social process between a child and adult, usually centered around storybook reading. One of the keys to early literacy is *joint attention*; that is, the child pays attention to the book and follows along with adult guidance.

Storybook reading is also considered a *reciprocal activity*, in which the child engages with the reading partner, takes turns, and maintains a balance of give-and-take in the interaction. While the adult reads, a young child does his or her part in a "communication partnership" by responding with words or actions, pointing to pictures, and turning pages.

- These steps in the interactive literacy process also stimulate a child's imagination.
- Early reading experiences help children learn to take the perspective of others and develop abstract thinking skills (Kaderavek & Rabidoux 2004; Bean, Perez, Dynia & Kaderavek 2020; Hou, Liang & Li 2025).

The "social construction of literacy" views the early interactive social activity of reading as the key to understanding that letters and words are symbols (Kaderavek & Rabidoux 2004, p. 241).

- "Alphabetic insight" occurs when a child realizes that each written letter is related to a specific sound and that letters the key to the code of written language (Hamilton & Hayiou-Thomas 2022).
- Completing the developmental cycle, exposure to reading contributes to further cognitive development in areas such as oral language comprehension, information processing, expressive language, attention, and memory (Levine 2002).

Literacy development is likely to be different for children with autism compared to typically developing children because of the developmental nature of autism and specific features of the diagnosis. Research indicates that:

- Problems with literacy development can relate to the impaired language and cognitive development that an individual with autism experienced as a young child, no matter how old they are when reading challenges are noted (Vukelich and colleagues 2020).

- Skills that are key for literacy development, such as joint attention, socialization, oral language and vocabulary may be underdeveloped due to differences in the learning profile, growth, and maturity of a child with autism (Kaderavek & Rabidoux 2004; Bean, Perez, Dynia & Kaderavek 2020).
- These factors can have a lasting, negative effect on reading comprehension (Willems, Loveall, Goodrich & Lang 2025).

The Reading Process

To understand *why* comprehension can be difficult for readers with autism, it is helpful to understand what reading *is* and what processes are involved. There are many definitions of reading. Let's begin with the definition from the No Child Left Behind Act of 2001 [NCLB].

Figure 1.2 NCLB Definition of Reading

Reading is "a complex system of deriving meaning from print."
NCLB 2001, Part B Sec.1208(5)

NCLB established the Reading First initiative as a cornerstone for providing quality instruction in reading by defining requirements, providing funds, and asking schools to create literacy partnerships. NCLB is explicit:

- To understand words and text, a reader must have **direct instruction** in five skill areas: phonemic awareness, phonics, vocabulary development, fluency development, and reading comprehension strategies (NCLB Part B Sec.1208(5)(A-E)).
- The five components of reading are summarized in Figure 1.3, based on descriptions in *Put Reading First* (Armbruster and colleagues 2003).

Figure 1.3. (Adapted from Armbruster and colleagues 2003)

Five Building Blocks of Reading

Phonics includes learning the alphabet and identifying the sounds the letters make (also called *sound-symbol correspondence*). Readers use their firm understanding of the relationships between sounds and letters to recognize familiar words accurately and automatically and to decode unfamiliar words. Without a solid foundation in phonics and phonemic awareness, a reader will struggle to sound out words, blend sounds together and recode or spell by writing the sounds they hear in a word.

Phonemic Awareness is "the ability to hear, identify, and manipulate the individual sounds-phonemes-in spoken words" (Armbruster and colleagues, p. 4).
- A person who has phonemic awareness can tell each sound that is heard in the word c-a-t *and* blend the sounds represented by the letters c-a-t to say "cat."
- S/he can manipulate the sounds, for example, deleting the 'c' sound in cat and instead saying the 'm' sound with -a-t, when asked to do so, saying "mat."

Fluency is "the ability to read a text accurately and quickly" (Armbruster and colleagues, p. 22). Building fluency creates a bridge between recognition and comprehension.
- A reader who is struggling to decode and recognize words will miss the flow of ideas behind the words. This is true whether the person is reading silently to himself or reading aloud to others.
- A fluent reader can recognize a word and understand what it means at the same time.
- Reading fluently is thought to free up the reader's attention and help them focus on the meaning of the sentence, paragraph, or passage.

Comprehension Strategies are sets of steps that help purposeful, active readers make sense of text. Reading comprehension skills help readers understand, remember, and communicate with others about what has been read.
- Comprehension strategies can be taught, and readers can learn to use different strategies before, during, and after reading.
- Most good readers use a combination of comprehension strategies, *such as asking questions about the text* and *summarizing*, depending on the material they are reading.

Vocabulary development is a comprehension skill necessary to gain meaning from text, starting at the word level. Readers learn and "store information about the meanings and pronunciation of words" (Armbruster and colleagues, p. 22).
- As children learn to sound out and recognize words, their vocabulary grows. They may begin to recognize words they have heard when they see them in print. They may learn to spell and write the words they can read.
- Gains in spelling and writing support reading and understanding of what is read. Students gain vocabulary indirectly when they engage daily in oral language, listen to adults read to them, and read extensively on their own.
- Students learn vocabulary directly when they are explicitly taught both individual words and strategies for learning new words.

Development of these five key reading skills does not necessarily follow a specific sequence. Instead, the processes may be simultaneous and intertwined.

- For example, the ability to recognize a word (phonics) and to learn what the word means (vocabulary) may be acquired at the same time.
- Any reader may need additional support in one or more of the five areas to become proficient, benefit from what they read, and enjoy reading.

In December 2015, NCLB was replaced by the Every Student Succeeds Act (ESSA) to address student achievement and achievement gaps. ESSA was reauthorized in 2021. This law continues the requirement for "age-appropriate, explicit, systematic, and intentional instruction in phonological awareness, phonic decoding, vocabulary, language structure, reading fluency, and reading comprehension" (Sec. 2221 [b][1][B]).

The Simple View of Reading

Decoding is attaching sounds to the letters in a word and then blending them to say the word.

- Good decoders demonstrate *automaticity* when they decode or recognize words quickly, with little or no conscious attention.
- It is assumed that someone who reads fluently understands what he has read.

Yet, just sounding out the letters or recognizing words is not reading; as NCLB states, the purpose of reading is to **gain meaning** from the words. A young reader's decoding skills at age six are typically considered the best predictor of future reading comprehension.

In the Simple View of Reading, made famous by Gough and Tunmer (1986), reading (R) is the **product** of decoding (D) and listening comprehension (C). Reading is the product of the ability to decode *and* understand what is read. This idea is expressed with the following formula:

$$R = D \times C$$

The Simple View of Reading can help predict why a reader is struggling. Either a reader has a problem with decoding (D), or has a problem with comprehension (C), or both. Knowing where the problem lies helps in designing interventions to address the issues.

- When a significant problem relates to D, or decoding, this type of reading disability is known as *dyslexia*. Direct instruction will be needed in phonemic awareness, phonics, and fluency (and perhaps some vocabulary building).
- When the difficulty involves C, comprehension, this type of reading disability is known as *hyperlexia*. Direct instruction will be needed in vocabulary development and reading comprehension skills. Support is likely to be needed in oral language and listening skills as well.
- Some struggling readers will need intervention for both D and C.

More about Hyperlexia (HPL)

The word *hyperlexia* is familiar to most people to describe a child who reads spontaneously and automatically at an early age. A more recent definition of hyperlexia is "strong mechanical word recognition with comparatively poor comprehension," whether it occurs in a young reader or an older reader (Grigorenko and colleagues 2002, p. 1079).

- Despite strong decoding skills, readers with hyperlexia **do not** automatically understand the meaning of what they are reading.
- For this reason, hyperlexia is also referred to as *word calling* to indicate that the decoding or word recognition process happens without understanding the meaning of the words being read (Truch 2004).
- Hyperlexic readers may have trouble understanding single words, sentences, paragraphs, and longer stories (Carnahan & Williamson 2012).

The Hyperlexia and Autism Connection

It's estimated that 7 to 10% of typically developing children have poor reading comprehension (Lucas & Norbury 2014). Hyperlexia is now linked to the autism spectrum because research reveals that study subjects who have good decoding with relatively poorer understanding **frequently have a diagnosis of autism**.

- Some people, including educators, may not be aware of current research and findings on this topic.
- Here is some of the evidence that supports the link between autism and hyperlexia.

Sorenson Duncan and colleagues did a meta-analysis of twenty-six research studies about reading comprehension and autism (2016). The studies involved 1,211 children with autism. **In all of the studies**, the participants' word-reading abilities exceeded their reading comprehension abilities.

- This was determined by comparing word-reading scores with reading-comprehension scores.
- This finding **represents a significant association between the hyperlexic profile and readers with autism** and confirms the hyperlexic profile of this population as a group.

Ostrolenk and her colleagues also wished to determine to what extent the hyperlexic profile is associated with autism (2017). The researchers systematically reviewed thirty-nine case studies of eighty-two readers with hyperlexia published prior to March 2017.

- The researchers concluded that 69 of 82 individuals with hyperlexia in the case studies had autism or several autistic features, a total of **84.15 %**.
- Their findings confirmed **"a strong association between autism and hyperlexia"** (p. 139).

Individual studies also support the finding that children with autism whose word decoding is intact have deficits in reading comprehension.

- Multiple researchers have documented that **38 to 73%** of readers with autism have above-average word-reading abilities but comparatively poorer comprehension.
- These include experts such as Davidson, Kaushanskaya, and Ellis Weismer (2014); Dyson (2015); Henderson, Clarke, and Snowling (2014); Huemer and Mann (2010); Jacobs and Richdale (2013); McClain and colleagues (2021); McIntyre and colleagues (2017); Nicolosi and Dillenburger (2024); Randi, Newman, and Grigorenko (2010); Ricketts, Jones, Happé, and Charman (2013); Singh and colleagues (2020); and Williamson, Carnahan, and Jacobs (2012).

The Autistic-Hyperlexic Cognitive Profile

Hyperlexic readers with autism have a distinct profile of challenges compared to readers who struggle for other reasons. The features of autism and related thinking processes result in a **unique cognitive profile** in autistic individuals (O'Connor & Hermelin 1994; O'Connor & Klein 2004).

- **Leading experts in the autism field recommend that the term** *hyperlexia* **be used exclusively for those with autism and a comprehension issue.**
- They recommend that the term *reading comprehension disorder* be used to describe others who struggle to understand but do not have autism (Grigorenko and colleagues 2002, p. 1079).

This distinction takes into account that hyperlexia in young readers with autism usually includes unique features such as these:

- The early and spontaneous ability to read words.
- An intense focus or preoccupation with numbers and letters.
- Repeated, **solitary** reading of preferred materials to the exclusion of other activities (such as imaginative play or engaging with other children).
- A significant gap between word-level decoding and comprehension.

Ostrolenk and her colleagues (2017) reviewed the traditional model for learning to read and understand, in which word recognition and word meaning are acquired together in three steps:

1. **Word recognition:** sight word reading and decoding skills
2. **Grapheme-to-phoneme conversion:** matching letters with their sounds
3. **Semantic access:** acquiring word meaning as words are read, storing this knowledge, and retrieving it when needed

The researchers found that due to "their extensive self-exposure to printed materials and thorough practice of reading," readers with hyperlexia are highly successful with the first two steps, yet "semantic access does not seem to be achieved" (2017, page 145).

- In other words, the fluent decoding of words is achieved *without* access to meaning.
- In light of this information, the researchers conclude, "The evidence showing differences in behaviors, brain activity, and connectivity in autism in general, and hyperlexia in particular, suggests that **hyperlexic reading is a substantially different process from typical reading**" (2017, page 145).

Logically, inherent differences in the reading process result in a need for tailored interventions to address comprehension problems in readers with hyperlexia. The authors continue, "The pattern of dissociation between decoding abilities and comprehension evident in hyperlexia results from the particular characteristics of autistic perception and learning modalities, the understanding of which is essential to adapt education and pedagogy to the special needs of autistic individuals" (2017, page 146).

In other words, readers with hyperlexia have a unique way or thinking and learning, which the authors call the *hyperlexic cognitive profile*. Learning more about this profile, including the **strengths** within it, can guide effective intervention.

- Linking the term *hyperlexia* specifically to autism may surprise some people who are not aware of the research and reasons behind this.
- Consistent with the findings discussed so far, readers with autism who have good decoding and relatively poorer comprehension are referred to as readers with *hyperlexia* in this book.

Is Hyperlexia a Reading Disability?

Dyslexia has been recognized as a learning disability and/or a specific reading disability for some time. It is logical to also view hyperlexia as a **reading disability** (Grigorenko Klin, & Volkmar, 2003). Literacy expert Dr. Timothy Shanahan concurs, saying, "Indeed, I do consider low comprehension with average or higher decoding to be a reading disability…" (Personal correspondence, May 22, 2025).

Therefore, I'm proposing a novel reading "equation," inspired by the *Simple View of Reading* and current research, to clarify this relationship, shown in Figure 1.4.

Figure 1.4 A Novel Reading Equation

Autism Spectrum Disorder - Comprehension = Hyperlexia

or

ASD - C = HPL

Iland, 2026

I propose that it's time to retire the common usage of the word *hyperlexia* as "precocious untaught reading" and move to a definition closer to that of Gough and Tunmer (1986), which is "failure in comprehension." Why retire the common definition? When hyperlexia is viewed as precocious untaught reading, it is estimated to affect only 5–10% of autistic individuals (Brown, Oram-Cardy, & Johnson 2013).

- The precocious reading gift is **temporary**. When the other kids catch up to precocious readers, the issue "disappears!"
- Then, there is no urgency to fully understand or address the causes of the precocious reading or the hidden lack of comprehension that come with it.

Hyperlexia is like a Trojan horse. Early, intense fascination with reading, letters, and numbers in a young child looks like a gift, and in many ways, it is. Hyperlexia is also *paradoxical,* meaning two things can be true at the same time:

- The child "reads" well, if reading means decoding (recognizing words).
- The child does **not** read well if reading means understanding.

Using the term *hyperlexia* to describe good readers with autism who have significant comprehension issues alerts us to the needs and vulnerability of this population.

- Hyperlexia is a *symptom* that needs attention. Hyperlexia signals that **the expected process of learning to read for meaning is disrupted.**
- While these readers quickly recognize words, they don't necessarily process the meaning of the words automatically.

Autistic researcher Dr. Jaime Hoerricks explains that for most individuals with autism, "language arrives in wholes," with tone and memory (2025). This language pathway is called Gestalt language processing, or GLP. The meaning of the parts is attached to language over time, through experience. Hoerricks emphasizes that GLP is not a deviant or broken way of processing language, but a different cognitive path (neurodiverse).

The educational system is built upon analytic language processing (ALP), where comprehension is built through the segmentation and recombination of language. This teaching approach is probably used because ALP is the most prevalent language pathway. Hoerricks believes that the structure of literacy education is a mismatch to GLP thinkers. Breakdowns in comprehension can result from the mismatch between autistic thinking and traditional teaching.

How to Identify Hyperlexia

Hyperlexic readers speed past comprehension at the word, sentence, and text level. Cain calls this "superficial reading" (2003).

- Because they are good decoders, their comprehension issues can go undetected until fourth grade or much later!
- The lack of recognition of the unique profile of hyperlexic readers can blind us from the start to how lasting and significant their comprehension issues are.

Here's one of the most important things to know about hyperlexia: It can be detected when a **significant discrepancy exists between the reader's ability to decode and their relatively lower level of comprehension, as well as their ability to decode compared to their developmental age** (Grigorenko and colleagues 2002; Newman and colleagues 2007; Chang, Menzies & Osipova 2020).

- At first, the gap between decoding and understanding is most noticeable within the person's own skill set: comparing their own decoding skills to their own comprehension. This is called an **internal gap**.
- After the primary grades, the discrepancy in understanding is likely to become noticeable when compared to classmates. This is called an **external gap**.

> Hyperlexia can be detected when a significant discrepancy exists between the reader's ability to decode and their relatively lower level of comprehension, as well as their ability to decode compared to their developmental age.

Many researchers have measured the degree of the internal and/or external discrepancy between decoding and comprehension with significant findings:

- Multiple researchers found **internal gaps** of one to two standard deviations (15 to 30 points) between a reader's own decoding skills and comprehension skills. These findings are statistically significant with many practical implications, including a lack of benefit from reading, despite an excellent ability to decode.
- Researchers also found **external gaps** of one to two standard deviations between the comprehension skills of readers with autism and those of their same age peers. Again, these findings are statistically significant with many practical implications, especially for learning in the classroom.

Two studies are highlighted here to illustrate the comprehension discrepancy. The first study focused on children with an average age of ten years, and the second study included older teens.

- The research supports the idea of "hidden" difficulties and the discrepancy between the ability to decode and the ability to understand.

- The findings also suggest that learning can become more difficult for readers with hyperlexia around fourth grade.
- Figure 1.5 summarizes key information from these two studies.

Figure 1.5

The Comprehension Discrepancy Internal & External Gaps

Nation, Clarke, Wright, & Williams 2006

A study of 41 children with autism with an average age of 10.33 years found that 65% of the students with autism had poor comprehension, defined as a deficit of at least one standard deviation compared to peers.

More than one-third of the study subjects (38%) had *severe* impairments in comprehension, scoring more than two standard deviations below their peers.

The **internal gap** was also seen *within* study participants, with as wide a gap as two standard deviations between an individual's word accuracy reading compared to their own comprehension scores.

Saldaña & Frith 2007

A study about inferencing included 16 male adolescents with autism who had poor comprehension and sixteen typically developing readers without autism, ages 11 to 19.

Students with autism and controls were matched for age, vocabulary, and word reading accuracy.

The students with autism differed *significantly* in reading comprehension from the controls.

Internal and **external** gaps were documented with a discrepancy of 19 points, or 1.5 standard deviations in comprehension compared to their peers, and compared to their own ability to read words.

Switching to Another Perspective: The Dynamic View of Reading

In contrast to "the simple view of reading" ($R = D \times C$), the process of reading can be broken down into specific interwoven skills and actions. When you see the demands of the reading process spelled out in this section, it's clear how comprehension breakdown can occur for readers with hyperlexia.

Shanahan defines reading as **"a form of active and dynamic thinking"** (2006, p. 28). Snow (2002) described the **highly complex cognitive processes and abilities** that readers use to understand what is read:

- Attention.
- Memory.
- Critical analysis.
- The ability to visualize.
- The ability to infer.

In addition, the reader needs a certain level of knowledge to understand text:

- Vocabulary.
- Knowledge about the topic.
- The knowledge of comprehension strategies to use while reading.
- Real-life experiences.

The National Reading Panel (NICHD 2000) also views reading as **an active thinking process**. They emphasize that to understand while reading, readers must engage in the following **cognitive actions**:

- Read with purpose and motivation.
- Use the author's organizational plan to think about information (or impose organization on the ideas).
- Interpret information through the filter of their own knowledge and beliefs.
- Infer what the author does not tell explicitly.
- Monitor their own comprehension actively and effectively.

What Good Comprehenders Do

Good comprehenders **read with purpose** and know what they are trying to get out of the material (Shanahan 2006). For example, when reading a recipe, the reader needs to know if they will use the information to make a shopping list or to assemble the ingredients. Attention and focus differ, depending on the purpose.

Good comprehenders are **motivated** to read and **interested** in the material (Snow 2002). People who read well and enjoy it may be more motivated to read than those who struggle.

- Everyone has preferred and non-preferred subjects and interests.
- The desire to read can vary greatly, depending on the type of material.
- It's important to find ways to interest a reluctant reader and help them understand the purpose or how they can benefit from the material.

Background Knowledge

Background knowledge, or general knowledge about the world, is necessary to understand and relate to written words. For this reason, background knowledge is also called *world knowledge.*

- Background knowledge is typically acquired though personal experiences, conversations with others, and exposure to media, including books, television, film, the Internet, and even video games.
- Exposure to many different experiences can expand vocabulary and word meaning, and improve reading comprehension (NICHD 2000).

Expanding background knowledge and **connecting relevant information** to the material to be read is considered an effective pre-reading comprehension strategy for most readers. However, common methods of stimulating prior knowledge are not always successful for readers with hyperlexia.

- Typical teaching techniques need to be modified for readers with autism.
- **Direct instruction** can help readers with hyperlexia expand their background knowledge. The reasons for this and carefully "tailored" methods designed for these learners will be discussed in the chapters on interventions

Infer and Connect

Good comprehenders go beyond the text to **infer** meaning, relate to the material on a **personal level**, and **make connections** with other experiences and ideas.

- Reading comprehension skills help readers **understand, remember, and communicate** with others about what has been read.
- The ability to write a cohesive, on-point essay or report is an example of a written **demonstration of comprehension**.
- Struggling **writers** may actually be **struggling comprehenders!**

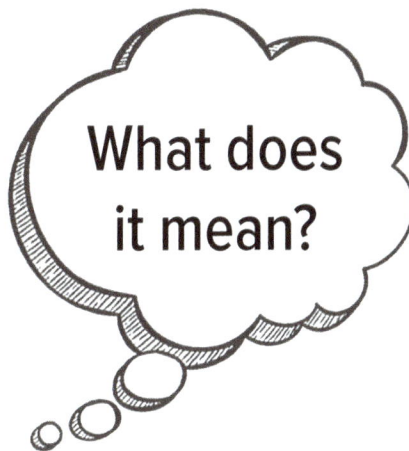

What does
it mean?

Self-Monitoring

Good comprehenders are aware of their own understanding (or lack of it) and **monitor** understanding while reading. When they realize that understanding has broken down, they use "fix-up" strategies to keep understanding on track. They:

- Use certain strategies to repair understanding during and after reading, such as re-reading, looking back, restating what they have read in their own words, or comparing text to known information.
- Use a combination of comprehension strategies, depending on the material they are reading.
- Are flexible and switch from one strategy to another as needed.

Figure 1.6 summarizes what good comprehenders do during **the active, dynamic thinking process known as reading.**

Figure 1.6

Reading as a Process of Active and Dynamic Thinking	
Demand of Reading	**Skills and Actions**
Get ready to read	Have purpose, motivation, and interest
Prepare for the task	Know the meaning of vocabulary words and have/ can relate relevant background knowledge
Use cognitive functions	Pay attention Recognize and remember important information
Use higher-order thinking skills (HOTS)	Analyze, visualize, infer, interpret, relate to personal experience, and integrate, or connect to other information
Use strategies while reading	Look for the author's organization of ideas Monitor comprehension Use repair strategies when understanding breaks down
Remember, store, and retrieve	Remember important ideas and recall them as needed Relate new ideas to known information

The graphic below, in the form of a mind map, expresses many of the complex actions that are involved in reading comprehension.

Link word meaning and world knowledge

Want to read with purpose, motivation and interest

Construct meaning

Pay attention, focus

Reading is an Active, Dynamic Thinking Process

Recognize & remember important information

Understand author's perspective and text organization

HOTS

Analyze, visualize, infer, interpret, integrate ideas, relate to personal experience

Monitor & repair understanding

The Mismatch Between Cognitive Skills and Reading Demands

A proficient reader is "one in whom multiple neurodevelopmental functions and relevant educational factors have worked together to promote the acquired ability to extract meaning efficiently from written language" (Levine 2002, p.183).

It is a primary premise of this book that the demands of the dynamic reading process present a mismatch with multiple cognitive skills and "core deficit areas" often seen in autism and, therefore, are at the root of comprehension problems.

- The foundational skills, abilities, and knowledge needed in the dynamic reading process may be underdeveloped or missing.
- This affects both comprehension and learning *how to* comprehend.
- As a result, the needs of readers with autism are **unique**, particularly when compared to those of other struggling readers.

Clearly, multiple cognitive actions are involved in reading comprehension, and many of them may be challenges for readers with hyperlexia. Understanding where comprehension breakdown occurs for a particular reader is essential to address or remediate it.

Five Types of Reading Comprehension

To discover how to assess "comprehension," I referred to textbooks by Salvia, Ysseldyke and Witmer, leaders in the field of educational assessment (2004, 2017).

- The authors indicate that there are actually **five types of reading comprehension**.
- The five types of comprehension clearly align with the active, dynamic thinking processes of reading that were just described, as shown in Figure 1.7.

Figure 1.7

	Five Types of Reading Comprehension	
	Type	**Meaning**
1	**Literal**	Understanding explicit material in text.
2	**Lexical**	Making sense of text by knowing the meaning of key vocabulary words.
3	**Inferential**	Understanding ideas beyond the literal text by interpreting, synthesizing, and extending meaning.
4	**Critical**	Meaning derived by evaluating, analyzing, and making judgments about material that was read.
5	**Affective**	Relating to the material at a personal and emotional level.

Readers with autism and hyperlexia often have **success with literal comprehension**, meaning that they can find or recall factual information and answer the basic "Wh-questions" (who, what, where, and when) very well.

- It is important to consider that a hyperlexic reader may be able to find or remember information that is explicitly stated in the text, but this can be done without truly understanding the meaning.
- Take for example a sentence in a passage, "The bride wore a beautifully beaded red sari." A reader can correctly answer many factual questions, such as the color of the sari, or what the bride wore, without having any idea of what a *sari* is.
- **This situation can result in overestimating the reader's comprehension.**

Despite genuine or relative strength in literal comprehension hyperlexic readers are likely to have difficulty with the other four types of comprehension: lexical, inferential, critical, and affective (Dennis, Lockyer, & Lazenby 2000; Nation & Norbury 2005; O'Connor & Klein 2004; Wahlberg 2001a, 2001b).

- Salvia, Ysseldyke and Witmer point out that **no one assessment measures all five type of comprehension**.
- The writers who create a standardized assessment define what comprehension is. They spell out how their assessment tool proposes to measure "it" in the test manual.

Many popular standardized assessments **do not** reveal the comprehension gap that is characteristic of hyperlexia. Assessments will be discussed further in Chapter 5 and Appendices B and C, but I want to mention them here, so readers know that truly understanding comprehension issues involves identifying the reader's abilities and challenges **in all five areas** of comprehension. Do you think this is happening routinely for good decoders with autism?

The Matthew Effect

As discussed, the reading problems of students with autism are not always obvious. In primary grades, comprehension issues for students with hyperlexia may be masked by strong decoding skills, good memory for facts, and understanding of concrete content (Doyle & Iland 2004; Nation & Norbury 2005; Beckerson and colleagues 2024).

Students with autism may become more at-risk in elementary school, from about fourth grade on, for reasons such as these:

- Students are required to "read to learn." In other words, students' own reading abilities, including comprehension, directly affect their progress in the curriculum.
- Reading demands move from narrative material (such as fiction and non-fiction stories) to expository material (informational non-fiction, such as social studies and science textbooks). Expository material is more difficult for almost all students.
- Grade-level content and curriculum become increasingly complex and abstract.
- The material presented goes well beyond the personal experience and knowledge base of the typical reader with autism.

Stanovich described the "Matthew effect" in reading, based on the Old Testament tenet that, "The rich get richer, and the poor get poorer" (1986). For students with hyperlexia, the Matthew effect often begins around age ten as they lose motivation and interest in reading because of their weak comprehension.

- This can start a cycle of weaker vocabulary, less comprehension, less motivation to read, and less time spent reading (Nation & Norbury 2005; Newman and colleagues 2007).
- **It's very difficult to motivate someone to read who has experienced failure. In this case it is not failure to read (decode), but failure to understand.**
- Withdrawing from the reading experience means that students do not gain the rich information available from text. They don't expand their vocabulary and world knowledge.
- They are less prepared to read and to benefit from reading (Erhen 2005).

Deceleration of Word Reading and Comprehension

Several studies have documented the decline in both word reading and comprehension for readers with autism and hyperlexia after the primary grades.

- One research team found that children under the age of five with both autism and hyperlexia outperformed typically developing five-year-old children *and* ten-year-old children with autism and hyperlexia for single word reading (Newman and colleagues 2007).
- In fact, single word reading that was far above average at age five declines to the normative average around age ten, or fourth grade (Grigorenko and colleagues 2003; Newman and colleagues 2007).
- Other researchers documented a decline in reading comprehension scores for readers with hyperlexia around age ten. Scores continued to decline or decelerate in upper-elementary grades to below age-level norms (Myles and colleagues 2002; Wei, Blackorby, & Schiller 2011; Wei, Christiano, Yu, Wagner, & Spiker 2014).

The internal gap between a reader's own ability to decode and understand *may* be noticeable in early grades, depending on how it is evaluated (and whether it is evaluated at all). In upper elementary grades, the external gap appears when readers with hyperlexia fall behind their peers in the area of comprehension, which can noticeably begin to interfere with learning.

- In fact, relatively poor reading comprehension is identified as the **most common area of weak academic achievement** for autistic students (Jones and colleagues 2009).
- **It can affect learning in all subject areas** in junior high, high school, and beyond.

Unexpected Frustration

According to the National Reading Panel (NICHD 2000), there are three levels of text difficulty when it comes to decoding words accurately, summarized in Figure 1.8. These levels of text difficulty refer to the ability to decode words and the number of words a reader finds challenging to recognize or call out.

Figure 1.8

Levels of Text Difficulty Decoding		
Type of text	Success rate	Level of difficulty
Independent-level text	No more than 1 in 20 words is difficult for the reader.	This text is relatively easy for the reader to read on their own.
Instructional-level text	No more than 1 in 10 words is difficult for the reader.	Material in this range of difficulty is considered appropriate for teaching or guided reading.
Frustration-level text	More than 1 in 10 words is difficult for the reader.	Too difficult to read successfully; extensive teacher support needed

The next graphic, Figure 1.9, summarizes the level of difficulty generally used to measure the level of overall comprehension.

Figure 1.9

Levels of Text Difficulty of Comprehension		
Type of text	**Success rate**	**Level of difficulty**
Independent-level text	Read with 90% or greater comprehension	Relatively easy for the reader.
Instructional-level text	Read with 75–89% comprehension with no teacher support.	Material in this range of difficulty is considered appropriate for teaching or guided reading.
Frustration-level text	Read with less than 75% comprehension.	Too difficult to comprehend successfully.

Text that can be read (decoded) with ease by someone with hyperlexia may be at the frustration level when judged by the *understanding* of the text.

- When less than 75% of the text is understood, the material is too difficult and will frustrate the reader.
- In this case, the difficulty is not in recognizing words (decoding or fluency of reading), but in understanding the meaning of the words (vocabulary and fluency of thought).

For a student with a comprehension problem, grade-level material may be too difficult.

- Below-grade-level comprehension interferes with the ability to understand their grade-level textbooks, novels, and other reading material.
- Silent and independent reading is an important instructional method used in the upper grades. Students who managed reading material in earlier grades may begin to struggle because they lack the skills to read independently or compensate for problems understanding.

This situation can depress students' performance and contribute to learning problems. This may be especially true if the individual was once considered a reading "star" but now feels lost or incapable.

- The difficulties can also cause and emotional issues, such as thinking they are "stupid" and experiencing the myriad of feelings that go along with this false belief.
- As a result, many students with hyperlexia experience anxiety about school as comprehension becomes more of a struggle.

The Profile of Hyperlexia

Good decoders with autism who can fluently read grade-level materials but fail to understand at the same level may share a common profile, no matter what their age. You can use Figure 1.10, The Profile of Hyperlexia, as a checklist for your child, student, or client.

The readers of concern to us will fit this profile in multiple ways, and in some cases, in every way.

- Parents and teachers should be alert to the uneven profile and comprehension difficulties in good decoders with autism of all ages.
- More research than ever is documenting the nature of comprehension issues of readers with this profile and the far-reaching effects it can have on their education and learning.

Good communication between home and school is needed to identify and support these students.

- It is especially important to fully understand how the features of their autism affect a particular student's development, learning, reading, and other skills.
- The chapters that follow explain why this is true and provide insight into how to understand, identify, and address comprehension issues for readers with hyperlexia of all ages.

Figure 1.10

The Profile of Hyperlexia	
✓	**Description**
	Has Level 1 autism, meaning they have some support needs (perhaps diagnosed in the past with Asperger syndrome or referred to as having high-functioning autism, terms you may still find in research)
	Has average or above-average cognitive ability
	Is in general education classes for all or much of the school day
	Tests in the "average" range on standardized comprehension tests
	Has oral language skills that appear intact, as measured by basic expressive and receptive vocabulary tests
	Is not formally identified as someone with a comprehension issue, reading difficulty, or learning disability
	Reads grade-level material at the frustration level (understanding 90% or less of the material)
	Has difficulty with higher-level interpretations and understanding
	Has a very different experience working at school (with structure and support) compared to working at home, where there is typically less structure and support
	Has comprehension issues with both written and spoken information,
	Is at-risk for having their needs unidentified, minimized, or unmet.

Call to action: It's time for widespread sharing of this information. Let's create momentum to understand, identify, and support these otherwise capable readers who are being disadvantaged by an unaddressed reading disability.

CHAPTER 2

Autism & the Comprehension Connection: Social-Communication & Language Features

Strategies used to teach learners with autism must be well-matched to the way the person thinks and learns (Nation & Norbury 2005). This chapter provides background information about the characteristics of autism to help readers understand the *features* of autism, the *impact* these features can have on comprehension, and the resulting *needs* in terms of reading and literacy. The chapter highlights:

- Simply-stated definitions of autism.
- The most recent official diagnostic criteria (2022).
- Explanations and examples of the potential impact that developmental differences can have on the learning and literacy of a learner with autism of any age.

Practical Definitions

Let's start with some non-medical descriptions of autism spectrum disorder. Especially when working with parents of newly diagnosed children or others unfamiliar with child development, here are the simplest ways I describe autism:

- A **pattern of differences** in socialization, communication, behavior, and sensory processing.
- An **uneven pattern of development**, with strengths in many areas, and difficulty with social-communication skills, repetitive behavior, and sensory regulation.
- **Asynchronous development**, that is, when a person's development in the specific areas affected by autism does not match their calendar age.

These descriptions suggest the types of difficulties that are shared by many autistic persons, linked to the diagnostic criteria. People with autism can have many learning challenges **due to their developmental differences and the features of autism**. The core features of autism are **closely interrelated**, each area affecting the others. This becomes clear in reading the most recent diagnostic criteria for autism from the *Diagnostic and Statistical Manual of Mental Disorders-V-TR; Text Revision* (known as the DSM-V-TR), as shown in Figure 2.1.

- The criteria are provided here as foundational information to link the features of autism with their effects on learning and literacy.
- Take your time. This information may be difficult to read and understand!
- The criteria are explained in simpler terms in the sections that follow.

Figure 2.1 Diagnostic Criteria for Autism

Autism Spectrum Disorder Diagnostic Criteria 299.00 (F84.0)

A. **Persistent deficits in social communication and social interaction across multiple contexts, as manifested by all of the following, currently or by history (examples are illustrative, not exhaustive; see text):**
  1. Deficits in social-emotional reciprocity, ranging, for example, from abnormal social approach and failure of normal back-and-forth conversation; to reduced sharing of interests, emotions, or affect; to failure to initiate or respond to social interactions.
  2. Deficits in nonverbal communicative behaviors used for social interaction, ranging, for example, from poorly integrated verbal and nonverbal communication; to abnormalities in eye contact and body language or deficits in understanding and use of gestures; to a total lack of facial expressions and nonverbal communication.
  3. Deficits in developing, maintaining, and understanding relationships, ranging, for example, from difficulties adjusting behavior to suit various social contexts; to difficulties in sharing imaginative play or in making friends; to absence of interest in peers.

Autism Spectrum Disorder Diagnostic Criteria 299.00 (F84.0)

B. Restricted, repetitive patterns of behavior, interests, or activities, as manifested by at least two of the following, currently or by history (examples are illustrative, not exhaustive; see text):

1. Stereotyped or repetitive motor movements, use of objects, or speech (e.g., simple motor stereotypies, lining up toys or flipping objects, echolalia, idiosyncratic phrases).

2. Insistence on sameness, inflexible adherence to routines, or ritualized patterns of verbal or nonverbal behavior (e.g., extreme distress at small changes, difficulties with transitions, rigid thinking patterns, greeting rituals, need to take same route or eat same food every day).

3. Highly restricted, fixated interests that are abnormal in intensity or focus (e.g., strong attachment to or preoccupation with unusual objects, excessively circumscribed or perseverative interests).

4. Hyper- or hyporeactivity to sensory input or unusual interest in sensory aspects of the environment (e.g., apparent indifference to pain/temperature, adverse response to specific sounds or textures, excessive smelling or touching of objects, visual fascination with lights or movement).

C. Symptoms must be present in the early developmental period (but may not become fully manifest until social demands exceed limited capacities, or may be masked by learned strategies in later life).

D. Symptoms cause clinically significant impairment in social, occupational, or other important areas of current functioning.

E. These disturbances are not better explained by intellectual developmental disorder (intellectual disability) or global developmental delay. Intellectual disability and autism spectrum disorder frequently co-occur; to make comorbid diagnoses of autism spectrum disorder and intellectual disability, social communication should be below that expected for general developmental level.

> ### Autism Spectrum Disorder Diagnostic Criteria 299.00 (F84.0)
>
> **Note:** Individuals with a well-established DSM-IV diagnosis of autistic disorder, Asperger's disorder, or pervasive developmental disorder not otherwise specified should be given the diagnosis of autism spectrum disorder. Individuals who have marked deficits in social communication, but whose symptoms do not otherwise meet criteria for autism spectrum disorder, should be evaluated for social (pragmatic) communication disorder.
>
> Reprinted with permission from the Diagnostic and Statistical Manual of Mental Disorders, Fifth Edition, Text Revision (Copyright © 2022). American Psychiatric Association. All Rights Reserved.

Levels of Severity

As indicated with the criteria, diagnosticians are asked to indicate the "level of severity," describing to what extent the individual being evaluated is affected by their autism. This corresponds to the concept of autism as a spectrum, affecting different individuals differently.

Needs Very Substantial Support • Needs Substantial Support • Needs Support

The information shown in Figure 2.2 helps diagnosticians rate severity and indicate the level of support an individual may need.

- Ratings are made separately for social communication and for behavior/sensory issues.
- An individual can be rated at the same level in both areas, or be rated as more severely affected in one area than the other.
- The severity scale includes more examples of the difficulties individuals with autism may experience, and can help clarify areas of need.

Figure 2.2 Levels of Severity

Severity Levels for Autism	
Level 3 "Requiring very substantial support"	
Social communication	Severe deficits in verbal and nonverbal social communication skills cause severe impairments in functioning, very limited initiation of social interactions, and minimal response to social overtures from others. For example, a person with few words of intelligible speech who rarely initiates interaction and, when he or she does, makes unusual approaches to meet needs only and responds to only very direct social approaches.
Restricted, repetitive behaviors	Inflexibility of behavior, extreme difficulty coping with change, or other restricted/repetitive behaviors markedly interfere with functioning in all spheres. Great distress/difficulty changing focus or action.
Level 2 "Requiring substantial support"	
Social communication	Marked deficits in verbal and nonverbal social communication skills; social impairments apparent even with supports in place; limited initiation of social interactions; and reduced or abnormal responses to social overtures from others. For example, a person who speaks simple sentences, whose interaction is limited to narrow special interests, and who has markedly odd nonverbal communication.

Severity Levels for Autism	
Level 2 "Requiring substantial support"	
Restricted, repetitive behaviors	Inflexibility of behavior, difficulty coping with change, or other restricted/repetitive behaviors appear frequently enough to be obvious to the casual observer and interfere with functioning in a variety of contexts. Distress and/or difficulty changing focus or action.
Level 1 "Requiring support"	
Social communication	Without supports in place, deficits in social communication cause noticeable impairments. Difficulty initiating social interactions, and clear examples of atypical or unsuccessful responses to social overtures of others. May appear to have decreased interest in social interactions. For example, a person who is able to speak in full sentences and engages in communication but whose to-and-fro conversation with others fails, and whose attempts to make friends are odd and typically unsuccessful.
Restricted, repetitive behaviors	Inflexibility of behavior causes significant interference with functioning in one or more contexts. Difficulty switching between activities. Problems of organization and planning hamper independence.
Reprinted with permission from the Diagnostic and Statistical Manual of Mental Disorders, Fifth Edition, Text Revision (Copyright © 2022). American Psychiatric Association. All Rights Reserved.	

Diagnosticians also assess a person's intellectual functioning when making a diagnosis of autism. This may range from cognitively impaired to highly gifted. Individuals with hyperlexia may be rated at Level 1 based on their cognitive ability, verbal skills, and level of independence. Despite their abilities, learners with hyperlexia still require support because the features of their autism are likely to interfere with their daily interactions, routines, and learning.

A Useful Mnemonic and Graphic

I devised a mnemonic, SBC Global, as a simple way to remember the four main "impairments" in autism, as described in the -DSM-V-TR. (The mnemonic is particularly helpful if you're familiar with this internet provider.)

- In the graphic shown below, *S* represents socialization, *B* is behavior, and *C* is communication.
- The *Global* metaphor, symbolized by the circle, represents the sensory issues seen in autism and refers to the person's reaction to sensory input from the world around them.

Figure 2.3. Four Essential Characteristics

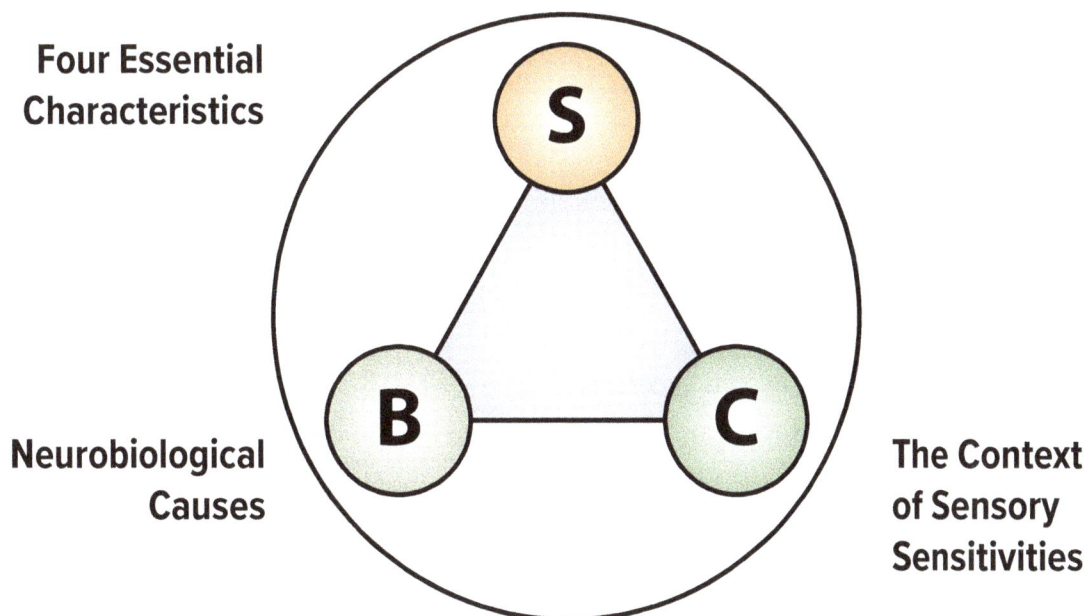

Four Essential Characteristics

S

B   **C**

Neurobiological Causes

The Context of Sensory Sensitivities

A note to avoid confusion from the start: *Behavioral differences* in autism does not mean "bad behavior." Behavior can be defined as anything that anyone does. In our context, *behavior* refers to restrictive and repetitive interests *and* repetitive actions. This will be discussed in detail in Chapter 3.

The Autism Spectrum

As indicated in Figure 2.2, Severity Levels, individuals with autism share the core features of social-communication, restrictive and repetitive behaviors, and sensory issues. Examples of these features can differ from one person to the other. Each individual may be affected more or less severely by the features of autism. This is why it is called a spectrum disorder.

The features of autism can look different in different phases of an individual's life.
- The features of autism must be present in the early developmental stage of life (roughly before age four), whether or not they are recognized at the time.
- Individuals with autism can learn, grow and make progress, particularly with appropriate instruction and supports.
- The DSM-V-TR specifically states that learning and progress can **mask** autistic features in an older child or adult that may have been more obvious at earlier ages.
- For a person of any age, features of autism that seemed to recede may "reappear" in times of stress, in response to high demands, and in situations involving change or transition.

Making the Connection Between Autism and Literacy

There's a clear connection between the developmental differences in autism with learning and literacy.
- This section connects the interrelated core social-communication features of autism and their potential impact on reading comprehension.
- These key points can guide efforts to identify, understand, and support readers with autism.

Social-Communication Traits

Medical and psychological jargon from a diagnostic manual can be hard to understand. Here's a simpler explanation of some of the **social-communication** differences that comprise autism. The information makes it clear why individuals with the same diagnosis can appear so different from one another.

Limited **social-emotional reciprocity** is a hallmark of autism. This means that the individual doesn't understand or engage in typical back-and-forth interactions and conversations.

- They may not initiate interactions with others, and they may not respond as expected when others try to engage with them.
- This feature is rarely seen in individuals with other diagnoses.

Some people with autism use little or no spoken language. This is now called being *non-speaking* (and used to be called *non-verbal*). At the opposite end of the spectrum is a talkative person who tends to have one-sided "conversations," downloading or monologuing on their favorite topics, without gauging the interest or reaction of the listener. This is another example of a lack of **reciprocity**.

Differences in **non-verbal communication** describe how an individual uses communication enhancements such as gestures and eye contact and includes:

- How the person uses non-verbal methods to manage or regulate social interaction.
- Engaging with others, and reading and responding to their body language and facial expressions.
- Interpreting whether other people are sending positive, negative, or neutral non-verbal signals.

Differences in social relationships describes how the person *interacts* with others and *reacts* to others. Their social style can be described on a spectrum from being withdrawn, to passive and aloof, to active "repetitive pestering" (Baron-Cohen, Leslie, & Frith. 1985, p. 38). Features can include:

- Stronger connections with parents or caregivers than other people (even if not typical).
- Struggling with play, relationships and friendships with peers their own age.
- Wanting to connect and interact with others, but not innately knowing **HOW** to do so successfully.

Social Development

A clear understanding of an individual's social development is relevant to every learner with autism, no matter how old they are. A comprehensive social-developmental history can be very helpful when assessing autistic students of all ages.

Keys to Social Development

Four key social skills are not acquired spontaneously in young children with autism: **joint attention**, **shared enjoyment**, **imitative play** and **imaginative play**. These skills were mentioned in Chapter 1. When you read the detailed descriptions of these skills, which are innate to most children, you can probably visualize just how young children with autism differ in this regard.

Joint attention means paying attention to a shared object or interest at the bidding of another. Joint attention includes looking in the direction that someone is pointing toward, and pointing at an object to direct someone else's attention.

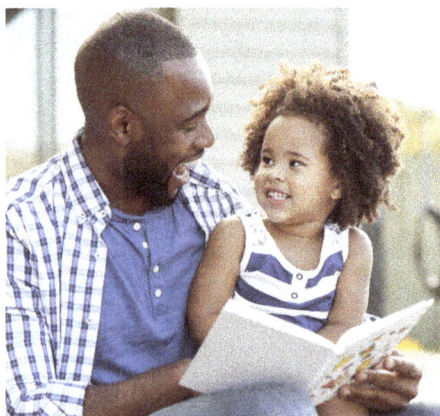

- An example is when an adult points to a bird in a tree and the child looks.
- A second example is a child pointing out a pretty flower to someone else and then checking to see if they're looking at it.

Shared enjoyment means increasing the child's enjoyment of a shared item or interest because of the reaction of the person with whom it is shared.

- An example is storybook reading, a shared activity that's fun for both people involved, and more enjoyable because it's shared.
- Another example of shared enjoyment is when a child looks at the face of the other person during the activity to "check in" on the reaction of their social partner.
- If the partner appears to like it, the child feels even more enjoyment.

Imitative play involves mirroring others, paying attention to, watching, and copying actions and words of others in the environment. Imitative play is a chance to practice for a variety of real-life social roles and language (Carpenter, Pennington, & Rogers 2002; Escalona Field, Nadel & Lundy 2002).

- Young children copy adults at home, imitating things that they see others doing. This includes chores like cooking or cleaning, self-care routines like shaving or combing hair, and daily activities such as talking on the phone.
- Children also watch and copy what other children are doing. They mimic what others do and say, and have to learn whether those things are appropriate or not.

Children invent **imaginative play** or **pretend play** together in the moment. It is novel, original and changeable.

- Children act out scenarios or take on roles based on imagination, not reality.
- Objects can represent anything at all, such as a stick becoming a magic wand.
- Pretend play usually involves a story that the child or children invent and act out. These play narratives can include complex events, dialog, ideas, and emotions.

Toddlers as young as 12 to 18 months demonstrate these four key skills, that are essential for developing relationships and interacting with others. It is possible to notice when these skills are *not* present. The lack of these essential foundational skills is cause for concern. In fact, these early skills are so important that the American Academy of Pediatrics (AAP) recommends that all children be screened for them at 18 and 24 months (AAP 2023).

Far-Reaching Effects

When children don't spontaneously develop joint attention, shared enjoyment, imitative play and imaginative play there can be lasting consequences on relating, thinking, and learning. Joint attention, shared enjoyment and interactive storybook reading are a clear foundation for the development of language and literacy.

For children with autism, the limited ability to watch and copy the behaviors of others (imitation skill) affects the child's ability to understand and practice new behavior and develop new interests (Pittet, Kojovic, Franchini & Schaer 2022). When children with autism have delays in watching, copying, and inventing play with other children, they miss out on learning social expectations, or "social thinking" (Escalona and colleagues 2002).

Play and imagination are keys to a child's intellectual development, enabling the child to "discover ideas, experiences and concepts, and think about them and their consequences" (University of Illinois 1998; Childcare.gov 2025).

- Child development experts believe that play is where learning and literacy really begin.
- Imaginative play can have far-reaching effects on social development, particularly forming relationships with peers.

It's important to note that some children with autism reenact something they've seen in movies or videos in a way that can appear imaginative, but is actually "borrowed."

- Autistic children may repeat their borrowed play using the same words and actions each time.
- This is a sign that the play is not original or truly imaginative.

Relationships

Social skills also affect learning directly. Interactions with teachers and peers in the social environment of early grade school are key to learning. People in the environment motivate typical children to come to school and share activities and enjoyment, especially when the classroom atmosphere is supportive and encouraging (Murphy, 2024; Pears and colleagues 2013; University of Illinois 2009).

- Children who engage in classroom tasks and participate with others establish lasting social ties and show greater gains in achievement than those who don't.
- Research suggests that children entering kindergarten who don't know how to interact with classmates and teachers may start on a pathway of low or declining school success.

As children grow up, peer relationships often become the center of their world. Children and teens have fun together, learn from one another, develop trust, communicate regularly, and support one another. Peer relationships contribute to a child or teen's social-emotional growth.

- Autistic individuals do not have an easy time with peer relationships.
- It's safe to assume that individuals with autism WANT to have friends but don't know how to make them.

Autistic individuals are likely to have the following social difficulties:

- Limited **social insight**, failing to understand the perspective, interests, motivations, and intentions of others.
- Lack of understanding of the **emotional states** of others, the intensity of those emotions, and a varied vocabulary of feelings (Gately 2008).
- Problems forming a mental concept about the beliefs or the internal states of others, known as *theory of mind* (ToM).

Social theorists believe that social impairments or social failure can cause a person with autism to withdraw from society.

- Isolation and the lack of social engagement limit what the autistic person can learn from others, share with them, and enjoy together.
- As a result of social withdrawal, the individual pursues their own restricted and repetitive interests, and fails to develop or enhance their communication skills, thus creating some of the symptoms of autism (e.g., Frith 1991; Happé 1993; Baron-Cohen, Tager-Flusberg & Cohen 1993).

Because of the clear impact on intellectual development, social inclusion, and learning, make-believe play and peer interaction must be explicitly taught and supported.

- Other children can be taught to engage with a child on the spectrum around their favorite interests and activities (think dinosaurs or building with LEGO® bricks).
- This can open the door to more play, shared enjoyment, and peer relationships, as evidenced by the Integrated Playgroups Model (Wolfberg & Schuler 1993).
- Once relationships are established, learners with autism can be taught ways to show interest in others, follow the lead of others in real-life situations, and expand their interests and activities, one step at a time.

The social complexity of peer relationships increases with age. Older children, teens and adults with autism usually need social skills training to figure out how to make friends. If they did not have support for social skill development during preschool or early elementary school, learners will need help in these areas matched to their stage of life.

- If it hasn't happened spontaneously, support and intervention are needed to create social and communication opportunities, expand language and vocabulary, and help the child or teen engage with others.
- As they become older, learners also need help to develop social cognition, which includes perspective taking, acquisition of socially acceptable problem-solving strategies, and understanding how the consequences of personal choices affect others.
- They also need to be taught about social expectations for different contexts, such as casual versus formal settings.

Hopefully these explanations clarify the social-communication features of autism mentioned in the DSM-V-TR. Figure 2.5 summarizes the key aspects of social development described, and the benefits of these experiences for individuals of all ages.

Figure 2.5

Key Aspects of Social Development in Children	
Developmental Feature	**Benefits and gains for development, comprehension, and literacy**
Play and imagination	Are keys to a child's intellectual development, enabling the child to discover ideas and concepts through their experiences, and think about those ideas and their consequences
Play with other children	Helps the child understand and practice new behavior, develop new interests, and form relationships
Joint attention	Forms social ties with others with others when one pays attention to a shared object or interest at the bidding of another
Shared enjoyment	Increases the enjoyment of a shared item or interest because of the response or reaction of the person with whom it's shared
Imitative play	Includes paying attention to, watching, and copying actions and words of others in the environment. • Mirroring others is practice for a variety of real-life social roles and the language that goes with them. • Social expectations are learned through imitation, including social thinking and empathy.
(Successful) social interactions with teachers and peers	• Gives motivation to go to school and share enjoyment • Provides opportunity for learning from adults and peers
Engagement in classroom tasks and participation with others	• Helps establish lasting social ties and interpersonal relationships, particularly with peers • Develops concepts and vocabulary

Key Aspects of Social Development in Children	
Developmental Feature	**Benefits and gains for development, comprehension, and literacy**
Social cognition **Social insight**	• Forms a mental concept about the beliefs or the internal states of others, known as *theory of mind* (ToM) • Helps in understanding the perspective, interests, motivations, and intentions of others • Helps in understanding how the consequences of personal choices affect others • Learning socially acceptable problem-solving strategies
Perceive and interpret social-emotional stimulation	Helps in understanding the emotional states of others, the intensity of those emotions, and a varied vocabulary of feelings

How Do Social-Communication Issues Affect Reading Comprehension?

Play is where children discover ideas, experiences, and concepts. Lack of social play can negatively impact cognitive development, literacy, and learning. A narrow range of social experiences can limit world knowledge, word knowledge, conversation, and perspective taking.

The **lack of imagination and perspective taking** can significantly affect social understanding of narratives, action, cause and effect, and understanding consequences.

- For example, an autistic child may not relate to unfamiliar social scenarios and interactions in a story, as s/he may not have personal experience to draw upon.
- This will cause a failure in **integration**, that is, comparing written material to known information and then creating and storing a new idea.

In addition, the **lack of imagination** often experienced by individuals with autism can impact their ability to visualize or picture unfamiliar characters, events, or fantasy elements in stories. This affects understanding, memory, and the ability to talk or write about these story elements.

44

Further, **limited social knowledge** means that readers with autism may miss the feelings, behaviors, and motivations of characters, as well as the interactions between characters, in stories they read. Therefore:

- The reader with autism may not identify with characters or the situations characters face. They may not understand words that describe or hint at the emotions that characters are feeling.
- The skill of inference is also limited by a lack of social understanding. Because individuals with autism often miss cues from the real-life environment, they are also likely to miss them in text.

Limited pretend play can affect children with autism in the earliest phases of reading (Vukelich and colleagues 2020).

- Emergent readers pretend to read books and imagine that they are reading.
- Children learn to adapt the way they speak and act in various situations when taking on different roles in pretend play.
- These foundational experiences may be different or lacking in learners with autism. This can affect interest in books and reading for some children, teens and adults.

Vocabulary growth is also clearly connected to socialization, as described in *Put Reading First*:

> Young children learn word meanings through conversations with other people, especially adults. As they engage in these conversations, children often hear adults repeat words several times. They also may hear adults use new and interesting words. The more oral language experiences children have, the more word meanings they learn (Armbruster and colleagues 2003, p. 35).

Reading this statement, one cannot help but make the connection between limited social-communication skills seen in autism and the effects on vocabulary development and literacy skills.

- Social-communication differences in autism may impact the quantity and quality of discussion and conversation with others, limiting the growth of vocabulary.

- Figure 2.6 summarizes the effects of social-communication differences seen in autism on comprehension and literacy.

Figure 2.6

Effects of Social-Communication Differences on Comprehension and Literacy	
Area of Development	**Possible Effects on Literacy and Comprehension**
Play skills	Impaired cognitive development, learning, and literacy
Shared enjoyment	Reduced shared social activities, including shared book reading with adults (and the associated benefits)
Joint attention	As attention is a prerequisite for learning, decreased attention to shared objects like books can limit the ability to follow another's lead or point out pictures and words
Imitative play	• Limited practice of words and actions related to real-life social roles • Hindered recognition and understanding of words and roles in stories
Imaginary play and imagination	• Literal interpretation of text at the word, phrase, sentence, and passage level • Weakened understanding of narratives, including plot, action, and cause-and-effect relationships • Diminished ability to imagine or create mental images while reading, especially with unfamiliar or fantastical material
Conversation with adults and peers	Fewer or less effective oral language experiences result in limited vocabulary development
Peer Relationships	Limited social insight, failing to understand the interests, motivations, and intentions of characters.

Effects of Social-Communication Differences on Comprehension and Literacy	
Area of Development	**Possible Effects on Literacy and Comprehension**
Social experiences	• Literal comprehension due to limited world and word knowledge • Reduced ability to infer the meaning of unknown words from context • Reduced ability to understand narratives, including plot, action, and cause and effect
Nonverbal Language	Disrupted recognition and interpretation of nonverbal cues, such as foreshadowing or contextual hints
Interpret social-emotional info	Impaired ability to perceive and understand the emotional states of characters, the intensity of those emotions, and the vocabulary used to describe their feelings.
Social Under-standing	Hampered ability to relate to characters and situations, integrate stories with personal experience, and assess the appropriateness of characters' actions based on social understanding
Social Cognition **Perspective-Taking**	• Impaired understanding of a character's thoughts, feelings, behaviors, and motivations, as well as interactions between characters • Limited ability to form a mental concept of the beliefs or internal states of characters (theory of mind) • Limited ability to understand and predict the behavior of characters • Reduced ability to understand an author's intention or bias

---

Author Insight: Ask *When*, Not *If*.

The feelings of the main characters are often central to a story. One of the most common language arts discussion questions is, "What do you think the character is feeling in this situation?" Or, "How would you feel if you were this character?" Autistic readers are likely to reply, "I don't know," because of developmental differences in socialization and imagination. The reader cannot imagine what the feeling might be, particularly if s/he has never been in a similar situation.

Some autistic readers are good at identifying basic emotions such as sad, mad, and glad. More complex emotions, such as envy or regret, are more difficult to perceive. One suggestion is to help the autistic reader identify a concrete example from their own experience that is similar to the character's situation. Maybe the reader has never felt the disappointment of losing a baseball championship described in a story, but might have been disappointed to come in second in a Spelling Bee. They might also have felt envious of the winner. The student may need help to find precise words to name their feelings. A word bank, or array of options, can be helpful for this.

Once the reader can identify their genuine feelings, they can transfer this understanding to the character's circumstances. The question, **"How did you feel when…"** is likely to help the autistic reader relate to characters and understand the emotions in a story. It's an excellent alternative to the unproductive prompt, "How would you feel if…"

Communication and Language Differences

Communication involves speaking, listening, reading, and writing, which are key aspects of literacy. Communication and language issues in individuals with autism can result in difficulties in any or all of these areas.

- Communication and language issues are no longer included as part of the diagnosis of autism per se. They can be co-diagnosed as a *specifier*, or a co-occurring feature.

- For this reason, this section systematically summarizes multiple communication and language issues often seen in autism, and their potential impact on literacy and comprehension.

How Can Communication and Language Issues Affect Reading Comprehension?

It is "universally agreed that reading is a language-based skill" (Nation & Norbury 2005, p. 24).

- Oral language and vocabulary are two key factors that support literacy.
- The differences in the development of lower- and higher-level language skills in learners with autism can affect many aspects of literacy development, including comprehension at the word, sentence, and text level.

Vocabulary and Concepts

The understanding of words and the way children learn what words mean can be affected by autism. Acquiring vocabulary and processing word meaning usually happens in a step-by-step process (Vogindroukas, Stankova, Chelas & Proedrou 2022).

- First, the child understands a word and combines it with the specific known object.
- Next, the child links objects to other objects and distinguishes *same* and *different* objects.
- Children learn to identify *categories* to which objects belong.
- They expand their vocabulary and language skills by learning to *label* and *describe* objects.

In contrast, children with autism may acquire words in a manner that is **absolute,** rather than connected or relational.

- It appears that while developing language, they do **not** develop a system to **organize concepts or word meaning** (Tager-Flusberg 1985).
- As a result, they often have problems using word meaning to organize, categorize, and recall, a difficulty known as *semantic breakdown.*
- This may be related to findings that individuals with autism tend to notice differences between items, words or concepts, but may not perceive **connections** and **similarities** (Floyd, Jeppson & Goldberg 2020).

- Semantic breakdown can also cause difficulties with **generalization** of meaning from one situation to another and understanding **multiple meanings** that a single word can have.
- When a reader with autism is not able to organize, categorize, and recall word meaning, **specialized teaching is required** to help develop vocabulary, relate concepts to word meaning, and learn to organize words into categories.

Context Clues

There are many reasons why a person with autism may have an underdeveloped vocabulary. A related problem is failing to use context to determine the correct meaning of words.

- **Homographs** are words that are spelled or written the same but pronounced differently depending on the context where they appear. An example is, "Gail was surprised when the **dove** circled in the air and then **dove** into the pool."
- When reading aloud, most readers decide on a correct pronunciation for a homograph based on the context.
- The reader self-corrects if an error interferes with the meaning of the text.

In a study about homographs, subjects with autism made significantly more errors compared to nondisabled peers when the reader:

- Does not self-monitor and self-correct when the wrong pronunciation is selected.
- Fails to realize that the text no longer makes sense and continues reading without using strategies to correct the breakdown (Wahlberg 2001a).

In addition, due to limited monitoring of their own comprehension, readers with autism are likely to keep reading without stopping to clarify the meaning of an unknown word, making it even less likely that the word will be added to their vocabulary or remembered. As a result, repeated exposure to the same word in different contexts does **not** ensure that they will understand the meaning of the word any better.

Problems with *inference* mean that readers with autism can have difficulty figuring out the meaning of an unknown word from context.

- Readers with autism in a study were less able than the other students to **integrate** information and words from the text with their own knowledge and experiences to make an inference that was appropriate to the context of the story (Norbury & Bishop 2002).
- Their ability to **infer** was also significantly lower than their ability to answer concrete questions.

Literal Interpretation of Language

Individuals with autism typically interpret language literally, or at face value. This form of black-and-white thinking results from several different aspects of the cognitive profile in autism. These include language and vocabulary development and limited ability to infer.

- The person believes that the words they hear or read are literally true, without realizing that the words may have an inferred abstract or figurative meaning.
- A real-life example is when a mother used an idiom, saying, "It's raining cats and dogs outside." Her daughter replied, "Great, I'm going to go out there because I want a kitten."

Literal interpretation of language affects a reader's understanding of text when they:

- Do not correctly interpret idioms.
- Do not know the relevant meaning of a word with multiple meanings.
- Miss the author's hidden intention or perspective due to difficulty with figurative language such as metaphors, hyperbole, and personification.
- Miss the nuance of an author's word choices or **connotation** (for example, describing a character as skinny, slender, or scrawny).
- Miss the inferred meaning behind sarcasm.

Pronouns

Difficulties with pronouns in spoken language may relate to problems understanding pronouns in print. The reader may also have trouble understanding to whom the pronouns refer. The reading skill called *anaphoric cuing* depends on the reader stopping to clarify meaning when reading sentences that contain subject pronouns (e.g., *I, she, he, we*) and possessive pronouns (e.g., *her, his, our*).

A sentence that illustrates the link between pronouns and the *referent*, the person or object that pronoun refers to, is, "Susan came into her mother's house and put her purse on her sofa." Whose house is it? Whose purse is it? Whose sofa is it?

- The difficulty with pronoun usage seen in autism may be a complicating factor in the reading task of pronoun clarification.
- This skill is also called *resolving ambiguity*, stopping to figure things out when pronouns make a sentence confusing.

Questioning

Another communication-related reading skill is *questioning*. Questioning is a skill central to comprehension. Good readers ask questions before, during, and after reading. Good readers can generate questions before reading to establish purpose and focus their attention on the most important information.

- They question text as they read to integrate the material with what they already know.
- While reading, they question themselves to monitor comprehension: "Am I understanding this material? Do I know what that word means?"
- After reading, good readers ask questions about the meaning of what they read and how to apply the information to their own lives.

The ability to question is a prerequisite for other complex strategies and thought processes. Many individuals with autism have great difficulty generating questions. This is seen when conversations break down or are not expanded due to a lack of questioning skills.

The inherent difficulty with questioning in autism can directly impact understanding. Many students with autism have educational goals of answering concrete "Wh-questions" about text (who, what, where, and when), particularly in the primary grades.

- Answering "why" and "how" is often not explicitly targeted or taught.
- Questioning skills must be addressed to support understanding and benefit from educational materials.

Auditory Comprehension of Oral Language

Listening to and understanding spoken language affects comprehension. Autistic individuals often have difficulties with auditory processing or auditory comprehension. They are likely to process what they hear more slowly than others. Therefore, they can miss the message in spoken language, including academic instruction.

- Recent brain imaging studies found that, compared to typical peers, children with autism had a response delay of 11 milliseconds in processing sounds heard in words.
- While the lag is brief, it means that the child with autism may still be processing the first syllable of a word when other students in class have already processed the entire word.

When students have problems getting started with work and following instructions, it is often a sign or symptom of difficulty processing auditory language quickly enough. They may have missed the meaning or message and, as a result, feel lost. Importantly, the auditory processing delays may cascade, and the child with autism may lag further and further behind when trying to capture the message during a longer conversation or lesson (Children's Hospital of Philadelphia 2010).

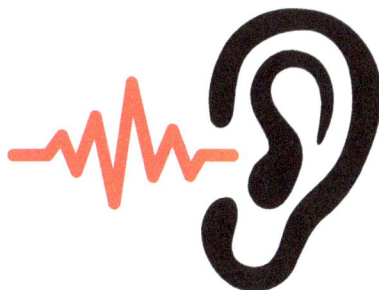

Typically, exposure to language helps children grow their vocabulary and word meanings. In the case of children with autism, exposure alone may not be enough if a processing problem interferes with their benefit from the exposure (Vogindroukas and colleagues 2003).

- The weakness in processing oral language can cause weakness in the development of vocabulary and word meaning.

- Such problems can also translate into limited understanding of written language. Words or concepts that were "missed" at the spoken level (for example, during an explanation prior to reading) can cause gaps in understanding when reading text.

- Figure 2.7 summarizes the effects of language and communication difficulties in autism on comprehension and literacy.

Figure 2.7

Effects of Communication and Language on Comprehension and Literacy	
Developmental Feature	**Possible Effect on Literacy and Comprehension**
Language development	Differences in the development of lower- and higher-level language skills affect comprehension at the word, sentence, and text level
Oral language	Weakness in spoken language translates to written language and to listening comprehension
Recognizing and responding to nonverbal language	Difficulty recognizing and interpreting nonverbal cues described in literature limits understanding of context cues and foreshadowing
Receptive and expressive vocabulary	Unfamiliar and unknown words interfere with understanding at the sentence and text level
Vocabulary development, semantic breakdown	Limited number of words or word meanings affects understanding of concepts, the generalization of meaning from one context to another, understanding of multiple meanings of a single word, and connotation, the implied meaning of words

Effects of Communication and Language on Comprehension and Literacy	
Developmental Feature	**Possible Effect on Literacy and Comprehension— Areas of Difficulty**
Understanding relationships between words and processing word meanings	When words are learned "distinctly" rather than in a relational fashion, it is difficult to organize and categorize words and recall information
Difficulty with context and inference	Problems using context, recognizing connotation, and identifying the author's perspective affect the interpretation of word choices
Difficulties with pronouns	Problems understanding pronouns in print and understanding to whom the pronouns refer (anaphoric cuing) causes confusion and loss of meaning
Difficulties in conversation skills, including asking questions	Problems with questioning, before, during and after reading limit comprehension
Literal interpretation of language	Limited understanding of idioms, connotation, and multiple meanings constrains language comprehension Difficulty with figurative language weakens understanding of metaphors, hyperbole, and personification
Listening to and understanding oral language **Auditory processing delays**	Inconsistent, delayed, or limited auditory processing and auditory attention impairs the understanding of spoken language, including academic instruction. This can result in limited benefit from oral explanations and preparatory lessons related to the text, or the analysis of the material after reading.

Effects of Communication and Language on Comprehension and Literacy	
Interpretative language abilities	Higher-level interpretive skills such as problems with conceptualization, reasoning, and logical analysis affect specific reading skills such as generating inferences, resolving ambiguity, understanding cause and effect, and monitoring comprehension

It's very clear that the complex and pervasive social, communication, and language features of autism have a complex and pervasive effect on reading comprehension and learning in general. With this knowledge, it is impossible to ignore the needs of these learners. The expertise of speech pathologists and other professionals to address growth in these areas is a natural fit.

As this description of language difficulties suggests, many of the challenges of readers with autism are similar to those of English learners (ELs). **Therefore, it might be helpful to think of a learner with autism being like an EL in his or her own language.**

> **"It might be helpful to think of a student with autism as being like an English learner in his or her own language."**

While the challenges occur for different reasons (i.e., developmental in autism and experiential or environmental for ELs), there are many parallels in the resulting needs.

- Therefore, **it is possible that techniques and strategies that help ELs may also improve the language and literacy of students with autism.**
- It is logical to think so, and future research may support the hypothesis.
- In addition, methods that help learners on the autism spectrum may help ELs and other diverse learners too.

Chapter 3 continues the discussion of the diagnostic criteria for autism and the effects on literacy and comprehension, focusing on the behavior category.

CHAPTER 3

Autism & the Comprehension Connection: Behavioral & Sensory Features

This chapter concludes the discussion of the diagnostic criteria, using a format similar to Chapter 2. This chapter will:

- Explain behavioral and sensory aspects of the autism diagnosis.
- Explore *the impact* these features can have on comprehension, and the resulting *needs* in terms of reading and literacy.

Restrictive and Repetitive Interests and Behaviors (RRBs)

To refresh your memory, Figure 3.1 highlights the behavioral features of autism, including sensory issues. This information is taken from the full listing of diagnostic features from the DSM-V-TR presented in Chapter 2.

To receive a diagnosis, the individual must have at least two of the four RRBs listed. The variable combination of possible features helps explain how individuals with the same diagnosis can appear so different from one another. The information and examples may bring to mind different individuals that you know, have met, have read about, or have seen in the media.

- It's worth paying attention to these explanations because you may be surprised to discover how directly restrictive and repetitive interests and behaviors (called **RRBs** in the rest of this section) can impact learning, literacy, and comprehension.
- The section that follows Figure 3.1 presents a plain-language explanation of these four **behavioral** differences.

Figure 3.1

> **B. Restricted, repetitive patterns of behavior, interests, or activities, as manifested by at least two of the following, currently or by history (examples are illustrative, not exhaustive; see text):**
>
> 1. Stereotyped or repetitive motor movements, use of objects, or speech (e.g., simple motor stereotypies, lining up toys or flipping objects, echolalia, idiosyncratic phrases).
> 2. Insistence on sameness, inflexible adherence to routines, or ritualized patterns of verbal or nonverbal behavior (e.g., extreme distress at small changes, difficulties with transitions, rigid thinking patterns, greeting rituals, need to take same route or eat same food every day).
> 3. Highly restricted, fixated interests that are abnormal in intensity or focus (e.g., strong attachment to or preoccupation with unusual objects, excessively circumscribed or perseverative interests).
> 4. Hyper- or hyporeactivity to sensory input or unusual interest in sensory aspects of the environment (e.g., apparent indifference to pain/temperature, adverse response to specific sounds or textures, excessive smelling or touching of objects, visual fascination with lights or movement).

1. Stereotyped or repetitive motor movements, use of objects, or speech

Many autistics seem to find purpose and/or pleasure from repeating particular actions, sounds, or words in just the same way. Whether or not the function of this type of RRBs is obvious to the observer, some of these *stereotypies* may be rooted in a need for extra sensory stimulation. Others may be self-soothing strategies.

- *Repetitive motor movements* means moving the body or parts of the body (especially hands) in a particular way. Classic examples are hand flapping, body rocking, toe walking, spinning objects, or sniffing objects in the environment.
- *Repetitive use of objects* is repeating actions with objects in just the same way.

Examples include lining up toys, spinning wheels on a toy car rather than using the object in the expected manner, or flapping their fingers across their peripheral vision.

- *Repetitive speech* means repeating sounds, words, phrases, or even songs. There is usually a purpose or intention behind this form of communication. It is up to the listener to understand the meaning and honor the message.
  - o *Vocal stimming* is when a person repeats specific sounds at apparently random times. Uninformed observers might call it "making weird noises."
  - o *Immediate echolalia* is when the person repeats back what someone just said to them, such as, "What's your name?"
  - o *Delayed echolalia* is when the person repeats something they heard at an earlier time, such as a line from a movie or part of a conversation, seemingly without context. An example is when a six-year-old randomly says, "Momma always said, life is like a box of chocolates ..." This is also called using *idiosyncratic phrases*.

RRBs can become problematic when they interfere with daily functioning and learning, become too intense, are extremely frequent, or are dangerous (such as head-banging).

- Many RRBs are considered socially inappropriate or stigmatizing and are targeted for replacement, so the person can get the input they are seeking in a safer or more socially acceptable way.
- An example is an adult who repeatedly picks their nose in public learning to use a tissue.

> **2. Insistence on sameness, inflexible adherence to routines, or ritualized patterns of verbal or nonverbal behavior.**

Kanner, who coined the term *autism,* described the insistence on sameness, rigid adherence to routine, and fascination with objects (or parts of objects) that are part of the diagnostic criteria today (1943). Examples of insistence on sameness include:

- A pressing need or desire to take the same route to school every day, and becoming highly distressed if a road is closed.
- Eating the same foods (and only those foods) repeatedly.

- Using verbal rituals in socialization, such as asking each person they meet, "What day of the week does the trash man come to your neighborhood?"
- Becoming very upset by changes in the daily routine that seem minor to others.
- Becoming very upset when asked to transition from one activity to another, especially when being asked to give up a preferred activity or being told to stop before completing a task.

The purpose of insistence on sameness for the autistic person may be to create predictability in a world that seems confusing to them. Relying on routines is most likely an effort to manage everyday life.

- If yesterday, today, and tomorrow are the same, the person knows what to expect and feels prepared.
- Unfortunately, the result is often black-and-white thinking, a dependence on following rules, not wanting to waver from them, and distress when things change or aren't the same as expected.

> **3. Highly restricted, fixated interests that are abnormal in intensity or focus describe the passion and fascination that autistic individuals may have for the things they love.**

Favorite interests can **preoccupy** an individual's mind. This "internal focus" can make them less attentive to other people and things around them.

- People who do not understand autism often say that a person on the spectrum is "obsessed" with a particular interest or activity.
- In fact, the highly focused interest in special "favorite things" is a core feature of autism, not an indicator of mental illness.
  - It's more accurate to refer to these interests as *restricted* and *repetitive*, rather than obsessive (Doyle & Iland 2004).
  - The terms *perseverate* and *perseveration* are also appropriate to describe engaging in repetitive, restricted, intensely focused interests.

- **Strong attachment to or preoccupation with unusual objects** includes a strong fascination with things that don't interest most children, such as vacuum cleaners, string, or trash containers. These interests may appear odd to others, especially when they are observed in young children.
- **Excessively circumscribed or perseverative interests** means that the individual has an intense focus on a narrow or small set of interests, in contrast to having a flexible, general interest in just about anything, as most children do. The interest may transform into specialized, useful expertise in teen and adult life.

> 4. **Hyper-reactivity or hypo-reactivity to sensory input or unusual interests in sensory aspects of the environment**

This section explains what is meant by this criterion by highlighting the meaning and importance of five common sensory issues in autism:
- **Sensory sensitivity**
- **Sensory defensiveness**
- **Sensory overload**
- **Sensory seeking and**
- **Sensory under-responsiveness**

Individuals with Autism Tend to Be Sensory Sensitive

Individuals on the spectrum range from being "somewhat sensitive" to "highly sensitive" to different types of environmental input. These including light, sounds, textures, and smells. They may also have sensitivity to **proximity**, being physically near other people or to particular objects.

- Each person reacts to specific sensory "triggers" to a greater or lesser extent, depending on their level of sensitivity *or* their ability to cope with the trigger at a given moment.
- When the person has difficulty processing and organizing sensory input, they can become upset, out of balance, or **dysregulated**.

- This can affect control of their emotions and behavior, with direct effects on attention and learning. Figure 3.2 explains more about sensory sensitivity.

Figure 3.2

Sensory defensiveness refers to being bothered by sensory input in the environment. Bothersome stimulation may be light, sounds, textures, and smells that others find normal or acceptable. Examples of **aversive** sensory input include a fire alarm, the texture of finger paint, food smells, and food textures.

The term *sensory avoidant* means that sensory-sensitive individuals usually **try to protect themselves** from things they find hard to tolerate (things they are aversive to).
- They may try to avoid them by covering their ears, not touching, not eating, etc.
- They may react with alarm when asked to engage with their aversive input or when they can't escape it.
- Aversive sensory input can be upsetting and distracting, taking attention and focus away from learning.

Sensory overload occurs when a person is overwhelmed by too much sensory input (even if it isn't bothersome to others). The result can be shutdown, meltdown, an emotional outburst (dysregulation), or an attempt to get away from the source.
- Some autistics may feel anxious just anticipating that they may be exposed to their aversive triggers.
- An example is not wanting to go to school on Wednesday because the fire alarm went off on Tuesday and it could happen again.
- Another example is getting agitated when driving past the hospital due to remembering a negative sensory experience there.

In contrast to sensory avoidance, some individuals with autism can also be highly **sensory seeking.** They can't get enough of specific lights, sounds, textures, smells, or movements that are highly pleasing to them or that satisfy a neurological need.
- Classic examples of actively seeking preferred stimuli include repeatedly watching the blades of a ceiling fan rotate or spinning the wheels of a toy car.
- Another type of seeking is physical movement, such as rocking or flapping, also called *motor mannerisms*. Some people seek certain types of movement, like swinging, or riding roller coasters repeatedly.

- Motor mannerisms are **self-stimulatory** experiences that can be gratifying and desirable, which explains why people with autism prefer these types of activities and want to repeat them. Some people call this *stimming*.
- As an adaptive strategy, especially when under stress, the individual may attempt to self-regulate by engaging in the self-stimulatory behavior.

A third type of sensory issue is called *sensory under-responsiveness*. This means that the person's nervous system does not appropriately "register" or respond to the level of stimulation coming from their environment.

- One example is not registering pain signals that the body sends after an injury, such as a sprain or a cut.
- Another example is not registering that their body is too cold, and putting on more clothes to keep warm.

In case you are wondering, yes, the same person can be **sensory avoidant, sensory seeking,** and **sensory under-responsive** at different times, in different circumstances. Imagine what it's like to find everyday environments so distracting, uncomfortable, and inhospitable!

- This is why sensory-friendly environments are becoming more popular and appreciated.
- It also highlights the importance of assisting learners with their sensory regulation in teaching environments.

The RRB and Comprehension Connection

There are multiple ways RRBs can interfere with reading comprehension! The first is **world knowledge**, "the general information shared by people in a given culture, as well as specific content domains, like biology, literature, and geography" (Ehren 2005, p. 312).

- Most people have a **shallow but wide** information base about a substantial range of topics, a general interest in most subjects, and the ability to converse easily for a few exchanges about just about any theme.

- Knowing a little bit about a lot of things is essential for preparing to read, and for understanding new information by relating it to known information.

Individuals with autism often have a restricted interest in a particular subject and may focus, read, and converse repeatedly on that topic. Or they may repeat the same activity time and again.

- As a result, individuals with autism tend to have a much smaller range of interests, experiences, and background knowledge than expected, despite being exposed to many stimulating opportunities.
- Their knowledge and experience base is **narrow and deep** instead of shallow and wide.
- This affects conversation, vocabulary, word knowledge, and world knowledge thus affects reading comprehension.

The conceptual understanding of facts, vocabulary, and general information is needed to understand what is read. This information, stored in long-term memory, can be activated and referred to while reading (Holman 2004).

- RRBs can limit the person's exposure to a wide range of topics and therefore limit their general fund of knowledge, facts, concepts, and vocabulary.
- While they may have access to a rich variety of experiences, their apparent lack of interest or engagement may limit the benefit of those opportunities.
- Persons with autism may, in effect, have a "poverty of experience," as if they have never been exposed, which can be a disadvantage in learning and understanding what they read.

Comprehension also involves relating new information to what is already known, and then storing it to be retrieved later (Levine 2002). If the fund of information is narrow, the process of connecting it to what is already known easily breaks down.

- As a result, the person will struggle to relate the something new to something known and store a new **schema** (or connected idea).

- Application of known material to new situations may also be difficult because information is not readily transferable. This is also known as failure to generalize from one context to another.

The Lions at the Zoo Analogy

My favorite analogy to explain restricted and repetitive interests is "the lions at the zoo." In this example, a highly-focused person with autism becomes an expert on just lions. The lion expert knows all the facts about lions and wants to talk endlessly about them, regardless of the listener's interest.

Image courtesy of Euro-t-guide.com Own work, CC BY-SA 3.0 https://commons.wikimedia.org/w/index.php?curid=2101541

- The lion aficionado only wants to visit the lion cage on each visit to the zoo and does not want to move on and experience the other animals or share the enjoyment of other animals that their companions like.
- The lion fan misses the chance to compare other animals to lions and recognize how they are the same or different.
- The lion expert has an extensive understanding of the specific topic. Their social interaction and vocabulary are centered around it.

This example illustrates how restricted and repetitive interests can significantly limit not only world knowledge and richness of experience, but also opportunities for socialization, communication, and word knowledge that have the potential to further broaden exposure, interests, and conversations with others.

- Fascination with a preferred subject can also result in limited play, leisure, or academic activities.
- A vicious cycle can occur when the autistic person does not develop a wide variety of activities and interests to share with others, and misses out on the enriching relationships and language that go along with them.

65

RRBs and Vocabulary

The restricted and repetitive interests seen in individuals with autism may limit the topics of conversation they engage in. As mentioned, many readers with autism have an extensive, sophisticated vocabulary in their area of interest. Repeated exposure to and practice of words that are known and understood builds strength in these areas.

But *not* talking with others on a wide variety of topics, *not* participating in play and social activities, and *not* following the interests and leads of others can limit exposure to new interactions, conversations, thoughts and relationships. This can have a direct and detrimental impact on vocabulary development.

- Thus, vocabulary may be affected in both spoken and written language in students with autism due to restricted and repetitive interests.
- Comprehension of text may break down at the word level because the learner knows fewer common words than expected for their age.

This situation can be confusing:

- The idea that the individual's vocabulary is comparatively limited may be resisted by those who've heard the learner using sophisticated language and vocabulary when speaking about their area of interest.
- The same is true if the learner tends to "borrow" complex language from movies, videos, etc. (echolalia) and the listener is not aware that the speech is not original.

As mentioned in the context of language development, readers with autism are known to have difficulties with multiple meanings of words (Vogindroukas and colleagues 2003, 2022; Wahlberg 2001a). This can be tied directly to their RRBs.

- Readers with autism are likely to stick with the familiar, single meaning related to their area of interest.
- One example is the meaning of *force* from *Star Wars*: "May the force be with you." A *Star Wars* fan might attach the "movie" meaning when reading, "He tried to force open the door."

Concrete, Black & White Thinking

Autistic readers may also have a rigid interpretation of what they read. The reader may try to fit the meaning of the story to particular axioms that they have learned, which causes confusion. For example, after reading Shakespeare's *Romeo and Juliet*, a young man with autism did not understand why Romeo and Juliet got married if it was against the rules (Roth 2007).

A related issue is how **specific and concrete** learners with autism can be. Wahlberg (2001b) suggested that concrete thinking and a black-and-white way of processing information result from restrictive and repetitive behavior.

- Understanding can become narrowly contextualized, or bound to direct experience.
- This can affect the generalization of knowledge from one setting to another.
- For example, the learner may develop a specific understanding of a lion in a zoo (from her experience) but fail to understand that a lion can roam free in its native habitat.

The literal and concrete interpretation of literature results in a difficulty with abstraction. Comprehension is negatively impacted when a reader does not understand concepts or ideas that are beyond the scope of their own concrete experience. As mentioned in the Introduction, my son, Tom, once said, **"If it hasn't happened to me, my mind is a blank page."**

Literalness can also relate to extreme difficulty understanding text that is imaginative.

- The lack of imagination can also affect the person's ability to write creatively and inventively as well as understand invented realities in text.
- Similar to "borrowing" spoken language, many learners with autism use a compensatory strategy when writing: relying on safe, practiced, or borrowed responses related to familiar or favorite interests that may appear novel or original to an unsuspecting reader (Doyle & Iland 2004).

Understanding of Narrative and Expository Text

Most readers understand narrative stories (such as fiction and non-fiction stories) more easily than textbooks. Another, perhaps surprising, way that restricted and repetitive behaviors or focus can affect comprehension is that some readers with autism understand certain expository (factual) material *better than* narrative text (stories).

- Concrete, familiar, and preferred subjects may be areas of strength.
- "Experts" with autism may have advanced vocabulary and factual knowledge in areas such as science or history due to avid study of their favorite topics.

Professionals as well as parents may engage the interest of the reader with autism by capitalizing on a strong focus or a favorite interest as an effective starting point for relating novel concepts or practicing new skills. For example, at our house, we used *Star Wars* analogies to explain so many things to Tom! It was a way to broaden his understanding by speaking his language.

Despite strengths in understanding of expository text in areas of interest, it should not be assumed that the reader with autism has similarly developed skills in understanding narratives.

- Stories are embedded with highly social content, including the thoughts, perspectives, motivations, and conversations of characters.
- Elements of the plot are also highly social, including the actions, interactions, and reactions of characters.
- For these reasons, autistic readers are likely to need explicit instruction and support to understand narratives.

In reading, familiar material is easier to understand than unfamiliar material (Leslie & Caldwell 2010).

- Things that are familiar to most readers may be unfamiliar to many readers with autism, due to restricted and repetitive behaviors!
- Textbooks from junior high school, through high school, and beyond are considered unfamiliar and more difficult for all readers.
- They may be even more challenging for autistic readers.

Interest and Attention

Intense focus or **perseveration** on favorite or preferred interests and activities can interfere with learning due to limited interest and attention. Restrictive interests can be an "internal distraction" for learners with autism, **limiting their ability to focus** on new information and experiences. Students with autism often have little motivation to focus on topics outside their area of interest.

- The focus on favorite interests may also affect how the person views pictures, photographs, or other images that accompany text.
- They may miss the big picture and focus on irrelevant details related to their interest, such as spotting a car in an image showing two people having an argument.

A Note about Reading as the Restricted or Repetitive Interest

For many young children with autism, a fascination with letters, numbers, words, and reading *is* the restricted and repetitive interest. The child enthusiastically seeks out letters and words, and often learns to read (or at least recognize words) spontaneously. Letters and words become the main focus of each day, and the activity selected at every opportunity.

It's important to note the risk underlying reading as a preferred, repetitive activity: **Reading can become a solitary, self-directed, and isolating experience.** For other young children, reading is a social, communicative, and developmental experience. Reading should expand joint attention, shared enjoyment, vocabulary, and meaning.

The more a child with autism reads on his own terms, the more he wants to read his own things his own way (repetitively, with limited understanding and conversation).

Adults may need to interfere early on to break the cycle and restore some portion of reading time to a reciprocal, interactive, adult-child experience. The goal is to build the length of time spent reading together, maintain joint attention, enable the adult to guide the process, and help the child respond as a balanced reading partner.

- Ideas for doing this include looking at family pictures or pictures of the child and talking about them, making customized story books about shared experiences of the caregiver and child, and focusing *together* on the topics of greatest interest to the child (Kaderavek & Rabidoux 2004).
- Another option is adding siblings or peers as reading partners. They will likely ask questions and stimulate conversation, creating give-and-take between the readers.
- The therapeutic Reading Education Assistance Dogs (R.E.A.D.) literacy program suggests reading to animals as a gratifying "social" experience! (Intermountain Therapy Animals 2025). With some guidance from adults, this might be a great idea for individuals whose special interest is animals (especially autistic girls).
- Another approach is trying to interest the reader in a wider subject area, rather than only reading about the favorite interest (such as trains, cars, or animals), by linking the area of interest to something new. (An example is linking a cat in a pet shop to a lion at the zoo.)

Figure 3.3 summarizes the effects of restrictive and repetitive behaviors (RRBs) on comprehension and literacy.

Figure 3.3

Effects of Restrictive and Repetitive Behaviors on Comprehension and Literacy	
Developmental Difference	**Possible Effect on Literacy and Comprehension Areas of Difficulty**
Limited general fund of knowledge	The person may understand less or may not understand concepts, facts, and vocabulary that is expected to be familiar (poverty of experience).
Narrow focus of interest or knowledge	• **Integration and memory:** The process of connecting new concepts with what is known and then storing it for later retrieval can break down • **Generalization:** the ability to transfer or apply known material to new situations

70

Effects of Restrictive and Repetitive Behaviors on Comprehension and Literacy

Developmental Difference	Possible Effect on Literacy and Comprehension Areas of Difficulty
Exposure to a narrow range of topics	**Level of difficulty:** Grade-level or general interest material is less familiar (and therefore more difficult) **Motivation:** Material may be less interesting and less motivating than preferred topics
Repeated exposure to a narrow range of topics	**Isolation:** Unexpected depth of knowledge in a specific area of interest may limit conversation and cause social isolation.
Restricted or repetitive play, leisure, or academic activities	• Limited activities and interests to share with others results in limited world knowledge, word knowledge, and social understanding • Restricted activities reinforce literal, concrete, and black-and-white thinking and cause problems with abstraction and flexible thinking
Reading as the restricted and repetitive interest	**Isolation:** Reading can become a solitary, self-directed, and isolating experience, compromising understanding. Reading together should expand joint attention, shared enjoyment, vocabulary, and meaning.
Literal, specific, and concrete understanding	• **Generalization:** Understanding may be narrowly contextualized, or bound to direct experience, limiting generalization of knowledge from one setting to another • **Imagination:** Material that is beyond the scope of the person's actual experience limits understanding
Restricted focus	A person with a narrow focus of interest assigns a single meaning to words and struggles to understand multiple meanings.
Over-selective attention	Strong focus on a specific interest or detail can interfere with the ability to shift attention or pay attention to more than one thing at a time.

It's helpful to recognize that restricted and repetitive behaviors and highly focused interests can also be **positive**, in addition to the pleasure the individual derives from them.

- First, preferred subjects or topics can be chosen to illustrate points and practice skills. Focusing first on preferred topics may be highly motivating and engaging.
- Second, many people on the spectrum love to follow rules and routines and make lists. These tendencies, related to their repetitive behaviors and highly focused interests, provide predictability and comfort. There are many ways that lists, rules, and routines can be used in comprehension instruction to benefit students with autism.

Sensory Issues and Comprehension

An unfortunate side effect of gratifying self-stimulatory behaviors (sensory seeking) and maladaptive reactive behaviors (sensory avoidance), which fall under the category of RRBs, is that they can be distracting, taking attention and focus away from learning.

- They can limit productive, engaging behaviors that would widen the person's scope of interactions, activities, and knowledge (Wahlberg 2001b).
- Therefore, individuals who have significant sensory issues are likely to be at risk for literacy and comprehension difficulties!
- Figure 3.4 shows some ways that sensory sensitivities can affect literacy and comprehension.

Figure 3.4

How Sensory Sensitivities Can Affect Literacy and Comprehension	
Self-stimulatory behaviors, seeking	• Can limit productive, engaging behaviors that would widen a person's scope of interaction, activities, and knowledge • May increase off-task behavior • Can negativity affect the benefit of reading, being read to, and discussing literature
Self-stimulatory behaviors, avoidant	• Can limit interest, attention, motivation, and focus. • Can negativity affect the benefit of reading, being read to, and discussing literature

Conclusion

Chapters 2 and 3 present clear information about how the diagnostic features of autism affect understanding in multiple, complex ways! Remember that all of the core features of autism affect the individual **simultaneously**, logically leading to obstacles in learning.

- This is why good decoders with autism are at risk for comprehension failure.
- This is also why additional support is needed to develop skills in all five areas of comprehension: literal, inferential, critical, affective, and lexical.

A foundational premise of this book was presented in Chapter 1: "The demands of the active reading process may present a mismatch with the cognitive skills and core features of autism and, therefore, are the root of comprehension problems."

- The explanations offered to this point about the specific features of autism demonstrate why this statement is true.
- As a result, the areas of need for readers with autism are **complex and unique**, particularly when compared to readers who struggle for other reasons.

The connection between all of the features of autism and comprehension problems in these areas is more than theoretical: it has been documented in research.

- Some studies describe specific cognitive processes that are interrupted or disordered in readers with autism.
- Other studies pinpoint where in the reading process a comprehension breakdown occurs.
- Difficulties are seen at the word, sentence, and text level, as well as in the use of comprehension strategies to repair meaning.
- This information will be explored in Chapter 4, along with "The List" of essential comprehension skills to teach, drawn from research findings.

CHAPTER 4

Putting It All Together: Cognitive Models in Autism

This chapter focuses on the cognitive profile and unique needs of autistic individuals. Understanding brain-based thinking and learning processes in autism can illuminate how, where, and why comprehension breakdown occurs. The ultimate goal is to tailor teaching to the way autistic individuals think and learn.

Neurology is illuminating! Science is shining a bright light on how the thinking and learning processes may be inefficient or break down for autistic individuals. This chapter presents clear, factual information to:

- Explore different cognitive models of autism, including autism as a disorder of complex information processing.
- Highlight important findings from neurological research that account for the many differences in thinking and learning seen in autism.
- Provide comprehensive lists of comprehension skills that are likely to challenge autistic readers due to their neurodivergence.

Note: Because neuroscience is a medical model, research in this area uses words like "normal" and "deficit." If you are sensitive to such language, be prepared for it in this part of the discussion, especially when referring to research studies.

Cognitive Models in Autism

In 1994, when Tom was diagnosed, my search for information about autism began. Since then, I've paid attention to all fields of science. I want to have at least a layman's understanding of what the brightest minds of our time continue to discover.

- This chapter presents some new information that I didn't have when I first published DaB in 2011.
- It was included in the textbook I used to teach a graduate-level college course (Buron & Wolfberg 2008, 2014).
- I've organized the information as clearly as possible to support *your* reading comprehension.
- As Tom says, **"This explains a lot!"** I hope you'll agree.

Revelations from Studies of Brain Functioning

As we've established, reading is an **active thinking process**. Therefore, it's important to understand **how people with autism think and process information**. This provides insights into their learning needs, especially in the area of comprehension.

Cognitive models of autism and recent advances in the study of **neurology** are worthy of attention, providing insight into the workings of the autistic brain. Cognitive models in autism:

- Integrate the different diagnostic features of autism into a whole.
- Answer the question, *"Why* do individuals with autism have a specific pattern of characteristics?"
- Explain characteristics that are not adequately accounted for by the diagnostic criteria alone.

Neuroscientists study brain functioning patterns to understand cognitive differences between typically developing and autistic individuals.

- Functional magnetic resonance imaging technology (fMRI) makes it possible to study the functioning of the brain while subjects are awake and perform tasks involving thinking, language, problem-solving, etc.

- fMRI images reveal how different regions of the brain react and interact in autistic study subjects, compared to study participants without autism (known as *controls*).

The results of such studies demonstrate just how clearly autism is a form of neurodiversity: **multiple brain-based differences affect the way autistic individuals think and learn, along a spectrum of human variation.**
- Some brain-based differences result in original thinking and creativity.
- Other brain-based differences can cause difficulties in perception, thinking, and learning.

Together, cognitive models and brain-based studies provide us with insights and understanding that was not available even a few years ago. **One of the most important reasons to understand the brain-based differences in autism is to select effective ways to meet the unique needs of each autistic learner.**

Autism as a Disorder of Complex Information Processing

How or *why* are the brains of autistic people different from those of others? Here is an explanation of what neuroscientists believe is happening, according to recent research (Litman and colleagues 2025).
- Inherited and/or new (de novo) disruptions in the genetic code for brain development affect how the brain develops.
- The resulting differences in development can include the size of the brain itself, the functioning of particular brain regions, communication between brain regions, and even differences at the cellular and molecular level (Dapretto 2006).
- Differences in the physical structure and functioning of the brain affect the individual's cognitive abilities.
- The final effects of this chain reaction are the observable characteristics of autism (the behaviorally diagnosed condition).
- Figure 4.1 illustrates this process.

Figure 4.1

The Biological Pathway of Autism

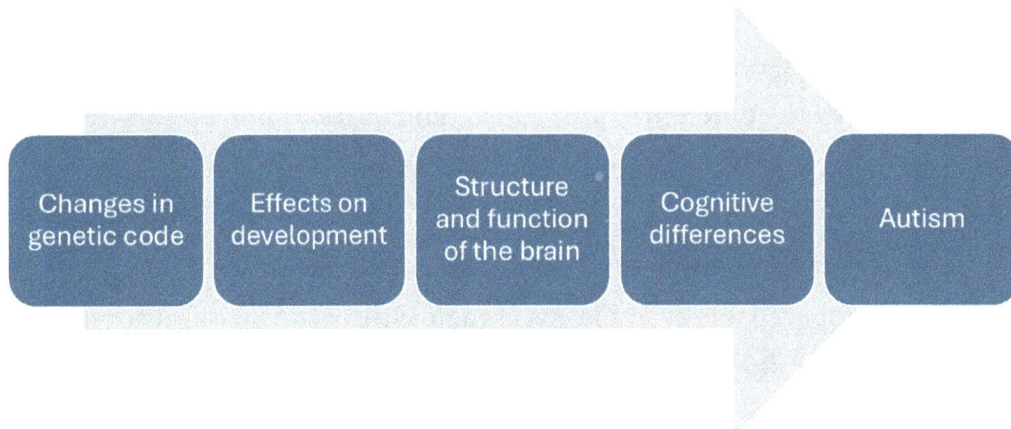

Changes in genetic code → Effects on development → Structure and function of the brain → Cognitive differences → Autism

Dr. Nancy Minshew has been a leading neuroscientist in the autism field for decades. Based on research findings from studies of the brain, she and her colleagues propose that **autism is a disorder of complex information processing** (Minshew Meyer, & Goldstein 1998).

- In early revealing research, they studied 33 verbal adolescents and adults with autism who had IQ scores above 80 and were considered high-functioning.
- Each person was matched with a typically developing adolescent or adult (control) for comparison.

Figure 4.2 summarizes the **unique profile of cognitive skills** that Minshew and her colleagues identified in the autistic subjects. Many basic skills were intact, but related higher-level skills were impaired. Based on their knowledge and experience, the researchers consider this cognitive pattern as **unique to the autistic population**.

Figure 4.2

The Complex Information Processing Model of Autism (From Minshew and Willliams 2008)	
Intact or Enhanced Skills	**Impaired Skills**
Formal language	Complex language
Simple memory	Complex memory
Rule learning	Concept formation
Elementary motor	Complex motor (movement)
Attention	Recognition of emotion in faces
Sensory perception	
Visuospatial processing	
Used with permission of the author	

Here are five key findings from this research:

1. The **acquisition of information was intact** in subjects with autism.
2. Information processing in autism **is reduced or constrained**.
3. Information processing is **negatively impacted by complexity** when multi-tasking is required or when multiple perceptions must be integrated simultaneously (such as listening while writing).
4. Information processing abilities are **disproportionately** affected for higher-order thinking demands, including **common sense, insight, abstraction, reasoning, and judgment**. *Disproportionately* means that the effects are more pronounced than expected relative to a person's general functioning and IQ.

5. Individuals with autism **process information more slowly** than non-autistic peers. Slower speed further hinders gaining meaning from information in both listening and reading.
   - o Figure 4.3 illustrates the effect of complexity.
   - o As complexity goes up, information processing goes down.

Figure 4.3

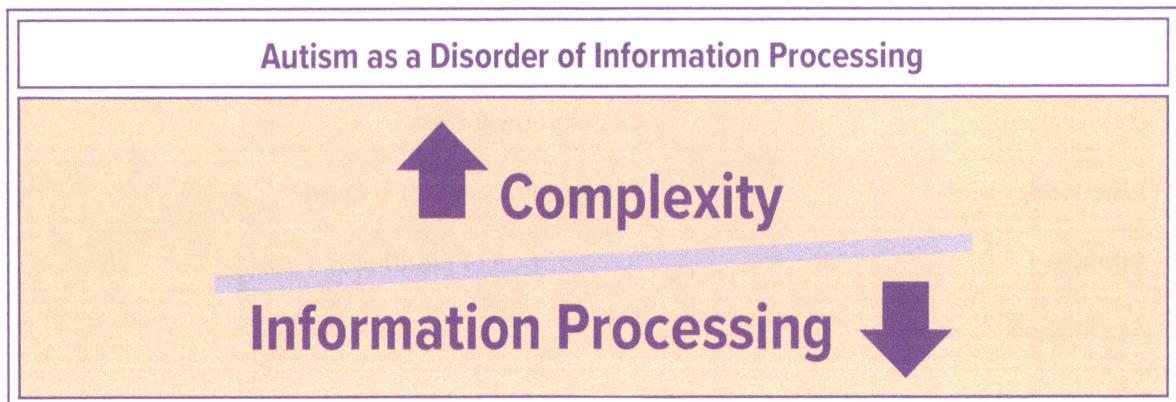

Autism as a Disorder of Information Processing

Complexity

Information Processing

In addition to this study, the researchers did a replication study with high-functioning, verbal autistic adults that confirmed the findings from the initial research.

- After that, in 2006, they conducted research with 56 high-functioning verbal autistic children, ages 8-to 15 whose Verbal IQ scores were between 80 and 120 (average to above average). The study included 56 matched "controls" without autism.
- Most of the findings about information processing for adults applied to the children.
- The findings about complex information processing and autism were also confirmed by different researchers using different methods (Dapretto and colleagues 2006; Harris and colleagues 2006; Turkeltaub and colleagues 2004).
- The replication of findings contributes to confidence in the validity of this work.

Examples of Complex Information

The first and best example of complex information is *life.* Just about everything we do every day is complex because it involves multitasking, or processing complex information quickly and efficiently.

- Multitasking can mean using different sensory modalities at once, such as seeing, hearing, touching and talking.
- Multitasking can mean thinking and doing something at the same time, such as driving a car.
- Complex tasks involved in driving include paying attention to the right things, anticipating what other drivers or pedestrians might do, planning the route, controlling the vehicle, etc. All this might be going on while you're also eating, listening to the radio, and/or talking with your passengers.

Social situations are complex and require a great deal of information processing. This includes:

- Understanding the social situation and your role in it.
- Perceiving verbal and nonverbal cues from people and the situation or context.
- Acting, interacting, and reacting to quickly changing, complex social information.

Communication and learning are two critical examples of highly complex daily activities. Most people can take routine complex information processing demands in stride, because our brains are wired to deal with them.

- Even with this neurological advantage, anyone can become overwhelmed by TMI (too much information), especially if it must be processed quickly.
- Our reactions can range from frustration, to anger, to withdrawal, to meltdown.

Now consider the mismatch between the continuous demand to process complex information and individuals whose neurological wiring can't keep up. Can problem behavior at school be related to the resulting frustration? Of course it can!

- Some autistic students use lots of internal energy to keep themselves together at school, but "fall apart" when they get home.
- Sound familiar?

Four factors can contribute to the *complexity* of information:

- Too much information.
- Disorganized information.

- Limited time to process, which can result in stress, confusion and anxiety.
- Required integration of ideas or multitasking.

Figure 4.4 illustrates these factors.

Figure 4.4

Autism and Information Processing
Inspired by Minshew & Williams, 2008

Complexity of Information			
Amount	Structure	Time Constraints	Multiple Simultaneous Demands

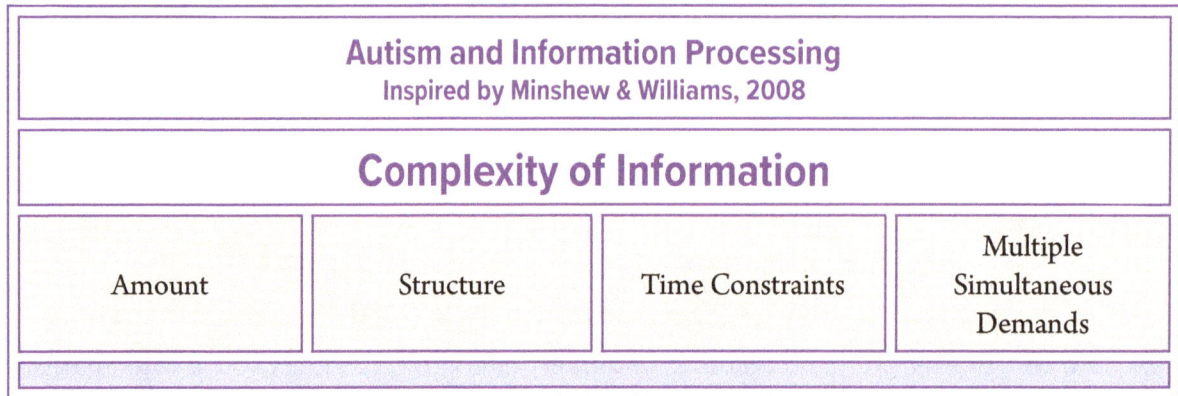

The theory of **autism as a disorder of complex information processing** makes sense of the clear patterns of strengths and needs seen often in autistic individuals, and may cause you to have your own "Aha!" moment.

The Complex Information Processing model of autism:
- Finds that certain cognitive processes are intact for individuals with autism, but related higher-order thinking processes are impaired.
- Explains why autistic individuals have many abilities yet face cognitive challenges with complicated tasks.
- Explains why students with autism may become frustrated with tasks that are too complex for them to manage, while other classmates can manage them.

Reducing Complexity

What if we can help address information processing problems by **reducing** the complexity of information? What if we can build on strengths, such as visuospatial processing and following rules, to assist with information processing?

- Minshew and Williams recommend communicating succinctly, using as few words as possible.
- They suggest getting to the point and overtly expressing main ideas, rather than having the learner integrate bits of information to draw their own conclusions.

Figure 4.5 illustrates four more ways to reduce complexity, including to:
- Manage how much information the person is asked to process at any one time.
- Add structure or impose order on the material to emphasize what is important.
- Give the person the time they need to think and process, rather than rushing (and stressing) them.
- Use one sensory modality at a time, such as talking *or* reading, but not both together.

Figure 4.5

Help with Information Processing			
Manage the Information Load			
Limit the Amount	Provide Organization & Structure	Extend Time	Reduce Simultaneous Demands

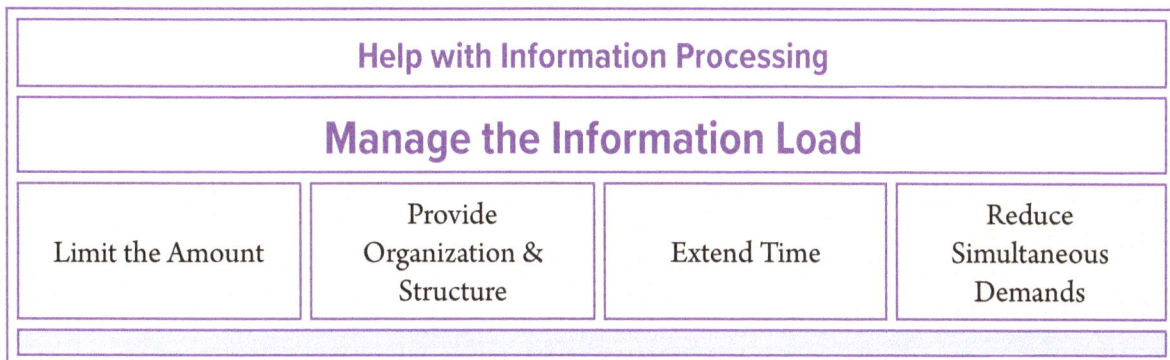

The Underconnectivity Hypothesis of Autism

Why do these functional differences in information processing occur in the brains of individuals with autism?
- Functional magnetic resonance imaging (fMRI) of the brain with subjects who were awake and thinking revealed differences in the **connectivity** of neurons (nerve cells that transmit information through the brain and body).
- Such findings led Minshew and her colleagues to propose the **underconnectivity hypothesis of autism** (2007).

The researchers found that:

- Study subjects with autism did not **integrate** information at neural and cognitive levels during higher-order thinking tasks in the same way that the control group did.
- Differences were observed in the **connections** between brain cells, the **timing** or synchronization of the connections, and the **interaction** between several parts of the brain.
- This **underconnectivity** results in needing more time to process information, **which is called impaired processing speed**.

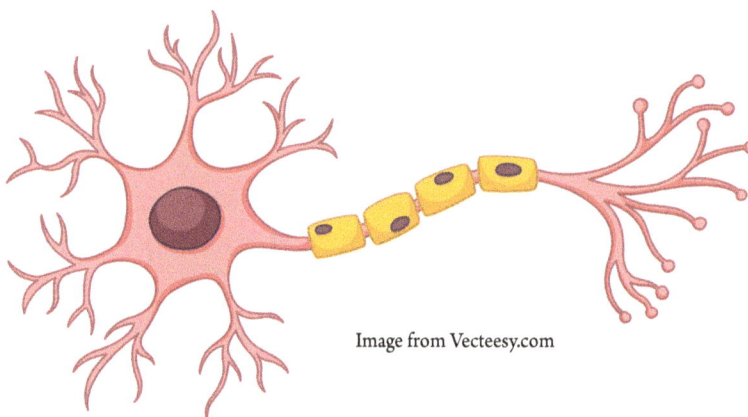

Image from Vecteesy.com

Concept formation is the cognitive process organizing objects or ideas into categories based on shared characteristics. The brain differences observed in the studies also resulted in **weak concept formation.** Weak concept formation includes difficulty in:

- Recognizing relevant similarities and differences.
- Developing or understanding abstract concepts.
- Generalizing information from one situation to another.

An example of weak concept formation is categorizing animals and a table together because they all have four legs. Weak concept formation makes it even more difficult to process information, especially as demands increase (Williams, Minshew& Goldstein 2015).

Figure 4.6 summarizes the four theories discussed to this point.

Figure 4.6

Theoretical Frameworks Based on Studies of the Brain

Complex Information Processing[1]

Complex information processing refers to the cognitive ability to handle, interpret, and utilize diverse and intricate data in a way that goes beyond simple recall or understanding.
- Many cognitive processes are intact for individuals with autism.
- The **higher-order thinking processes** are impaired.
- Complex information processing is crucial for various cognitive functions, including memory, language, and social skills.
- Complex information processing is needed for higher-order thinking skills like judgment, reasoning, problem-solving, and decision-making.
- The result is cognitive challenges with complicated or complex tasks, particularly those that require attending, encoding, storing, relating and retrieving information (such as reading!)

Impaired Processing Speed[2]

Impaired processing speed means that it takes a person longer than average to process information, think, and respond.
- In autism, processing time is especially slower or longer for complex social and communication tasks.
- The slowdown in understanding complex information in real life also translates to slower processing for academic demands.
- Impaired processing speed has nothing to do with intelligence. People of average or above-average intelligence can struggle to read, write, and understand due to slow processing speed.

Underconnectivity Hypothesis of Autism[3]

The *underconnectivity hypothesis of autism* refers to the lack of communication and integration between the frontal and posterior regions of the brain.
- This underconnectivity is thought to disrupt cognitive processes and lead to the characteristic symptoms of autism.
- In brain studies, subjects with autism did not integrate information at neural and cognitive levels during higher-order thinking tasks in the same way that the control group did.
- Differences were observed in the connections between brain cells, the timing or synchronization of the connections, and the interaction between several parts of the brain.

Theoretical Frameworks Based on Studies of the Brain

Weak Concept Formation (WCF)[4]

Concept formation is the cognitive process of grouping objects, events, or ideas into categories based on shared properties or characteristics.

- This crucial aspect of cognitive development allows individuals to make sense of the world and respond effectively to new information.
- Brain differences seen in autism can result in **weak concept formation**.
- **Weak concept formation** makes information processing more difficult as demands increase.
- Individuals with WCF rely on concrete understanding and rote memory.
- They struggle with cognitive skills such as abstraction and generalizing knowledge to new contexts.
- Note that weak concept formation related to vocabulary, as mentioned in Chapter 2, is also part of the language profile seen in autism.

Sources

1. Williams, Goldstein & Minshew, 2006a, 2006b; Williams, Minshew & Goldstein, 2015
2. Haigh, Walsh, Mazefsky, Minshew & Eack, 2018
3. Just, Cherkassky, Keller, Kana & Minshew, 2007; Just, Keller, Malave & Varma, 2012; Just, Cherkassky, Keller & Minshew, 2004
4. Williams, Minshew & Goldstein, 2015; Beck 2016.

Insights from Other Key Cognitive Theories

Other cognitive differences can negatively impact comprehension for autistic readers. The seven fascinating cognitive models summarized in Figure 4.7 include understanding relationships, mentalizing, theory of mind, emotional comprehension, central coherence, executive function, and control theory.

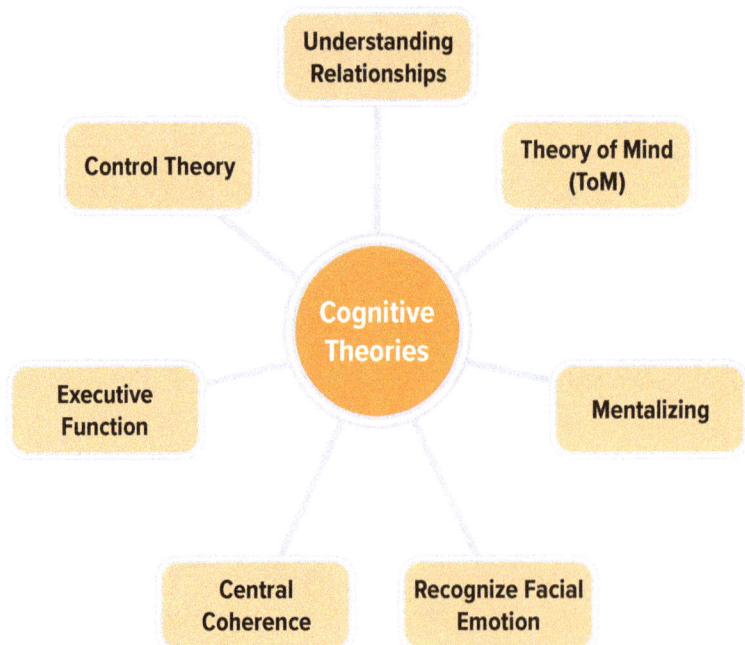

Figure 4.7

Seven Cognitive Theories of Autism
Understanding Relational Aspects[1] **of the environment, particularly relationships among people and objects**

People with autism can "miss" how people relate to other people and to objects.
- They have difficulty understanding what is likely to happen between them or what may happen next (probable event).
- This affects cognitive processing of problems such as understanding relationships, cause and effect, prediction, inference, generalization, and problem-solving.

Theory of Mind (ToM)[2]

ToM **refers to a person's ability to imagine and understand the feelings, beliefs, and perspectives of other people.**
- ToM is the ability to realize that other people have their own thoughts and beliefs about the world around them.
- Some people call ToM "mind-blindness." Problems with ToM create a "blind spot" in reading the minds of others, in person and in text.
- The lack of ToM can be a significant obstacle in predicting, inferring, and *interpreting* the thoughts, intentions, and actions of others, in life and in literature.
- A child's ToM ability at four years old *directly predicted* their reading comprehension 2.5 years later because the acquisition of ToM signals that a child is developing an awareness of their own thinking processes and learning to manage their thinking and learning. This is also called meta-cognitive development. In other words, delayed ToM is linked to delayed metacognitive development (Atkinson, Slade, Powell & Levy 2017).

"Mentalizing" or Forming Meta-Representations[3]

Mentalizing **is an intuitive understanding of the mental states of others.**
- Meta-representations arise through forming beliefs about another person's mental state by taking their perspective.
- A person with autism who cannot easily mentalize or create meta-representations may not be able to understand what other people or characters know, want, think, and feel.
- They may not understand and how specific feelings affect the actions and interactions of characters.

Seven Cognitive Theories of Autism

Emotional Comprehension: Recognizing and Responding to Emotion in Faces[4]

Many people with autism experience difficulties reading both genuine and deceptive facial expressions, especially reading complex emotions.

- Facial expressions do *not* provide clues to help the person with autism imagine what someone else is thinking or feeling in real life.
- The reader may miss clues about feelings based on context or the environment, for example, not knowing why someone is crying after falling down.
- This also applies to interpreting and understanding descriptions of facial expressions and emotions in text, understanding events, and recognizing the emotional causes or effects of those events.

Central Coherence or Weak Central Coherence (WCC)[5]

Central coherence **is the process of deriving meaning from a real-life situation or a literary context to create a global concept or an understanding of the whole.**

- Individuals with autism may have a *local bias* or superior ability for detail-focused processing.
- Because of the detail-focused way people with autism process information, they may miss main ideas.
- They often have difficulty integrating details or pieces of information to create the big picture.
- Problems with central coherence are sometimes referred to as *bottom-up processing*, where the person tries to make sense of different parts, rather than easily seeing how each of the different parts relate to a whole or a central idea.
- This processing difference affects understanding of the whole, whether it is understanding a real-life situation or the gist of a text.
- A man with autism once told me that he feels like he's standing too close to an impressionist painting. He can only see the dots, and he misses the meaning or message that everyone else can see.

Executive Function (EF)[6]

Executive function **is a cognitive process related to planning, organization and execution of plans, and self-monitoring of the process.** It also relates to the ability to bring prior knowledge or experience to bear on a situation or context, apply knowledge in a flexible manner, and learn from the past.

Seven Cognitive Theories of Autism

Problems with EF impact the ability to actively and efficiently process information:
- Difficulties in EF skills can affect all aspects of learning, especially reading. Reading requires an "organized" approach, including monitoring for understanding while reading, interpreting what was read, comparing new material to personal experience, storing relevant information, and retrieving information when needed.
- Readers with autism may also fail to **suppress irrelevant knowledge** that can result in a disorganized approach to making relevant connections before or during reading.
- Difficulties with EF can also result in difficulty with coherent retelling or writing due to issues with grasping main ideas and sequencing important events.

If this information seems familiar, EF difficulties are also seen in ADHD (attention deficit hyperactivity disorder).

Control Theory[7]

People with autism can find the world chaotic. As a result, they filter information in a *concrete manner* to impose order.
- Two core features of autism, insistence on sameness and repetitive behaviors, are part of the person's efforts to **exert control** as they process information.
- This style of processing information reinforces a strong focus on the concrete aspects of the world, rather than an interpretive response or understanding abstract information.
- This **literal perspective** can also be seen in response to literature.

Sources
1. Tager-Flusberg, 1985; Wahlberg, 2001b
2. Baron-Cohen et al., 1985; Happé, 1994; Wahlberg, 2001b; Atkinson et al., 2017; Randi et al., 2010.
3. Baron-Cohen et al., 1985; Fotheringham, 1991; Wahlberg, 2001b, p. 6
4. Dennis et al., 2000
5. Happé, 1997; Happé & Frith, 1996, 2006; Hoy, Hatton & Hare, 2004
6. Norbury & Bishop, 2002; Wahlberg, 2001b; Wahlberg & Magliano, 2004; Carnahan, Williamson & Christman, 2011; Ricketts et al., 2013
7. Wahlberg, 2001b

These descriptions and insights make it clear *why* readers with autism learn differently and *how* truly different their cognitive profile is compared to those of learners with other disabilities who don't have at least seven simultaneously occurring cognitive complications. In other words, the needs of autistic learners are different from those of learners who can rely on these cognitive processes to understand what they read.

- Unfortunately, no current instructional models, interventions, or evidence-based practices for comprehension instruction for this population have been identified that intentionally integrate these important cognitive factors in teaching (El Zein, Solis, Vaughn and McCulley 2013).
- This is an area begging for more study, research, answers, and results!

Cognitive Theories Link to Higher-Order Thinking Skills

The neurological findings about information processing in autism along with cognitive theories of autism explain some of the barriers autistic readers face in the process of comprehending text. As you read this information, **Bloom's Taxonomy** of human learning may come to mind. Rightly so!

Bloom's Taxonomy is a classification of learning skills, from simple to complex. This information is relevant to all types of learning, including the active reading process. It has been a part of teacher training in the US since the 1960's.

- The original cognitive taxonomy (1956) was revised in 2001 by David Krathwohl and Lorin Anderson (Wilson 2016).
- The 2001 Cognitive Taxonomy is shown in Figure 4.8 and is read from the bottom up.

Figure 4.8

Bloom's Taxonomy: Cognitive Skills

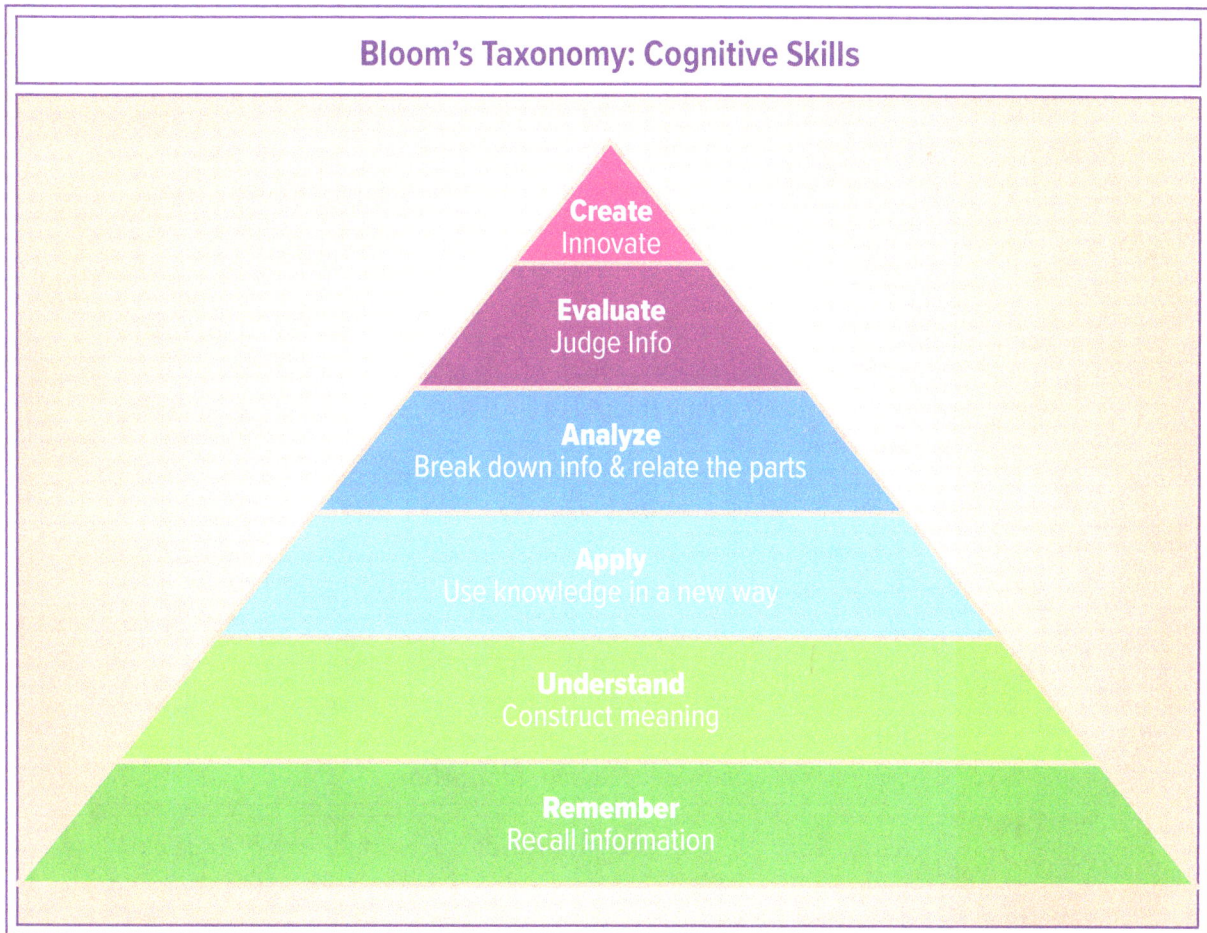

The explanations of Cognitive Theories and Bloom's Taxonomy also bring **HOTS** to mind, **h**igher **o**rder **t**hinking **s**kills (Johnson & Lamb 2007).

- HOTS are cognitive or complex thinking skills that go beyond basic knowledge.
- The categories in Bloom's Taxonomy match closely to different HOTS skills
- Figure 4.9 links higher-order thinking skills to each level of Bloom's taxonomy.

Figure 4.9

Synthesis of Bloom's Cognitive Categories and Higher Order Thinking Skills	
Bloom's Category	**Higher Order Thinking Skills Examples of What Students Are Asked to Do Including Complex Information Processing Demands**
Remember	Retrieve information, recall, name, identify, list, define, state, choose, or recite
Understand	Restate, discuss, explain, interpret, paraphrase, review, show, summarize, interpret, infer, classify, differentiate, recognize main ideas, draw conclusions
Apply	Use, solve, predict, explain, organize, relate, interpret, show, execute, demonstrate, illustrate, interview; create a presentation, dramatization, model, or simulation; problem solve
Analyze	Compare, contrast, distinguish, differentiate, discriminate, classify, categorize, organize, attribute, reflect, infer, deduce, experiment, inspect, dissect, detect, probe, understand perspective, separate fact from opinion, separate relevant from irrelevant information
Evaluate	Assess, check, judge, argue, defend, disagree, criticize or critique opinions or arguments, look for inconsistencies in information and faults in reasoning, reflect
Create	Combine, compose, produce, develop, synthesize, invent, hypothesize, construct a model, and role-play

The discussion to this point on the neurology and cognitive profile of autistic learners explains why HOTS are more difficult for learners with autism. How many of these skills are needed for reading comprehension, especially as students progress from elementary school through college and beyond? Yes, all of them.

Here's a reminder of the steps in the **active reading process** to view with a new lens:

- Access prior knowledge
- Recognize main ideas
- Summarize information
- Understand social situations and relationships
- Understand the emotions of characters
- Use text clues and cues to make connections, predict, and draw conclusions
- Monitor understanding while reading
- Create a *gestalt* or *whole meaning* of the text
- Store the information in memory
- Retrieve when needed.

Synthesis

A foundational premise of this book was presented in Chapter 1: "The demands of the active reading process may present a mismatch with the cognitive skills and core deficit areas often seen in autism and, therefore, be at the root of the comprehension problems." The explanations offered to this point about specific developmental and neurological features of autism demonstrate why this statement is true.

The areas of need for readers with autism are clearly complex and unique, particularly when compared to those of readers who struggle for other reasons. This is why hyperlexic readers need additional support to develop skills in all five comprehension areas: literal, inferential, critical, affective, and lexical.

From Theory to Reality

The connection between the cognitive features of autism and comprehension problems in all of these areas is more than theoretical: **it has been documented in research**.

- Some studies pinpoint where comprehension breakdown occurs in the reading process.
- Other studies describe specific cognitive processes that are interrupted or disordered in readers with autism.

- Difficulties are seen at the word, sentence, and text level, as well as in the use of comprehension strategies.
- Figure 4.10 summarizes key findings from research about documented comprehension breakdown in good decoders with autism.

Figure 4.10

Findings from Research about Readers with Autism and/or Hyperlexia	
Study	**Findings**
Brown et al. 2013	Readers with autism have difficulty understanding text with high social content, such as narratives
Emerich, Creaghead, Grether, Murray & Grasha 2003; Treichel, Dukes, Barisnikov & Samson 2021	• Readers with autism did poorly in understanding humor because humor requires inference, abstraction, and the integration of information across a narrative to create a new, coherent meaning • Several processes are involved in getting a joke, including thinking flexibly to reinterpret the original understanding of the information • When a punch line is delivered, individuals with autism had difficulty understanding the surprise ending, also called *resolving incongruity*
Lucas & Norbury 2014	Skilled word recognition and oral language skills are not sufficient to support comprehension for children with autism
Nation & Norbury 2005	Readers with autism failed to integrate information within the context of the text or from external knowledge
Grigorenko et al. 2003	There is a link between poor comprehension of written material seen in hyperlexia and poor comprehension of oral language (a double disadvantage)
Holman 2004	Readers with hyperlexia do not use oral language (or listen to themselves when reading) to help process meaning
Holman 2004	• The readers with hyperlexia did not follow the second step in the decoding process • The reader needs to *recode*, or "activate the word meaning in memory," and then apply his or her own knowledge

Findings from Research about Readers with Autism and/or Hyperlexia	
Study	**Findings**
Holman 2004	• Readers who do not integrate fail to form meaningful ideas, or achieve comprehension • The failure to integrate meaning through recoding may cause problems with long-term memory, or lack of knowledge
Minshew, Goldstein & Siegel, 1995	Individuals with autism were significantly impaired in tasks that required them to use complex or interpretative language abilities.
Myles et al. 2002; Nation 2005	Difficulties were documented with **semantics** (word meaning), **morphosyntax** (rules of word formation and word relationships), and **vocabulary**
Myles et al. 2002; Nation 2005	Difficulty understanding figurative and abstract language, including idioms
Sadoski & Paivio 2007	• Comprehension is enhanced when information is "dual coded," that is, stored simultaneously in both the verbal and nonverbal language systems • Individuals with autism may not dual-code or cross-reference information efficiently
Sorenson Duncan et al. 2021	Oral language, vocabulary, morphology, syntax, pragmatics, and listening comprehension are essential elements to support reading comprehension in good decoders with autism
Truch 2004, p. 10	The breakdown seen in hyperlexia is "the inability to link language with mental imagery and/or the inability to recode those images back into language in an appropriate fashion."
Vogindroukas et al. 2003	• Subjects focused on details in a picture and missed the meaning of the big picture • Readers with autism have problems using word meaning to organize, categorize, and recall words
Wahlberg 2001a	Limited vocabulary, problems with homophones, only knowing one meaning for words with multiple meanings, and failing to use context to understand the meaning of a word were part of a problem in interpreting ambiguous language

Findings from Research about Readers with Autism and/or Hyperlexia	
Study	**Findings**
Wahlberg 2001a	• Readers understood sentences in isolation. • They appeared unable to incorporate previously learned knowledge as they read. • As a result, they failed to derive appropriate meaning from a sentence.
Wahlberg 2001a	Readers with autism failed to clarify the meaning of ambiguous text
Wahlberg & Magliano 2004	Readers with autism were able to use cues in text (like an informative title) to activate general background knowledge, yet they could not put the knowledge to use to interpret or remember specific information

Teaching Methods

Many readers with autism **do not benefit as expected** from classroom instruction, even when evidence-based practices are used (Vaughn & Fletcher 2012; Al Otaiba & Fuchs 2002). This is likely due to the effects of the core symptoms of autism and related difficulties, including complex information processing.

- Students with autism go through whole and small group classroom activities just like everyone else.
- While the other students have taken in the information, the student with autism may have gaps in processing and understanding.
- These gaps may not be obvious in lower grades. However, the gaps can affect the student's foundation and readiness for independent reading tasks in upper grades.
- This may be especially true for hyperlexic readers in general education classrooms.

Our discussion and a review of the key research literature leads to a clear conclusion: **To be successful readers and gain meaning when reading, exposure to the curriculum is not enough.** As reading expert Joseph Torgesen advises regarding all at-risk readers, **"the instruction must be more explicit, more intensive, and more supportive than instruction typically is"** (2004 n.p.).

Students with hyperlexia need explicit instruction and individualized interventions to support the development of specific, essential comprehension skills. I extracted the skills listed in Figures 4.11 through 4.14 from findings from the research and literature available on this topic, including many of the studies mentioned in multiple chapters.

Basic Foundational Skills

Language-Based Skills

HOTS

These skills, organized into three categories, lead to true literacy: the ability to gain meaning and benefit from what was read. In addition, these areas are clearly areas of concern for readers with autism who struggle with **both** comprehension and decoding.

Figure 4.11

Areas in Need of Explicit Instruction for Readers with Hyperlexia		
Basic, foundational comprehension skills (prerequisites for many other comprehension skills and strategies)		
Find factual information	Identify the main idea	Separate relevant from irrelevant ideas
Summarize main ideas or plot (retell)	Organize main ideas or plot in order (sequence)	Paraphrase
Understand cause and effect	Draw conclusions	Predict
Ask questions about the text	Infer ideas not stated explicitly	Answer questions about text

Figure 4.12

Areas in Need of Explicit Instruction for Readers with Hyperlexia		
Language-based skills		
Build vocabulary	Understand double meanings (jokes, irony, sarcasm)	Categorize objects in terms of concepts
Know and use multiple meanings of words	Understand figurative and non-literal meaning (idioms, metaphors, indirect requests)	Use context clues to understand unknown words
Recognize the connotation of synonyms	Use context to read homographs	Recode, or activate word meaning in memory
Note: In addition to vocabulary, developing the language components of morphology, syntax, pragmatics, and listening comprehension is critical for reading comprehension in autism.		

Figure 4.13

Areas in Need of Explicit Instruction for Readers with Hyperlexia	
Active, higher-order thinking/comprehension skills	
Self-monitor understanding	Interact with the text
Use different comprehension strategies while reading	Activate and draw upon relevant prior/background knowledge
Preview/prepare to read	Clarify/resolve ambiguity
React/relate/identify personally to the material	Read purposefully in an organized manner
Integrate the meaning of one idea with the next to create a coherent message	Shift thinking while reading (revise understanding)
Code information in the nonverbal system—create mental representations (*imagens*)	Code information through the verbal system (*logogens*); create representations of text in words
Use organization of text and story structure	Synthesize: tie details together to get the big picture or gist
Separate facts from opinions	

Image from Easy-Peasy.AI

Figure 4.14

Explicit Instruction in these HOTS Is Needed to Understand Narratives	
Create a situational model of a story	Track the goals and plans of characters
Visualize (create an internal representation of the material)	Understand the relationship between characters
Understand the author's intention	Analyze characters and their intentions
Understand how story events relate, including cause and effect	Apply known information to the story to interpret the action or characters
Sequence story events	Understand plot twists
Recognize false beliefs	Recognize deception in characters
Understand characters' feelings and perspectives	

Summary

Hyperlexia is a reading disability closely associated with autism. Students with hyperlexia are likely to have multiple areas of need and require more support and explicit instruction than is often recognized.

- It's reasonable to propose that young readers with autism and hyperlexia should, at a minimum, be considered **at-risk learners** in the area of reading comprehension and vocabulary.
- In addition, hyperlexic readers of all ages are likely to need tailored support in the related areas of writing and organization of ideas.

After reading this, the following question may come to mind: "Don't most readers with disabilities have some kind of trouble with comprehension? Why all the concern for readers with autism and hyperlexia?" Here's why:

- Autistic readers are flying under the radar and rarely ring alarm bells!
- As described in this chapter, autistic individuals have challenges in thinking and learning due to **multiple** features of autism.

- The cognitive profile seen in autism is brain-based, multifaceted, and rooted in cognitive and developmental differences.
- These differences can pose unique, complex challenges for autistic students, both in learning and using higher-level thinking skills.

The field of reading intervention is primarily tailored to the needs of readers with learning disabilities. This area has been established and well-researched over decades.

- Most educators are very informed about the literacy needs of these students. They're trained and ready to use proven intervention methods based on extensive research (particularly for dyslexia).
- The same thing **cannot be said for** intervening with readers with autism, including those with hyperlexia.

Understanding, research, and training are out of sync with the tsunami of students with autism now attending school. There has been unprecedented growth in the number of documented cases of autism spectrum disorder (CDC 2025). This situation creates a problem of **focus and timing**.

- Universities and teacher training programs tend to have a minimal focus on the unique profile of autistic readers or proven comprehension interventions for them.
- Educational professionals are recognizing the need for more research and attention to this group of learners (Nation & Norbury 2004).

Conclusion

This discussion, together with all that is known about autism and findings from research on reading comprehension, **verifies a genuine cause for concern**. We all need to raise awareness and find appropriate, effective ways to help these struggling readers, who do not benefit from the strategies used to teach reading to other populations.

The link between the diagnostic and neurological features of autism with language, literacy, and comprehension makes another hopeful and positive point clear: **All efforts to address the challenges in autism may also have a positive impact on reading**

comprehension! Gains made in socialization, communication, language, behavior and even sensory processing can improve literacy and comprehension.

- Gains in language concepts and processes can have a positive effect on understanding what is read.
- Therapies to address cognitive issues, such as theory of mind, organization of thought, executive function, and central coherence, may produce gains in reading comprehension.
- The suggestions and activities for intervention in this book, found in Chapters 6 through 9, are designed to effectively address the multiple complex needs that have been identified for readers with autism and hyperlexia.

A key step remains before remediation begins: identifying and defining the needs of an individual reader. Even when poor comprehension is masked by strong decoding, there are numerous ways to pinpoint specific difficulties. Careful assessment will help identify each learner's profile of strengths and needs. This subject is explored in Chapter 5.

CHAPTER 5
Masking and Unmasking: Identifying Comprehension Issues

It would be wonderful to be able to point to a specialized, standardized reading test designed to get to the bottom of the complex comprehension and vocabulary challenges experienced by readers with autism. Unfortunately, the ideal assessment does not yet exist. In the absence of such a tool, this chapter provides guidance to help with the identification and evaluation of individuals with autism and comprehension issues.

This chapter explores these topics:
- How to identify signs and patterns of comprehension difficulty.
- Concerns that appear from about fourth grade up.
- Informal, formal, and novel assessment ideas that may be used by teachers, reading and resource specialists, educational therapists, speech pathologists, other educational professionals, and parents to gather more information.

Masking and Unmasking Comprehension Issues

One might think that assessment in the area of comprehension would be clear-cut. However, when it comes to readers with hyperlexia, the reality is far from it. One of the reasons is the uneven profile of development in autism.
- Comprehension issues might be suspected in dysfluent readers who struggle to decode, but *not* in students who appear to be strong readers and on track in the early grades.
- **Strong skills in some areas can mask or hide weaknesses in others.**

Students with hyperlexia often test in the average range on many types of language or academic tests, yet still have a comprehension problem. The result is a "masking effect." (Griswold, Barnhill, Myles, Hagiwara & Simpson, 2002; Holman 2004; Nation and colleagues 2006; Newman and colleagues 2007).

- Students who decode well but have comprehension problems can fly under the radar for a long time when task demands match the learner's level of decoding abilities, memory, and comprehension of basic facts (especially in the early grades).
- In other cases superficial understanding is hidden when students give short or limited responses to questions, and when they are retaught at home or in private tutoring.

The way comprehension is measured can also hide some issues, rather than highlighting them. This includes practices such as:

- Asking mostly literal comprehension questions on classroom tests.
- Averaging scores in class work or assignments.
- Measuring general reading skills rather than specific comprehension skills.
- Averaging subtest scores or using composite scores on standardized tests.

In a real-life example, a student once took a standardized reading test where her reading vocabulary scored at the 81st percentile. This meant that her vocabulary was equal to or higher than 81% of the population and 19% of the population had a higher score than she did on that measure. Her passage comprehension score was at the 1st percentile, meaning that 99% of the population had a higher score than she did on that measure.

- When these two numbers were averaged together, the resulting score was 41, which was considered in the "average range."
- Therefore the student's reading was not considered a problem for someone of her age and grade level.

Unmasking Comprehension Issues from Fourth Grade and Up

The heightened demands that begin in fourth grade help explain the shift from apparent ease to more of a struggle for good decoders with comprehension problems.

- There are a number of reasons why this is the case.
- Twelve key ideas are summarized in Figure 5.1, The Fourth-Grade Turning Point.

Figure 5.1

The Fourth-Grade Turning Point
1. Learn to read vs. read to learn 2. Reading better, reading more (or not)
3. Mismatch between skill sets and task demands 4. Complexity
5. Developmental timelines 6. Peers catch up
7. More homework 8. Demand for independence
9. Changes in instruction/setting 10. Need to respond to instruction
11. Reading affecting math 12. Social aspects of group work

Students who are currently beyond fourth grade may have experienced difficulties with the factors listed here. If earlier difficulties were not understood and addressed, they will continue to affect comprehension and academic skills for a person of any age.

- The difficulties may intensify in junior high school, high school, and college.
- A learner with autism can feel stressed or frustrated when the demands of school suddenly become too much for them.

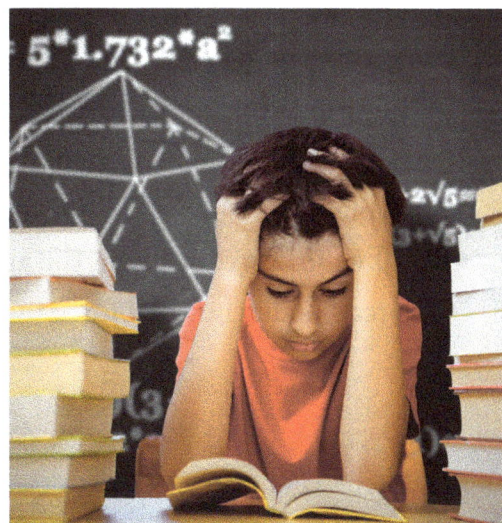

An older student or an adult reader may present with limited understanding compared to their level of decoding skills, cognitive potential, or strong performance in certain subject areas.

- The difficulties detected through close examination of the person's fourth-grade reading experiences may be revealing.
- Appendix A provides an expanded explanation of these factors.

Insights into Unmasking

As a reminder of the discussion from Chapter 1, **there are five types of reading comprehension, and no one standardized test measures them all.** In fact, some assessments don't actually measure up when it comes to measuring comprehension, especially for this population (Cutting & Scarborough 2006).

- For students in fourth grade and up, the assessment of reading must go beyond tests of word recognition.
- In fact, Nation and her colleagues (2006) offer a "cautionary note," explaining that "reliance on tests of word recognition is likely to overestimate children's reading competence in other areas, most notably reading comprehension skills" (p. 918).
- Therefore, determination of understanding should be at the **passage** or **text level**, which is most revealing of true understanding, as compared to the word, sentence, or the paragraph level.

A study by Newman and colleagues (2007) compared readers with autism and hyperlexia to readers with autism and no hyperlexia and to typical peers.

- They found that readers with autism and hyperlexia did well on many standardized tests of reading achievement and that these results **masked** their comprehension problems.
- To be more precise about the areas of difficulty, the researchers suggest using tests of reading fluency that force the reader to **access meaning while reading**.

Several comprehension measures use a procedure called *cloze*, where the person being tested is asked to fill in a missing word in a sentence or paragraph from a choice of several options.

- Surprisingly, Newman and colleagues (2007) found that adults with autism **could fill in the blank correctly**, but when probed, it was clear that they **did not actually understand** the meaning of the completed text.
- The resulting test scores were in the normal range, **despite known comprehension difficulties**.

Given this reality, **there is a need to develop new, cohesive comprehension measures that examine working memory, higher-level language skills, the use of comprehension monitoring, and understanding ideas across text** (Newman and colleagues 2007).

Formal and Informal Assessment Methods

Various informal and formal ways to identify, define, or measure comprehension difficulties may be used, depending on the needs and circumstances of the learner and the adults working with them. Evaluation must go beyond the surface of good decoding or basic writing, to understanding the skills that are and are not intact in the meaningful processes of reading.

The next sections of this chapter present ten options for unmasking comprehension issues, shown in Figure 5.2.

- Some of the methods can be used by parents or professionals.
- Other options require specialized training or materials, as noted.

Once comprehension issues begin to reveal themselves, it requires creativity, sensitivity, and cooperation on the part of those who will be gathering information to address the students' needs.

Figure 5.2

Ideas for Unmasking Comprehension Issues
5A. Documenting and reporting concerns 5B. Homework trials 5C. Curriculum-based assessment
5D. Use of state standards 5E. Retelling 5F. Measures of vocabulary 5G. Reading inventories
5H. Diagnostic reading tests from remedial programs 5I. Community college placement tests 5J. Standardized measures

5A Documenting and Reporting Concerns

Many struggling students with autism keep themselves glued together at school but come apart at home. Difficulties are often seen when the student has to work independently, such as doing homework.

- Many parents have to make extraordinary efforts to help the student complete their homework on a daily basis.

- Parents may wonder why their bright child is having such a hard time and may even hire a tutor.

Educators need to know about parental concerns and what is going on at home. Parents should speak up about changes and challenges in the student's ability to work independently, problems with book reports and projects, and the amount of time and support needed to complete homework. Parents can:

- Provide teachers and other professionals with examples of material or assignments that are problematic.

- Present before-and-after work samples, showing what the student could do independently and what s/he was able to accomplish once the parent intervened.
- Track the number of minutes or hours the student needed to finish their work.

Any new emotional or behavioral issues related to school or schoolwork, or worsening of behaviors at home, should also be brought to the attention of school staff, including the school psychologist.

- A change in the student's frustration level, anxiety, anger, self-esteem, mood, and so on may be side effects of the underlying comprehension difficulties.
- Concerning signs include crying over homework or projects, refusing to do homework, saying, "I'm stupid," losing sleep, or ruminating (excessive worrying) about assignments.
- Some children may begin to say that they hate school and don't want to go. In some cases, they get headaches or feel ill from stress.

Sometimes students are able to talk about what is bothering them.

- They're often aware of their lack of understanding and may be able to describe it.
- This information should be shared, and the student voice should be listened to.

In some cases, the classroom teacher or other school staff notice the signs of a comprehension issue and want to make an appointment to speak with parents.

- This may be done in an informal conference or an IEP (individualized education program) meeting.
- Staff can share information about their concerns, present specific examples, and find out more about the homework situation to determine where the student is struggling.
- Parents and staff can share feedback on a more frequent basis using email or texting (if possible).

Sometimes parents go to a private specialist outside the school system in an effort to get to the bottom of their child's difficulties.

- They may consult with a psychologist, reading specialist, speech pathologist, educational therapist, or other professional.
- Specialists can collect information, conduct various types of assessments, and work with the school and parents to identify and address the student's issues.

Importantly, when signs of distress begin to appear, they should not be minimized. Rather, attention should be given to an unexpected or surprising pattern of learning as soon as it is noticed. Recognizing difficulties and remediating them through explicit instruction is the key for readers who need help to acquire higher-level comprehension skills.

5B Homework Trials

Often there is a difference in what a student with autism can do in a structured setting, such as school, and the work s/he can produce independently at home, no matter how helpful parents try to be. When parents describe a stressful, laborious daily routine for homework or project completion, the teacher or school team can set up a "homework trial."

Here are three suggestions for how a homework trial can be used to help identify comprehension issues.

1. **Twenty-minute limit.** The parent uses a timer (quietly or overtly) and has the student work as independently as possible on an assignment, offering minimal assistance.
   - The parent or student marks the paper after the 20 minutes are up to show how much work the student was able to complete independently.
   - This can be done in any or all subject areas for about a week, so the teacher can review the content to determine what material was not understood.
2. **Homework at school.** Sometimes seeing is believing. In a homework trial at school, a teacher, resource specialist, or reading specialist agrees to watch/help the student to do his homework in one subject area for 20 minutes a day for a week.
   - This can be done during the school day or after school, depending on schedules.

     o The educational professional should intervene in a limited manner.

     o The goal is to see where support is needed and find out why the student struggles to work independently.

3. **Projects at school.** Some students can manage homework but cannot handle independent projects assigned as homework, such as book reports.

     o Many times parents relate that they have to reread and explain the meaning of an entire book to the student, page by page, even though the student is able to decode the material.

     o A teacher, resource specialist, or other specialist can agree to do an in-school project for diagnostic purposes.

     o The student can work with the teacher or in a specialist's room to do the project so the educator can observe the nature of the struggle (understanding instructions, understanding content, organizing ideas, understanding steps of the process, staying on task, etc.).

To conduct a homework trial, the team can decide which option to use, the length of the trial, and other logistics.

- The team should agree that the student's grades will not be penalized for any incomplete work during the trial period.
- The student will also need reassurance to know that the teacher gives permission for the plan. The student needs to know that s/he will not "get in trouble" in any way during the homework trial.

5C Curriculum-Based Assessment

In curriculum-based assessment, work samples from daily instruction are reviewed to identify which skills have been learned and which are underdeveloped.

- Materials from language and literature, such as daily class work, chapter tests, and writing samples, can be reviewed to pinpoint the material and tasks that are difficult for the student.
- A student's work from the fall can also be compared to work from the spring , to see if the student is struggling as the academic year progresses and the material becomes more difficult.

- Figure 5.3, Finding the Pattern of Errors, provides some insights into using curriculum-based assessment with hyperlexic students.

Figure 5.3

Finding the Pattern of Errors
One key to a qualitative review of work samples is to "undo" the averaging of scores to identify a particular **pattern of errors**.
• This involves breaking apart measures of reading and literature by separating scores that demonstrate clear mastery or consistent strength (such as spelling, mechanics, etc.) from content scores that are lower.
• Look **separately** at scores for tasks requiring comprehension skills, such as finding the main idea, separating main ideas from details, drawing conclusions, inferring, comparing, understanding the motives of the characters, recognizing the intention of the author, and so on.
• Chapter tests in literature often delineate skill sets that are being tested. Separating out the scores for comprehension tasks and examining them separately is a good opportunity to see the pattern of errors.
Teacher-made reading quizzes also offer an opportunity to take a closer look. The teacher may generate ten questions about a story, with seven to eight factual questions and two to three inferential or higher-order thinking questions.
• A student with autism may consistently score 70% or 80% on such quizzes by getting **only** the factual questions correct.
• **The passing grade can hide the fact that the student misses 80% to 100% of the inferential questions, 100% of the time!**
• If a student gets an inferential question correct after explanation and discussion in class, it becomes a question of recall rather than inference; this needs to be kept in mind when looking at the student's success with these types of questions.
• Parents, teachers, and specialists who are wondering about the comprehension skills of a student can go back and review tests and quizzes to see if this pattern is present: correct answers for literal or concrete questions and errors in questions of inference or HOTS.

Finding the Pattern of Errors

Examining the quality, complexity, and cohesion of writing tasks when the student writes about something that was read can be revealing.

- First drafts, in particular, can show what the student understands on his or her own.

- This can reveal gaps in understanding, such as finding the main idea or drawing conclusions.

5D Using State Standards

Each state department of education creates state standards, that are guidelines that define the skills, knowledge, and concepts that students should acquire at each grade level in all academic areas. As part of an informal assessment process, parents and professionals can use the state standards for reading and writing to do a "skills inventory."

- Forty-three states have adopted Common Core State Standards, which are designed to create consistency in what is taught in schools across the country.
- The remaining seven states created their own standards.

Reviewing the standards is useful for identifying the comprehension skills students are expected to acquire each year, including those for literature, language, and vocabulary.

- Most school districts provide the standards to parents each school year.
- Report cards are often tied to students' progress toward the standards.
- Some schools do regularly-scheduled computerized tests to track each child's progress toward the standards, using a system such as **I-Ready**.

As an informal assessment, it's often a good idea to start with the standards for kindergarten, to check mastery of skills that students are expected to learn when they start school, regardless of the age of the person of interest.

- Parents and teachers can check off skills they have seen the student demonstrate and mark skills they think the student struggles with.
- An objective way to confirm these perspectives is to collect information (e.g., report cards, work samples, or interactive questioning) to determine if the student demonstrates mastery of the standard in question.

Every state posts its standards online, so be sure to check the standards for your state.

- Figures 5.4 and 5.5 are examples of the Common Core English Language Arts standards for narrative literature for Kindergarten and fourth grade.
- These examples illustrate how basic skills from an early grade are built upon and expanded as school progresses.
- Additional examples of standards for Informational Text, Vocabulary, and Speaking and Listening are found at the end of Appendix B.

Figure 5.4

Common Core Standards for English Language Arts

Kindergarten Standards for Literature

Key Ideas and Details

1. With prompting and support, ask and answer questions about key details in a text.
2. With prompting and support, retell familiar stories including key details.
3. With prompting and support, identify characters, settings, and major events in a story.

Craft and Structure

4. Ask and answer questions about unknown words in a text.
5. Recognize common types of texts (e.g., storybooks, poems).
6. With prompting and support, name the author and illustrator of a story and **define** the role of each in telling the story.

Integration of Knowledge and Ideas

7. With prompting and support, describe the relationship between illustrations and the story in which they appear (e.g. what moment in a story an illustration depicts).
8. (N/A- Parallel skill for informational text is not applicable to literature).
9. With prompting and support, compare and contrast the adventures and experiences of characters and familiar stories.

Range of Reading and Level of Text Complexity

10. Actively engage in group reading activities with purpose and understanding.

Figure 5.5

Common Core Standards for English Language Arts
Grade 4 Standards for Literature

Key Ideas and Details

1. Refer to details and examples in a text when explaining what the text says explicitly and when drawing inferences from the text.
2. Determine a theme of a story, drama, or poem from details in the text; summarize the text.
3. Describe in depth a character, setting, or event in a story or drama, drawing on specific details in the text (e.g., a character's thoughts, words, or actions).

Craft and Structure

4. Determine the meaning of words and phrases as they are used in a text, including those that allude to significant characters found in mythology (e.g., Herculean).
5. Explain major differences between poems, drama, and prose, and refer to the structural elements of poems (e.g., verse, rhythm, meter,) and drama (e.g. cast of characters, settings, descriptions, dialogue, stage directions) when writing or speaking about a text.
6. Compare and contrast the point of view from which different stories are narrated, including the difference between first- and third-person narrations.

Integration of Knowledge and Ideas

7. Make connections between the text of a story or drama and a visual or oral presentation of the text, identifying where each version reflects specific descriptions and directions in the text.
8. (N/A- Parallel skill for informational text is not applicable to literature).
9. Compare and contrast the treatment of similar themes and topics (opposition of good and evil, patterns of events, the quest) in stories, myths, and traditional literature from different cultures.

Range of Reading and Level of Text Complexity

10. By the end of the year, read and comprehend literature, including stories, dramas, and poetry in the grades four to five text complexity band proficiently, with scaffolding as needed at the high end of the range.

Following Up on a Standards Review

Needs for a particular student can be defined as skills or standards that should have been mastered but are not consistently demonstrated.

- Once there is agreement on what the student's needs are, the focus should be on explicitly teaching the *earliest* skills that are missing.
- Addressing basic skills such as "finding the main idea" will create a foundation of essential prerequisite skills that can be used to build more complex skills (such as writing a summary).

If the student has an IEP (individualized education program), goals may be written for any standard that was not mastered from a previous grade level. In most states, a computerized goal bank is available to teachers, with an array of suggested goals tied to each state standard.

- These are excellent starting points for writing a precise goal for a particular student.
- Goals are not usually written for skills that are worked on during the course of the current grade level because all students are expected to learn the grade level standards with a minimum of 70% mastery.

5E Retelling

Assessment experts Salvia, Ysseldyke and Witmer cut to the chase about assessing comprehension. In essence, they say if you want to know if someone understands, ask them to read and then tell you about what they read (2017). **Retelling** requires the use of higher-level, integrative language and thinking skills, making it one of the best indicators of comprehension difficulty (Thorne & Coggins 2007).

- Depending on the age of the student, interrelated comprehension skills needed to retell a story include recognizing the main idea, separating relevant from irrelevant details, sequencing events, paraphrasing, summarizing, drawing conclusions, and inferencing.
- Retelling tasks can also show whether the reader can identify elements of a plot, describe character interactions, take the perspective of the characters, and recognize the intent of the author, compared to expected skills for the grade level.
- In addition, expanded responses often include important details or insights.

Looking closely at a student's ability to perform retelling tasks in school and at home can be revealing. Probing for understanding by asking additional questions during retelling is a chance to go beyond factual or superficial understanding.

- Even if the student can give a correct answer, when probed, s/he may have difficulty explaining *why* it is correct, or *how* s/he knows it is true.
- Additional probing can also verify whether the reader understood the gist or message of the story.
- Comparing the quality of the responses to other children in the same grade who have similarly developed verbal skills can also be helpful.

Basic or limited responses during retelling indicate a possible comprehension issue.

- If the response is a **simple restatement** of the facts, this can indicate that the student can repeat back things that s/he remembers.
- Repeating what was read is not a guarantee that the person actually understood what was read, particularly if s/he is parroting back the words or sentences.
- **Paraphrasing, or retelling in one's own words, is a more reliable indicator of understanding than restating.**

Retelling may also reveal issues such as the literal interpretation of language or difficulty with **non-literal meaning,** including idioms, sarcasm, humor, or figurative language. A reading specialist, language specialist, resource specialist, or educational therapist should be consulted when a student has difficulties retelling.

Retelling and Visualization

One study that included students with autism showed that while they were able to retell, the **quality of their retelling was significantly different** compared to that of controls.

- The children with autism included more "bizarre" elements in the retell than other children in the study.
- The researchers concluded that "some autistic subjects appeared to have difficulty grasping the story as a representation of meaningful events" (Loveland, McEvoy, Tunali, & Kelley 1990, p. 21).

Readers who have difficulty retelling may also have problems visualizing while reading or being read to. Remember that the reader with autism may *not* create and store a visual or mental image while reading or listening.

- A lack of visualization skills can cause processing delays, interfere with understanding text, and limit what the reader can remember and describe when retelling or writing.
- As my son Tom describes it, with no visual images in mind when asked to retell, the reader with autism may **draw a blank**.
- Paivio calls this the **failure to create visual images, or imagens** (Sadoski & Paivio 2007).

Temple Grandin is an autistic professor and author who is famous for describing how she thinks in pictures. I listened at a conference when she shared her process of "visualization" during reading.

- When she reads the word *tree* she opens the visual file in her brain and pulls up a Christmas tree. She holds this image in her head as she reads, until she comes across a description like *colored leaves*.
- This causes her to realize that a Christmas tree is not the correct visual. She puts the Christmas tree back in the image file, pulls up a tree with colored leaves, and continues reading.
- This unique method of visualizing is definitely different than creating a custom-made mental image or **situation model** to match a specific description in text (which is what most readers do).

Appendix E describes the Lindamood Bell Visualizing and Verbalizing (V/V®) Program, which is designed to teach visualization. This commercial option may be appropriate for some readers with autism and/or hyperlexia.

Figure 5.6 suggests ways that speech and language professionals can help assess retelling skills. **Identifying language-based areas of need is critical for improving comprehension of text!**

Figure 5.6

How Speech and Language Professionals Can Help
Speech and language pathologists (SLPs) can be of great help in the assessment of oral retelling.
• Retelling can be measured informally in conversation, including prompting with the phrase, "Tell me more," to see whether the retell is superficial or based solely on memory. • Analyzing the language produced during an oral narrative can reveal both *coherence* (how informative the retell is) and *cohesion* (the integration of the information) (Thorne & Coggins 2007).
Two assessment tools for retell favored by many SLPs are the Test of Narrative Language (TNL) (Gillam & Pearson 2004, 2017) and the SNAP, the Strong Narrative Assessment Procedure (Strong et al. 1998).
• The TNL includes picture cues that can be used for narrative retelling, along with literal and inferential comprehension questions to determine how children use language to retell. • The SNAP can be used to determine if a student can retell a story in his or her own words after hearing it on tape while reading along. The quality of the retell and responses to comprehension questions are analyzed according to specific guidelines to reveal language and other difficulties.
Asking a student to make up and tell an original story to go along with a series of pictures can also be a useful evaluation tool because creating a new story (an oral narrative) is a complex and cognitively demanding task.
If the language and concepts are very simple, if the student does not expand on ideas, and/ or if the sequence is disorganized, there is likely to be cause for concern.

Be aware that some students may give elaborate responses when retelling, especially when using photographs or pictures.

- Autistic individuals sometimes borrow from a video or movie they like and weave it into their story.
- Check with parents or others who know the student well before assuming that a long and complex explanation is original.

For example, one parent saw a red flag when it was reported that her son's retell about pictures was mostly about a Miner and a Jeweler.

- The person doing the evaluation was very impressed with the complexity, creativity, and originality shown in the retelling.
- The parent knew that the characters and plot were borrowed from the child's favorite video game.

In cases like this, it should **not** be assumed that the student is intentionally misleading or plagiarizing.

- It is more likely that the student made a connection between something in the picture and something preferred and familiar, and takes the story in that direction.
- The bottom line is that this type of retelling can create a false impression of competence when in fact the student wasn't able to create a cohesive story without borrowing.

Writing as Retelling

For upper-grade students or even adults, retelling through writing can be as useful an indicator of comprehension as oral retelling.

- Difficulty with prewriting activities, such as brainstorming and completing graphic organizers, can indicate limited understanding of the material that was read.
- First-draft work samples and independent efforts with book reports and story analysis can be reviewed for complexity, coherence, and cohesion of writing.

5F Measures of Vocabulary

Gathering information to understand how evenly a student's vocabulary is developed can help assess the risk of comprehension problems. Several informal ways to measure vocabulary are described here. Some approaches require special tools or materials, as mentioned in the text below.

Curriculum-Based Assessment of Vocabulary

Determining whether a student understands the words in the material read in school is a good starting point to measure vocabulary. Teachers may do a pre-reading quiz in any subject to see how many grade-level words the student knows and understands.

- The results can be informally compared with the scores of other classmates with similar cognitive development.
- Rechecking for gains in understanding of the same words after class instruction can show if instruction was beneficial.

Parents can make a list of any unknown words encountered in homework or independent reading and share it with the teacher. It is helpful to note any surprising unknown words that other children the same age seem to know and use.

- An example is a junior high school student who asked her father what a *plot* was!
- Another teen did not know what the word *patriot* meant after completing the final project for a unit on the American Revolution.

It takes careful observation and discriminating assessment to identify the vocabulary issues in students with hyperlexia. This includes noting differences between test scores and the real-life use or applications of vocabulary.

- It is particularly important to go beyond the reader's superficial understanding to probe for meaning.
- Informal information gathering and concrete examples sometimes yield more useful information than formal testing.

Students with hyperlexia are likely to have particular difficulty understanding words with **multiple meanings** (like *lean* or *force*), words that can be nouns or verbs (*waste, pound,* and *batter*), words that look the same but mean different things depending on the context (homographs like *lead* and *read*), and words with connotation or implied meaning (like *slender* and *scrawny*).

Vocabulary Screening Using Homographs

Homographs are words that are spelled or written the same but pronounced differently depending on the use and meaning. An example is, "She had a *tear* in her eye because she had a *tear* in her dress." Problems with understanding words in context can be detected using homographs.

She had a *TEAR* in her eye...

...because she had a *TEAR* in her dress.

- When reading aloud, most readers will decide on a correct pronunciation for a homograph based on the context.
- They will self-correct if an error interferes with the meaning of the text.

One study found that individuals with autism fared poorly in identifying the correct pronunciation of homographs while reading sentences.

- The results suggested that "individuals with autism **do not use sentence context** in order to correctly identify which meaning of the homograph is correct" (Wahlberg 2001a, p. 19).
- A teacher-made screening using homographs can show whether a reader is integrating the words in the sentences, self-monitoring their comprehension, and using corrective strategies when a mistake is made.

Conversation Skills, or Social Pragmatics

Children grow in knowledge and understanding through interaction with others.

- They expand their vocabulary from talking with and playing with other children.
- Children with autism are less likely to experience this boost in learning and vocabulary from other children due to the social, play, and communication features of autism (Vukelich and colleagues 2020).

To learn more about a child, observe their play, interaction, and conversation with other children.

- Notice if child's engagement is minimal, or if they are just an onlooker, watching other children play.
- Notice whether other children are trying to connect, and whether their efforts are successful.
- Consider what supports may be needed to help children expand their social interaction to expand their personal growth, language, and literacy.

5G Reading Inventories

An authentic way to assess a person's ability to determine the meaning of text is to listen while s/he reads text aloud, retells the story, and answers questions.

- This method is considered authentic because it involves an interactive reading task with grade-level literature, rather than the use of materials specially designed for testing.
- Many different **informal reading inventories** (IRIs) have been designed that provide a framework for a teacher or specialist to document and understand difficulties that occur during the reading process.

The use of a reading inventory may come close to what assessment experts Salvia, Ysseldyke and Witmer describe as the ideal way to understand what someone else understands: ask them to read and then tell about what they read in their own words (2017).

- This section describes a particular reading inventory that I've used, the QRI-5 (Leslie & Caldwell 2010), as an example of what IRIs may include and how they may be used for readers with hyperlexia.
- The QRI-5 provides passages to measure oral reading, silent reading, and listening comprehension.
  - The test passages are graded, or matched to readers' reading level from pre-primer through high school.
  - Passages become longer and more complex, matching increasing grade-level demands.

Measures in the QRI-5 include:

- **Concept questions** to ask before reading to determine whether the passage content is familiar or unfamiliar.
- A **pre-reading prediction test** to see how well the reader can predict what the story will be about based on the title. Guidelines are provided to score the predictions.
- **Retell scoring sheets** to record and count the number of factual and inferential ideas retold in unaided recall as a qualitative measure of comprehension.
- **Comprehension questions** to use after the passage is read, with clear distinction between explicit and implied questions, to help indicate the pattern of errors and any weakness in inference.

Observing how readers interact with the material when reading aloud is another way to directly experience their active reading process. This can provide insight into what strategies (if any) the reader uses to gain meaning, resolve ambiguity, or clarify.

- If readers do not "fix up" comprehension breakdowns or self-correct, it may indicate that they are not monitoring understanding or paying attention to context.
- Asking an upper-grade or secondary-school reader to "think aloud" and tell about the thinking processes s/he is using while reading helps evaluate the reader's monitoring of understanding and the quality of their comprehension.

Another benefit of an informal reading inventory such as the QRI-5 is that the understanding of passages with and without pictures can determine if the student is relying on external clues to support understanding. Finally, the QRI-5 measures unaided recall by providing checklists that can be marked to show what main ideas and details the reader can retell after hearing or reading the passage.

The QRI-5 can also help determine a reader's independent, instructional, and frustration levels for different types of material (like *narratives*, or stories, and *expository* text, such as content material in science and social studies). Figure 5.7 describes the reading levels, paraphrased from the QRI-5.

Figure 5.7

Reading Levels for QRI-5 Scores	
Independent Level *The student reads successfully with no assistance.*	Word accuracy in oral reading – 98% correct Comprehension questions – 90% correct or better
Instructional Level *The student reads at least at grade level.*	Word accuracy in oral reading – 90–95% correct Comprehension questions – 70% correct or better Student reads successfully with teacher assistance
Frustration Level *Grade level material is too difficult.*	Word accuracy in oral reading – less than 90% correct Comprehension questions – less than 70% correct Student is unable to read with accuracy or understand

For struggling readers with hyperlexia:
- Word accuracy in oral reading may be at or greater than 90% correct, while comprehension may be below 70%.
- The reader is likely to function at the frustration level with daily demands even when decoding is better than expected.

Informal reading inventories usually rely on the assumption that narrative material (like stories with a beginning, middle, and end) are easier to read than expository material (like textbooks and fact-based material).
- For readers with autism, however, the opposite is likely to be true.
- Depending on the subject area, readers with autism may be more familiar and have more ease with expository material.

The QRI-5 and similar measures may allow or prompt the reader to "look back" to find an answer in the text when s/he cannot answer a question about the passage. The comprehension score may be higher when the reader can search for the answer, but being able to find an answer is not necessarily the same as understanding the meaning of the passage.

- Therefore, allowing look-backs can overstate the reader's understanding.
- When discussing scores of reading inventories, it is best to be clear whether the score is reported **with or without look-backs.**

5H Diagnostic Reading Tests from Remedial Reading Programs

Diagnostic tests of reading comprehension tied to specialized remediation programs may be useful for readers with hyperlexia. Resource specialists, reading specialists, and educational therapists are often familiar with commercial programs designed to help readers with comprehension issues. Remedial programs usually include specially designed screening materials and test materials to pinpoint reading problems.

Diagnostic testing can identify areas in need of remediation or intervention. Based on the results of the diagnostic testing, the reader is placed into the level of a remedial program for direct instruction that is most suited to his or her present level of performance and needs.

The **Corrective Reading program**, also known as SRA Corrective Reading, is an example of a specialized remediation program that includes testing materials to screen and identify reading problems, including comprehension issues (Engelmann, Hanner & Johnson 1989). The program includes placement tests to determine the student's current level of skills and needs. This provides a specific starting level for direct instruction. (There is more information about SRA Corrective Reading in Chapter 7.)

5I Community College Placement Tests for High School Students and Adults

One of the goals of education, including special education, is to prepare students for success in postsecondary options like higher education. For college-bound students with autism, reading comprehension **must** be strong enough to manage college-level material.

Most communities offer free community college placement tests to help determine if a person is ready for the pace and demands of college-level academics, including reading comprehension and writing.

- **Placement tests** are free, generic tools that may be used by a person from about junior high school age through adulthood, usually administered on a computer.
- The results compare the person's skill level to the level needed for college success.

It's a good idea to determine exactly how prepared students with hyperlexia are to meet college-level comprehension standards before they enroll. It's especially important to know where the student stands during high school while s/he still has access to special education services and supports to develop the skills needed.

- One idea is for high school students to take the community college placement exam every year.
- When to start would be up to the educational team, but the ninth grade would be a good time to try this process, to identify gaps in comprehension and related concerns with writing skills.
- The results may be used as a general indicator to monitor progress, adapt instruction, and provide remedial services.

For adults who are not enrolled in special education (after receiving a high school diploma, or age 22, whichever comes first),* community colleges offer several levels of remedial courses in reading comprehension and writing that must be completed before a student can enroll in a degree course, like English 101.

*Remember that a high school diploma is an exit document. It terminates all special education services and supports, even if the student with an IEP is only 17 or years old, unless a specific transition plan is arranged that specifies something different.

5J Standardized Measures

In addition to informal and formal measures, standardized assessments are often used to try to define an individual's reading abilities and difficulties.

- Standardized tests are **normed**, which means that the person's decoding, comprehension, and vocabulary scores can be compared to those of others of the same age or grade level.
- The scores can also reveal peaks and valleys, or a pattern of strengths and weaknesses in the same person.

It might be surprising that standardized tests for comprehension have not been discussed until this point in the chapter. However, standardized tests that are specifically designed to measure comprehension may *not* be the best tools to use to understand the comprehension of a reader with autism.

- After intensive study and review of assessments used in education at the request of the U.S. Department of Education, reading expert Catherine Snow warned that "the widely used comprehension assessments are inadequate" to provide the data needed about a person's ability to comprehend when reading.
- A major drawback is that the tests try to "sort children on a single domain using a single method" rather than create an understanding of the dynamic, active process of comprehension (2002, p. 53).

Another critique of commercial tests of reading comprehension is based on the fact that the tests intend to measure "comprehension," which a very complex construct, but **there no commonly agreed-upon definition of "comprehension"** (Clemens & Fuchs 2021).

- Many interactive cognitive processes are involved in comprehension: attention, working memory, reasoning, inferencing, sensitivity to the structure of language, background knowledge, vocabulary development, motivation, and the use of comprehension strategies.
- The issue is that "**authors of commercial tests choose which dimension(s) to measure and which to ignore**" (Clemens & Fuchs 2021, p. 4).

Many education professionals are frustrated by the lack of valid, useful test instruments to measure comprehension and lament the drawbacks of those that exist (Snow 2002). Salvia and Ysseldyke concur, based on their own critique of standardized diagnostic reading measures.

- In their 2004 text on assessment, Salvia, Ysseldyke only listed **a single diagnostic comprehension test** (the Test of Reading Comprehension-3, or TORC-3) that the authors believe to be "sufficiently reliable for making important individual decisions about students" (p.468).
- The authors stated, "Most of the norm-referenced devices clearly lack the technical characteristics necessary for use in making specific instructional decisions" (p. 479).

Thirteen years later, in the 13th edition of their text on assessment, Salvia, Ysseldyke and Witmer reiterate that the best way to assess comprehension, in their opinion, is to ask a reader to paraphrase or restate what they read (2017).

- The updated textbook mentions the TORC-4, as an update of the TORC-3.
- Only one diagnostic reading assessment is described in detail, the Gray Oral Reading Test-Fifth Edition (GORT-5). It measures the decoding skills of reading rate and accuracy, and includes material to assess reading comprehension. The authors conclude that the GORT-5 is "sufficiently reliable for making important decisions about individual students" (p.219).
- Appendix C provides more information about these assessments.

Key Things to Know about Standardized Measures

Griswold and her colleagues were troubled by the fact that students with Asperger syndrome in their study tested in the average range on achievement tests (including reading comprehension) while having actual deficits in particular skill areas as great as two standard deviations (2002). **The problematic skill areas (i.e., reasoning and inference) were only revealed using specialized assessments**.

An awareness of the limitations of available comprehension assessments can help parents and professionals make a conscious decision to gather information in more than one way, and not rely on standardized tests alone. Figure 5.8 provides eight important considerations to keep in mind about standardized measures.

Figure 5.8

Eight Key Points about Standardized Measures

1. *Comprehension* **means different things to different people (including test designers) and can be tested in different ways.** Each test manual defines comprehension and describes how a particular test measures it.

   Read the manual to decide if you are on the same page with the test author(s). You can confirm whether the test design is a good match to what you are attempting to measure.

2. **Some students with known comprehension issues score in the average range on many standardized tests.** It can be helpful to focus on subtest scores rather than average scores or composite scores.

   Averaging several scores or creating a composite score can erase the discrepancy between decoding and comprehension, or hide other areas of need that you are attempting to identify.

3. **Standardized measures alone may not be sufficient to get to the bottom of comprehension issues.** Decisions should not be made based on the results from a single standardized measure.

   It's reasonable to question the results from standardized measures if the results conflict with other concrete signs of a comprehension problem.

4. **Language testing may be particularly useful** for understanding higher-level, complex, and interpretative language abilities related to comprehension.

5. An individual **item analysis of skills and deficits** within each subtest of an evaluation can be extremely valuable for identifying skills to teach.

6. **Some standardized tests are not sensitive enough to detect qualitative differences in reading skills.** Some standardized tests are more likely to reveal comprehension difficulties than others.

7. **Standardized tests are revised and updated regularly.** Various versions of the tests may be quite different from one another. Subtests can be added or removed, and scoring instructions may be changed.

   When reviewing records, it is helpful to be aware of the subtests that were included at a particular point in time. When selecting tests, newer or older versions may contain the most appropriate subtests for a particular purpose.

8. **Note whether individuals with autism were included in the norming of the assessment.** How can you rely on an assessment to reveal comprehension issues if the questions were not tested with individuals with autism during test development?

   This information is found in the test manual. It can shed light on whether test questions are sensitive enough to pick up on the reading difficulties of hyperlexic readers. If the normative group includes individuals with autism, the results may be more accurate.

A Revealing Profile

McIntrye and colleagues analyzed the literacy and comprehension performance of 81 children with high-functioning autism, ages 8 through 16 (2017). They identified four reading profiles, one of which was *comprehension disturbance* (CD), which is consistent with our use of the word *hyperlexia*. Approximately 20% of the readers in their study had the CD profile.

Here's the really important thing: The extensive testing done in the study revealed a very specific response to standardized testing for this group. Good decoders with comprehension issues shared this **testing profile**:

- **Average** rapid automatized naming, phonological awareness, word decoding and word recognition, text reading accuracy, and expressive vocabulary.
- **Low-average** phonological memory, sentence-level syntactic skills, expressive language skills, and story recall.
- **Deficits** in auditory reasoning, auditory inference, and reading comprehension.

This information is new and telling. It's also useful for comparison with student records, especially if standardized testing did *not* reveal a comprehension issue for a struggling autistic reader.

- Maybe the hyperlexic reader was only tested in areas where readers with this profile tend to perform in the average or low average range.
- After all, there is no cause for concern when scores are in the average range.

What to Measure

It's reasonable to focus standardized testing in recognized areas of deficit, including auditory reasoning and inference. Remember that comprehension problems seen in autism and hyperlexia relate particularly to higher-level, complex, or interpretative language abilities, such as conceptualization, reasoning, and logical analysis (Snow 2002).

As explained in Chapter 4, these types of cognitive actions are called *higher-order thinking skills*, or HOTS (Johnson & Lamb 2007). Difficulties with HOTS often translate into a poor understanding of text.

- They can affect reading skills, such as generating inferences, resolving ambiguity, understanding cause and effect, and making comparisons.
- Problems with HOTS also affect the reader's ability to respond to text when asked to evaluate, synthesize, explain why, and so on, or to apply new information to different situations (Johnson & Lamb 2007).
- Evaluations that measure inference skills, problem-solving, and logic may be helpful in understanding higher-order thinking skills.

Sometimes language-based tests are ideal to accurately define the nature of the comprehension problem. Language measures conducted by speech-language pathologists, including language samples, are often helpful in identifying problems with vocabulary.

- Language-based tests can also reveal problems with more complex language skills, such as telling how words are related, giving definitions, and expanding on answers.
- Based on the results, speech-language pathologists often play a role in improving comprehension through therapy focused on remediating multiple weaknesses in language.

As Mcintyre and her team found, another area to measure is listening comprehension, which can be problematic in autism (2017).

- Poor listening comprehension can relate to poor oral comprehension and vocabulary, which are known to affect reading comprehension.
- Listening comprehension tests can be administered by psychologists, speech-language pathologists, and educational therapists, among others.

It's logical to consider using the same standardized measures of reading comprehension that the researchers did, because they were revealing! Of course, this has to be decided on an individual basis, but the tools selected by researchers can provide guidance on the issue.

Appendix C describes some tests and subtests that can be useful to understand the nature of the comprehension issue in an individual with hyperlexia. Some of these have been mentioned in the text thus far, and others have not. The tests used by McIntyre and her team, along with tests used by many other researchers mentioned in this book, are also highlighted in Appendix C.

- Given that the research and literature on this topic are so limited, this list of tests represents an effort to bring promising possibilities from different disciplines together in one place.
- It is merely a starting point; there are no guarantees that one of these measures will hit upon the nature of the difficulties or be appropriate for a particular reader with hyperlexia.

The list of assessments is not an endorsement of particular products or companies, but shows how one might use available resources in an informed and discriminating way. The tests and subtests in Appendix C were selected in four ways:

1. They're mentioned in the literature on reading research for people with autism as the evaluation tools used to **accurately identify reading difficulties**, when other testing instruments used with the same study subjects did not. An example is the GORT-4 (used in the 2024 study by Beckerson and colleagues.).
2. They were **suggested by language specialists** with extensive experience with this population, one who is also an educational therapist (K. Schnee & L. Legler, personal communication, January 2010).
3. They are a good match for **assessing known areas of difficulty** related to autism.
4. In an informal private review of the records of my advocacy clients, they provided the **breakthrough scores** that identified needs for specific individuals.

A Personal Discrepancy in Scores: A Telling Result from Standardized Measures

As mentioned, one of the best reasons to use standardized measures to detect reading comprehension issues is the following: **In hyperlexia, a significant discrepancy exists between the ability to decode and the relatively lower level of comprehension, as well as the ability to decode compared to the developmental age** (Grigorenko et al. 2002).

Standardized tests can be used to compare a student's decoding and comprehension scores to those of other students, and to compare differences in skill development **within the same student**.

- Typically, an individual's ability to decode and their ability to understand are similarly developed, or "even."
- Comparing the ability to decode to the level of comprehension may show the discrepancy between an autistic student's ability to read and the ability to understand.

Data reported in several studies suggest that from about third grade, the individual score discrepancy within readers with autism may be one standard deviation or more, which is statistically significant (McIntyre and colleagues 2017; Norbury 2004; Ricketts and colleagues 2013).

- Even if all scores are in the average range, the discrepancy between scores can signal hyperlexia.
- For many, this will be the first concrete sign, and the discrepancy may indicate the need to delve deeper into comprehension issues.

To be able to detect differences or discrepancies among skill sets, it is important to review subtest scores, rather than only focusing on scores based on averages.

- Broad reading scores are often calculated by averaging various subtests in a particular area to come up with an overall score.
- When highs in decoding are averaged with lows in comprehension, the important discrepancy that needs to be identified is erased.

Some standardized tests are scored by computer.

- The computer-generated report often **automatically averages subtest scores** to generate the scoring report.
- Remember to view the scores and results with a discerning eye.

Assessment Results Matter Because Needs Become Goals

Shared concerns, observations, informal assessments, and standardized tests can reveal areas of need to address for a particular learner.

- Many students with autism and hyperlexia are already eligible for special education services.
- Goals and focused instruction to build vocabulary and fundamental reading comprehension skills can be added to their IEP based on the areas of need identified through testing and other relevant information.

If the student who was evaluated is not yet eligible for special education, assessment findings can help determine if the needs interfere with educational progress. Since comprehension is essential for academic achievement, there is an obvious relationship to educational progress.

- IDEA 2004 added a provision that IEP teams must address the **developmental needs** of students.
- Autism is a developmental disability, and reading comprehension issues are directly related to it.
- Therefore, it is reasonable to address comprehension issues as both a developmental and academic need.

Remember: In special education, needs drive goals. Goals drive services (Doyle & Iland 2004). Identifying needs is the first step in deciding which priorities should be addressed with special education goals. The next decision is to determine what special education services are needed to help the student reach their goals.

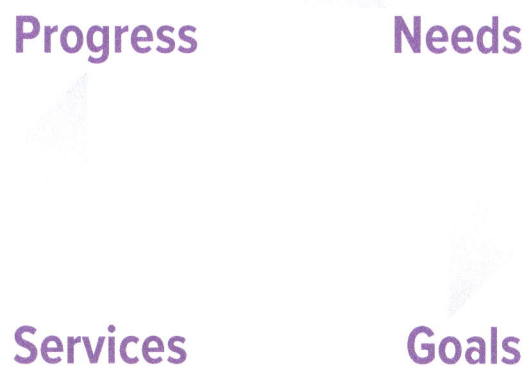

Progress   **Needs**

Services   **Goals**

- The type of goal established gives direction to the type of service to help meet the goal.
- The service or additional support selected to meet needs and related IEP goals in comprehension and language may be provided through the classroom teacher, a resource teacher, a reading specialist, a speech-language pathologist, an educational therapist, another specialist, or a provider the team deems appropriate.

Often, reading remediation programs in school focus on children who cannot decode quickly or fluently.

- Seldom do reading groups focus mainly on good decoders who lack understanding.
- Therefore, an individualized approach is needed to support readers with hyperlexia.
- Support may also be necessary in the related areas of writing and organization of ideas.

Establishing small groups or delivering individual remediation in these areas may be pioneering work at a particular school. It's necessary to support the unique literacy needs of students with hyperlexia.

- In special education programs, the explicit instruction of comprehension and writing skills can be integrated into the curriculum or resource classes.
- Outside of school and for adult readers, educational therapists, tutors, and commercial learning centers may assist in the process of skill building.

Failure to address comprehension deficits results in a heavy burden on students with autism who already struggle in many domains.

- These problems can be prevented or remediated by using effective instructional methods and reading strategies.
- Many researchers suggest that future study of interventions should maximize the strengths seen in students with autism, such as strong visual discrimination, good rote memory, and interest in computers (Frith 2004; Williams and colleagues 2002). The idea of "fit" is a recurring theme in Chapters 6 through 9.

Next Steps

You've been a dedicated reader, developing a thorough understanding of the many developmental reasons that good decoders with autism struggle with comprehension. Your expertise on the topic is growing by the page!

- You understand the body of research that documents specific areas of comprehension breakdown and how they are related to the developmental and cognitive profile of autism.
- You have comprehensive lists of the skills that need to be explicitly taught.
- You know why this problem can be masked and ways to unmask it.

Knowing this information makes you a powerful ally of hyperlexic readers! The solid foundation of knowledge can guide you in the next steps of this process: determining how to teach, including using research to guide practice. The rest of the book is dedicated to this subject.

CHAPTER 6

The Search for Evidence-Based Practices to Improve Comprehension in Readers with Autism

The unique learning profile and needs of readers with autism and poor comprehension have been discussed in depth. Two questions remain: "*What* methods are effective to help readers with autism improve comprehension?" and "*How* can I teach key skills and strategies?"

This chapter discusses evidence-based interventions to improve comprehension in readers with autism. The chapter:

- Defines what makes an intervention "evidence-based."
- Describes the status of research on this topic.
- Describes how interventions were selected for this chapter, and the focus of studies that were excluded.
- Explains seven best practices, three from the first edition of *Drawing a Blank*, and four from more recent research.

This chapter also provides answers to these key questions:

- What can educational professionals do in instructional or remedial sessions to help readers with autism improve reading comprehension before, during, and after reading?
- How can parents, including homeschool parents, support reading comprehension?
- Which intervention methods and strategies best match the pattern of strengths and needs of readers with hyperlexia?

Evidence-Based Practices

There is specific emphasis in the field of education to use evidence-based practices (**EBP**s) or **proven techniques** for instruction (Ehren 2005; Ohnemus 2002).

- Teachers and students only have so much time in a day. Teaching techniques need to be **effective** so that all students can make gains.
- EBPs are instructional strategies and interventions that have been **rigorously researched** and **proven to be effective**.

Research studies need to have an *experimental design* to conclude that the resulting intervention is effective and evidenced-based. This includes:

- Study subjects who are **randomly assigned** to receive the intervention or be on a waitlist for it.
- Having a well-matched **control** (comparison) group.
- Results that can be **replicated** or **repeated** by different researchers to verify effectiveness.
- Being **peer-reviewed**, that is, evaluated for quality, validity and accuracy by other experts in the field before the research is published.

Teachers are using evidence-based practices in general education classrooms now more than ever. Yet it is critical to note that students with disabilities were usually **not part of the research** on the effectiveness of those practices! Evidence-based practices are most often designed for and researched with typically developing students. Therefore, the findings of effectiveness may only apply to typically developing students.

Students with autism, who are already behind their peers in comprehension, need to close their learning gaps to benefit from their education, especially as they move to middle school and high school.

- That means that teaching methods for these students need to be *really* effective!
- There is limited research on this topic with this population.
- The variability among study participants makes it difficult to generalize findings.

Researchers Vaughn and Fletcher found that students with disabilities, especially in general education classrooms, **are not responding well to current evidence-based practices** (2012). This is critical information in the current era when Response to Intervention (RTI) or tiered instruction is a widespread classroom practice.

- The educational community is challenged to create and investigate targeted interventions to meet the needs of students with autism and comprehension issues (El Zein and colleagues 2015).
- My informal review of the literature indicates that research in autism and comprehension in good decoders is about 40 years behind the research focused on students with learning disabilities or the reading disability of dyslexia.

What Research Is Available?

A 2007 review of the literature on improving reading comprehension found that of 754 potentially relevant articles, only 11 were peer-reviewed studies with an **experimental design** that had at least *one* participant with autism (Chiang & Lin).

- Only 49 individuals with autism were represented in the 11 studies reviewed.
- Seven of the 11 studies focused on comprehension of single words, but *not* understanding at the sentence, paragraph, or text level.

Let's compare this to recent research focused on interventions to improve reading comprehension for individuals with autism.

- I read and reviewed seven meta-analyses or literature reviews that analyzed recent published research (Accardo 2015; El Zein and colleagues 2013; Fernandes and colleagues 2016; Finnegan & Mazin 2016; Singh and colleagues 2020; Solis and colleagues 2016; Whalon, Al Otaiba & Delano 2009).
- The literature review by Singh and colleagues stood out because it analyzed studies using the high **standards for quality research** established by the What Works Clearinghouse (WWC) from the US Department of Education (2020).

Singh's team used an **evaluative framework** to assess each of 220 peer-reviewed articles published prior to 2018. Of 220 articles, the researchers identified **13 studies** to evaluate further. All of them had the following qualities:

- Had at least *one* participant with autism.
- Included K–12 students.

After their analysis of the 13 articles, Singh and her colleagues stated clearly that **"None of the interventions reviewed achieved the status of evidence-based."**

- In other words, as of 2020, the date of the Singh review, **there were no new studies about reading comprehension intervention for autism with a rigorous experimental design and an outcome that can qualify as an evidence-based practice.**
- That's because only a randomized, controlled study with comparison groups can earn evidence-based status.
- Similarly, a literature review by El Zein et al. (2013) reported, "We were unable to identify any studies that used experimental research design."

Now What?

Readers with hyperlexia **don't have time to wait** or **waste** while the educational community designs and conducts randomized, controlled studies to discover interventions that qualify as evidence-based! Therefore, we need to:

- Use the information from recent research to *maximum* advantage.
- Use what you know about comprehension, autism, and the readers with autism in your life to find individualized solutions for your students, clients, or child.

In light of this situation, I looked for peer-reviewed journal articles about comprehension intervention for autistic readers that were published after the Singh review (2020).

- I looked for interventions to help good decoders with autism improve comprehension at the sentence, paragraph, or text level.
- I excluded studies if the results were mixed, and studies about preschoolers.
- I expanded the search to adults with autism and completed doctoral dissertations.

This chapter presents a **research summary** for each of seven relevant studies selected.

- The introduction to each research summary explains information that's needed to understand the study better.
- Insights about the research and information about teaching (translating research into practice), are provided after the summaries.
- Figure 6.1 identifies the studies highlighted in this chapter.

Figure 6.1

Evidence-Based Practices to Improve Comprehension for Students with Autism		
Evidence-Based		
6.1	Explicit Instruction	Roux, Dion, Barrette & Fuchs 2014
6.2	Reciprocal Teaching	Turner, Remington & Hill 2017
6.3	Primer Passages and Informative Titles to Provide Relevant Background Knowledge	Wahlberg & Magliano 2004
Evidence-Based with Study Design Reservations		
6.4	Anaphoric Cueing	O'Connor & Klein 2004
6.5	Reciprocal Questioning Strategy	Whalon & Hanline 2008
Quasi-Experimental		
6.6	Multiple Thematic Exposure Related Narrative Stories	Coalescent & Griffith 1998
Established Through Evaluation of Quality Indicators		
6.7	Computer-Assisted Instruction (CAI) to Teach Academics (Including Literacy)	Root et al. 2016

To help clarify the jargon and acronyms commonly used in research you may want to skim over the information in Figure 6.2 and refer back to it as needed to read and understand the studies described in Chapters 6 and 7.

Figure 6.2

A Primer Passage to Spot Key Information When Reading Studies

Does an intervention work? How well does it work?

That's what we want to know when we read studies.
- Unfortunately, the formal language, jargon, and unfamiliar acronyms in research articles can be intimidating.
- To help you quickly answer these two questions, this Primer Passage explains important **signal words** and **terms** used in the research summaries.

What Is PND?   Banda & Therrien (2008)

PND is a method that determines the effectiveness of an intervention by measuring the **progress of each participant**.
- PND is calculated using data collected before, during and after an intervention.
- PND stands for *the percentage of non-overlapping data points*.
- PND scores report effectiveness for each participant as follows:

Highly effective = a PND of 90 % or higher
Moderately effective = a PND of 70 % to 90%
Minimally effective = a PND of 50 to 70 %
Little or no effect = a PND below 50%

What is PEM? *The Percentage of data points in the intervention phase that Exceeded the Median of baseline*

PEM is another method to calculate the effectiveness of an intervention.
- It is expressed as a percentage, with 100% as the best score.
- PEM is used in single-case studies and is considered more stringent than PND.
- A higher PEM percentage suggests that an intervention is resulting in a positive effect, as follows:

Very effective = Scores over 90%
Effective = 89 to 70%
Questionable = 69 to 50%
Ineffective = Below 50%

A Primer Passage to Spot Key Information When Reading Studies
What Is Effect Size? **Borenstein and colleagues 2009**

Effect size (ES) is a statistical measure of effectiveness to describe the **impact** of an intervention on learning or progress. ES is rated as small, medium, or large:
Large = ES of 0.8 or above
Medium = ES ranging from 0.3 to 0.8
Small = ES below 0.3

Let's begin with the **three studies** with results that can be considered evidence-based, with sound study design and reliable results.

6.1 What Is Direct, Explicit Instruction?

This method of instruction emphasizes direct teaching, explicit explanations, and immediate feedback.

- Complex concepts are broken down into smaller, more manageable parts.
- Teachers provide clear learning objectives, modeling, and step-by-step guidance.
- Teaching is often scripted for consistency.
- Students are highly engaged and have multiple opportunities for guided practice and teacher feedback.

What Is Anaphoric Cueing?

Difficulties with pronouns in spoken language, as discussed in Chapter 2, may link to problems understanding pronouns in print. Even when the word is a simple, recognizable pronoun (such as *he*, *she*, or *it*) meaning is lost if the person does not **link the pronoun to the person or thing it refers to**.

The reading skill called *anaphoric cueing* depends on the reader stopping to clarify the meaning of pronouns and understand to whom or what the pronoun refers.

- The reader must make the link between *subject pronouns* (such as *he, she, it,* or *they*) and the person or thing those words represent, called the *referent*.

145

- The same **linking process** also applies to:
  - *Possessive pronouns* (such as *his, her,* and *their*),
  - *Object pronouns* (like *him, it,* and *them*),
  - And the person or thing those words represent.

Readers with hyperlexia are **unlikely** to pause and clarify a word or phrase they do not understand while reading, also called *repairing meaning*.

- They read on, without realizing they do not understand.
- This is a clear sign that the reader is **not** self-monitoring for comprehension.

Research Summaries

Research Summary 6.1 provides details about a Canadian study that used explicit small-group instruction to teach key comprehension skills: finding the main idea, learning vocabulary through definitions, text structure (organizational patterns) for summarization, and anaphoric cueing. Please refer to the original article for more information.

Research Summary 6.1
Direct, Explicit Instruction

Use of Visual Boards for Vocabulary, Main Idea, Text Structure, and Pronouns
Efficacy of an Intervention to Enhance Reading Comprehension of Students with High-Functioning Autism Spectrum Disorder
Catherine Roux, Eric Dion, Anne Barrette, Veronique Dupere, and Douglas Fuchs 2014

This randomized, controlled Canadian study was conducted in French. The researchers taught multiple skills concurrently, including expanding vocabulary through definitions, finding the main idea, anaphoric cueing, (stopping to clarify the meaning of pronouns and understand to whom or what the pronoun refers) and text structure.

Participants

Forty-five students with autism, ages six through twelve, across six elementary schools, were randomly assigned to an intervention group or a control group. The majority, 88%, were boys.
- Twenty-four children were in the intervention group.
- The 21 children in the control group received regular instruction and no explicit comprehension instruction.

Research Summary 6.1
Direct, Explicit Instruction

What the Researchers Did

A research assistant used a script to provide explicit, structured instruction with groups of two to four students outside the classroom.

- Sessions of 30 minutes each were held three times per week for sixteen weeks.
- This totals 24 hours of intervention.

Visual boards were used in 42 sessions to target vocabulary through definitions, identify the main idea in a text, and identify text structure (summarization). Four activities were conducted in each session.

Activity 1: Vocabulary Instruction

- Eight words were taught in each session. Five were new and three were review.
- A total of 201 "second-tier" vocabulary words were taught over the 42 sessions.
- The words were chosen because they're often encountered in texts, but may be unfamiliar to many students.

Each word was presented on a board with a drawing showing the meaning of the word.

- Under this, the word was divided into syllables.
- Complex graphemes were underlined, and silent letters appeared in a lighter font.

After decoding the word, the researcher read it normally. Then the students reread it.

- The researcher provided a simple definition of the word, described the illustration, and gave a sample sentence that included the word.
- Next, each student repeated the definition and formulated a new sentence using the word. The routine was repeated for each word.
- The activity concluded with a review, in which students matched definitions to the words and illustrations on a visual board.

Activity 2: Story Reading

A text with a total of about 350 words was presented on a board.

- Current lesson vocabulary words were **bolded**, and the researcher defined each of these words while reading.
- Review words were <u>underlined</u>, and students defined them during reading.

Activity 3: Main Idea Identification

This activity used the text from Activity 2. Each paragraph in the text had a clear main idea.

- The activity began with a reminder of what a main idea is.
- The researcher repeated the two questions needed to identify a main idea: "Who or what is the paragraph about?" and, "What happens in the paragraph?"
- Each student took turns rereading a paragraph, answering the two questions, and using their answers to describe the main idea in one sentence.
- The researcher assisted as needed and wrote the responses and main ideas on a board.
- After each main idea was identified, the group was shown a drawing to illustrate it.

Research Summary 6.1
Direct, Explicit Instruction

Activity 4: Identification of Text Structure
The researcher showed drawings that illustrated the main ideas to the group, one by one, following the sequence of paragraphs in the story.
- Each student took a turn to restate the main idea.
- The goal of this activity was to help students create a coherent representation of the central aspects of the story for themselves (summarize), which is key to comprehension.

Six Pronoun Sessions
In the first two introductory sessions, the researcher explained the use of nine personal pronouns (for example, that *I* refers to the person who is speaking).
- Next, she modeled a strategy to identify the referent of the pronoun in the text.
- Students were instructed to ask themselves, "Who is [pronoun]?" and look for the answer in the preceding sentence.
- The strategy was written on a board that the group could refer to.

To start each of the last four pronoun sessions, the assistant reviewed the use of personal pronouns and the strategy to identify the referent of the pronoun (anaphoric cueing).
- The strategy was then put into practice in two read-aloud activities.
- The first activity used paragraphs in which pronouns were underlined. When it was their turn, the student read it normally. They then reread it and demonstrated the strategy to identify the referent of each underlined pronoun.
- The second activity used paragraphs in which each pronoun had been replaced by a blank and a choice of three pronouns. As each student read a paragraph, they tried to select the correct pronoun.

Results

The researchers designed the assessment measures. Pre-tests were done before the intervention began. A post-test was given one week after the intervention ended. A follow-up assessment was carried out five months after the post-test.

The intervention was highly effective for vocabulary, as measured by the students' vocabulary assessment scores (effect size = 1.0)

The intervention was effective for identifying the main idea as measured by improvements in scores (effect size =.89).

Students made **significant improvements in resolving anaphoric cues**.

In addition, the intervention group made **small but significant gains in a summarization task** created by the researchers.

The activities used in this study appeared well planned, starting at the word level, building to the sentence and paragraph level, and finally helping students get the gist of the whole text. This sequence supports the integration or cohesion of ideas.

- Gains from each activity contributed to students' success with the next.
- The researchers reported that the students seemed engaged and liked the clear information.
- The participants may have also liked the repetitive routine.

6.2 What Is Reciprocal Teaching?

This structured, explicit teaching method improves reading comprehension with direct, targeted instruction. **The instructor engages small groups of students in a dialogue about the text. Students receive direct teaching to predict, clarify, question, and summarize.** As they master the skills, students can take the lead in the discussion.

Research Summary 6.2 provides extensive details about a study using reciprocal teaching done in the United Kingdom (UK), and the results. Please refer to the original article for more information.

Research Summary 6.2
Direct, Explicit Instruction: Reciprocal Teaching
Developing an Intervention to Improve Reading Comprehension for Children and Young People with Autism Spectrum Disorders   **Horatio Turner, Anna Remington & Vivian Hill 2017**
This study tested the effectiveness of using the reciprocal teaching method (Palincsar & Brown 1984) to help students learn and practice four key comprehension strategies: **prediction**, **clarification**, **questioning**, and **summarizing**.
Participants
Twenty-nine students with autism, ages 11 to15 (mean age 13 years, 6 months). Fifteen students received intervention, eight boys and seven girls. The 14 autistic students in the control group were predominantly male.

Research Summary 6.2
Direct, Explicit Instruction: Reciprocal Teaching

Participants attended a total of seven schools. Two were schools specializing in autism. Five were mainstream schools, two of which had an autism unit within them.

The majority of participants who received the intervention (11/15) attended special education classes or received special education support. The majority (10/14) of the control group attended mainstream education.

- Some students from each school type had a high degree of adult academic support, and some students had very little.
- There were no significant differences between the two groups on the baseline measures of expressive vocabulary, age, non-verbal reasoning, reading accuracy, rate, or comprehension.

What the Researchers Did

The intervention plan was adapted from the reciprocal teaching method developed by Palincsar and Brown (1984).

Popular teen fiction, *The Fault in Our Stars* by John Green (2012), was used as the reading material for the intervention.

- None of the students had read it, and it was not part of the school curriculum.
- It was easy to read with few unfamiliar words.
- The text was challenging from a social-communication perspective because to make sense of the story, readers had to make numerous inferences and relate story events to their personal experiences.
- Readers also had to interpret some idioms.

The researcher facilitated two 45-minute group sessions weekly, for six weeks, for a total of 12 sessions.

- Each group had three to four students of mixed ages.
- Students were only required to attend 75% of sessions, to work with schedules.
- The first ten minutes were used for relaxation and to build rapport with the researcher and other group members.
- Next, the facilitator introduced and modeled the four key strategies while reading a text.
- Students used starter sentences to scaffold their use of the strategy in group discussion.
- Students became more independent in strategy practice over time.

To measure effectiveness, participants read two passages (one non-fiction and one fiction).

- After reading, they responded verbally to factual and inferential questions.
- In addition, participants were asked to summarize the passages from memory.

Research Summary 6.2
Direct, Explicit Instruction: Reciprocal Teaching

Results

Improvement in comprehension was measured using the standardized York Assessment of Reading Comprehension (YARC). This test has a normative group from the UK.

Based on the age equivalent data provided by the YARC manual, students in the intervention group made 36 months of progress in their reading comprehension. **The increase in scores was equivalent to three years of progress with just 100 minutes of intervention per week for six weeks**.

The improvement of the intervention group supports the view that reciprocal teaching is an appropriate intervention to develop the comprehension skills of adolescents with autism.
- Semi-structured interviews with participants indicated that many learned to focus on their comprehension when reading.
- Participants also reported that the intervention supported their speaking and listening skills

The comprehension score increased significantly more in the intervention group than in the control group.
- The mean score of the intervention group increased by 9.80 standard scores over the course of the intervention. The effect size was significant, at 1.57.
- The control group's mean score **decreased** by 4.57 standard scores over the six-week period of "treatment as usual." Their scores represent a decrease of 11 months.

The majority of the intervention group made at least some progress with their reading comprehension (13/15) and summarization (11/15).

In contrast, very few of the control group demonstrated an increase in comprehension (2/14) and summarization (4/14), with the majority demonstrating a decrease in comprehension (8/15) and summarization (8/15).

The most exciting sentence in the research summary may be, "The increase in scores was equivalent to three years of progress with just 100 minutes of intervention per week for six weeks."
- The intervention appears efficient and easy to implement.
- Success was reported for students from ages 11 to 15, suggesting that educators can use the method with students in several different grades.
- Independent replication of the findings of this study, and in particular conducting research in the United States, would be ideal.

Something that was concerning but not included in the research per se was the decrease in scores of the autistic readers in the control group. More study would be needed to understand the reasons for their regression. One thought is that the skill loss aligns with the idea that "treatment as usual" is not enough to meet the needs for comprehension intervention for this population, especially as students progress beyond elementary school.

Preparing to Read: What Doesn't Work

Several researchers looked for ways to help readers with autism understand text through the *activation of prior knowledge*, relating what they were going to read to information they already knew (O'Conner & Klein 2004; Wahlberg 2001a; Wahlberg & Magliano 2004). Students need to draw upon their background knowledge or associate their world knowledge with the text to be read.

To activate prior knowledge, teachers typically ask students, "What do you know?" about a subject. For many readers with autism, this is likely too broad of a question.

- A student with autism may know too much or too little and have difficulty coming up with **the right amount of appropriate information**.
- For this reason, traditional methods used to stimulate prior knowledge may be ineffective for readers with autism.

For example, a *K-W-L* chart is a tool that is often used to prepare readers to read (Ogle 1986). Three columns on a page are marked "Know," "Want to Know," and "Learned."

- Before reading, the student is asked to fill in the first column, "Know," with facts or information relevant to the material to be read.
- The student is asked to fill in the "Want to Know" column by generating questions expected to be answered when reading, things the reader would like to know about the topic.
- Finally, after reading, the student fills in the last column, marking what was learned.

Just reading the steps involved in using a KWL chart (questioning, coming up with the right amount of relevant information, and drawing conclusions) makes it clear why a tool like this is less than optimal for learners with autism. In fact, when using a KWL chart, readers with autism may **draw a blank** when asked what they know about an unfamiliar topic or what they want to learn about a topic!

What DOES Work

The following pre-reading methods were successful in the limited studies with this population:

- Relating the title to the text.
- Primer passages with basic factual concepts.
- Anaphoric Cueing.

Information from two studies that used these interventions is presented next.

6.3 Noticing and Relating the Content to the Title and Primer Passages

Wahlberg found that a single method of preparing students with autism to read was **not enough** to stimulate sufficient prior knowledge. He concluded that readers with autism need **multiple cues** before reading to help them take advantage of background knowledge (Wahlberg 2001a).

- For example, a passage with no title that describes multiple steps in a task can seem strange and confusing to any reader.
- When a title is provided that reveals that the passage is about doing the laundry, the passage is *disambiguated*, or clarified.
- The title helps the reader relate the ideas to one another and relate all of the ideas to the main concept.

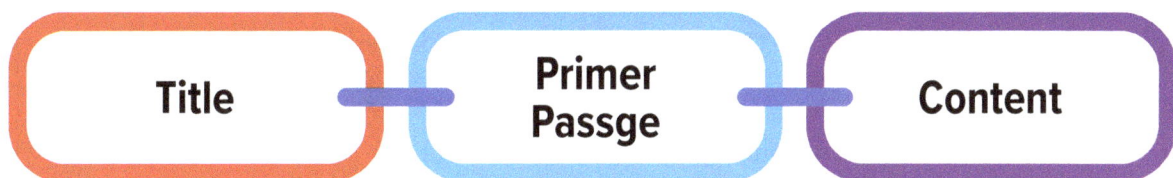

Title ▬ **Primer Passge** ▬ **Content**

Using Primer Passages to Pre-Teach Basic Factual Concepts

The idea of pre-teaching basic factual concepts is as straightforward as it sounds. Familiar material is easier to read and understand. Providing key information in advance can improve familiarity by shifting foundational ideas from "unknown" to "known."

A primer passage is **a basic, facts-only passage** that creates a concrete understanding of the main elements of a story or text.

- The primer passage is a summary of the material to review before reading the text.
- Primer passages can "prime" or prepare the reader to understand the material by explaining central concepts and clarifying the meaning of key vocabulary words.

Research Summary 6.3 provides details about a study that used informative titles and primer passages together.

Research Summary 6.3
Informative Title and Primer Passage

The Ability of High-Functioning Individuals
with Autism to Comprehend Written Discourse
Timothy Wahlberg and Joseph P. Magliano 2004

This study measured the ability of readers with autism to integrate background information from a primer passage to understand ambiguous or unclear text.

Participants

- Twelve high-functioning college-age students with autism, two females and ten males. Their age range was 18 to 53. Their IQ scores ranged from 81 to 127, with a median of 105.
- Twelve readers without autism, five males and seven females, were matched on IQ as control subjects. They ranged in age from 18 to 27.

Materials

- **Factual primer texts** of 256 words, about well-known events in history, such as the Wright brothers' first flight or Paul Revere's ride, written like an encyclopedia page
- **Ambiguous short passages** of 172 words on average that described the same events but had unclear meaning
- **An informative title** that announced what the text was about
- **Uninformative titles** that did not shed light on the text

---

Research Summary 6.3
Informative Title and Primer Passage

What the Researchers and Students Did

Participants read ambiguous short passages on a computer screen. Sometimes an informative title and/or a primer (factual) passage were presented, and sometimes they were not.

- The study measured understanding by asking the participants to try to recall as much as possible about what they read.
- Analysis of their responses measured how well readers could **integrate information** from the different sources in their recall.

Results

Recall of the material was improved for students with autism when both an informative title *and* a primer passage were used before reading the ambiguous text.

Reading instruction to facilitate the ability to activate and use relevant background knowledge may benefit readers with autism.

- Cues need to be **explicit**, and the **relevance** of the cues needs to be made clear.
- Compared to controls, readers with autism were *less able* to integrate background information from a primer passage into the understanding of the unclear text.
- Their understanding was more closely related to the explicit, factual text than the interpretation or recall of ambiguous text.

Understanding at the word and sentence level must be mastered before inference is introduced.

Readers with autism are disadvantaged when they don't have the right amount of relevant background knowledge.

- Primer passages are a structured, controlled way to provide relevant information.
- Primer passages simplify complex information to improves understanding.
- The key to using primer passages is to keep the primer material *succinct* and *relevant*.

Primer passages help students pay attention to and remember important main ideas. This is the purpose of reading and supports learning. In fact, Wahlberg and Magliano found that the **readers remembered information from the primer better than from the more complex text**.

- Creating a primer passage is similar to pre-teaching facts, but does not necessarily use numbers or a list form.
- Primer passages used in the research were about 275 words (Wahlberg & Magliano 2004).
- Please refer to the section in Appendix D, "How To Teach Reading Comprehension using Primer Passages and an Informative Title" for more information, including examples for teaching.

> Primer passages are often used in programs for English learners (ELs) to improve comprehension of material that may be unfamiliar. Many instructional programs for ELs **include ready-made primer passages**. Be sure to take advantage of these materials if they are available to you and otherwise seem appropriate.

Research Summary 6.4 provides details about a study that compared the effectiveness of three different interventions that could possibly improve comprehension, including anaphoric cueing.

Research Summary 6.4
Anaphoric Cueing, Cloze Procedure, and Pre-Reading Questions

Exploration of Strategies for Facilitating the Reading Comprehension
of High-Functioning Students with Autism Spectrum Disorders
Irene M. O'Connor and Perry D. Klein 2004

This study investigated ways of supporting high school students' understanding of text and their use of background knowledge.
- Three *facilitative techniques* were selected to prompt executive processes.
- Each strategy addressed a recognized comprehension issue for students with autism.
- The hypothesis of the study was that one or more of the three techniques would "produce significantly greater comprehension of text passages than a control condition in which students did not receive facilitation" (p. 118).

Research Summary 6.4
Anaphoric Cueing, Cloze Procedure, and Pre-Reading Questions

Participants

Twenty students with autism, 19 males and 1 female, ages 14 to 17 years, who fit the profile of high-functioning autism.

- All of the students had at least average decoding skills, but their standardized comprehension scores were significantly lower than their word-identification skills.
- Four students were in a self-contained classroom, six attended general ed classrooms with resource support, and ten were in partially integrated programs.
- Six students participated in the study at school, and 14 chose to do so at home.

Materials

Five stories for the SRA Reading Lab Grade 6 reading series were adapted for the study.

- Two stories were unaltered and were the control materials.
- The other three stories were tailored to the comprehension strategies. To measure comprehension, a series of 12 questions was created for each text.
- These included free retelling, identifying the main idea of the story, generating a title for the story, and detecting an incongruous sentence from a story paragraph.
- Four inferential *why* or *how* questions were included, along with four literal *who, what, where,* and *when* questions for recall of explicit information.

What the Students and Researchers Did

The intervention was conducted with each student individually. The student read two unmodified control passages and three modified passages aloud during the study session, which lasted about one hour.

- The researcher read 12 comprehension questions aloud after each story, and the students responded verbally.
- The students were not allowed to look back at the passage to answer.

The researcher explained that she was going to ask a few questions before the student read one of the stories. **Five pre-reading questions** were asked to stimulate prior knowledge.

- The questions were designed to aid understanding by helping students keep important information related to the main ideas of the story in short-term memory.
- Respondents answered verbally to the pre-reading questions.

Research Summary 6.4
Anaphoric Cueing, Cloze Procedure, and Pre-Reading Questions

The second technique was **anaphoric cuing**, which prompted the student to relate 12 underlined pronouns in a passage to their antecedent nouns. Before reading, the researcher discussed pronouns (or "shortcuts") and referents, or "the long way to say the same thing."
- A practice question was provided so the student understood what s/he was being asked to do.
- The visual cuing of underlined pronouns helped the student pause to clarify the referent noun of a pronoun while reading.
- Then they circled one of the three options provided under each identified referent.

The third technique was a **cloze task**. The students in the study were familiar this fill-in-the-blank format.
- While the student read the modified passage, s/he filled in the blank with a word to complete the sentence, choosing from a small array of words provided.
- As with the anaphoric cuing intervention, the blanks inserted in the text were intended to cue the student to stop, monitor their understanding, and choose an appropriate word to complete the sentence.

Results

Based on scores from the post-reading questions for the three methods, **only anaphoric cuing significantly increased students' passage comprehension**.
- It appeared to be most beneficial for students with low grammatical ability.
- The effects of anaphoric cueing were statistically significant (medium effect size, ES = 0.42).

Pre-reading questions **did not improve comprehension scores**.
- In fact, the researchers assert that due to the cognitive profile of autism, students sometimes **activated and perseverated on irrelevant prior knowledge** that may have distracted them during reading, causing them to miss important information.
- The authors contend that this technique might be successful **if it could be modified to help students activate relevant information**, such as using graphic organizers to stimulate and organize relevant prior knowledge.

Students were successful using the cloze procedure (filling in a blank by choosing one of the words provided). **However, it did not have a significant positive effect on the post-reading comprehension scores**.

Some recent research that analyzed the O'Connor and Klein study categorized it as **inconclusive**, because two of the three methods used did not improve comprehension (El Zein et al. 2013). Other critics note that a one-hour session is hardly an intervention.

- In their defense, the researchers' goal was to identify **one** or more strategies that worked to improve comprehension.
- The study is included here because it verifies the effects of anaphoric cueing, and the negative results are as valuable and important as the positive one!

First, the common classroom practice of using five pre-reading questions to stimulate prior knowledge **didn't work**, and even backfired. This supports the use of Wahlberg and Magliano's alternative method: providing the right amount of relevant prior knowledge using primer passages and an informative title, methods that are tailored to readers with autism.

Second, the study participants could choose the correct word to fill in the blank in a sentence **without genuine understanding**. Even though they chose the right words, their comprehension scores did not improve on related testing.

Students with autism often test in the average range on reading assessments that use the cloze procedure. One example is a commonly used and highly-regarded academic assessment, the Woodcock-Johnson Psychoeducational Battery IV Tests of Achievement (also called the WJ-IV-ACH).

- In light of what O'Conner and Klein learned, assessments such as the WJ-IV- Test 4 Passage Comprehension Subtest, which uses a cloze procedure, may actually **overestimate** a reader's abilities and mask comprehension difficulties.
- While additional research is needed, it is reasonable to be cautious about using assessments with cloze procedure to assess hyperlexic readers.
- Appendix B suggests numerous additional options for evaluation.
- Appendix D provides some teaching materials for anaphoric cueing.

Two More Comprehension Interventions

This section summarizes two studies involving subjects with autism with poor comprehension. The studies may have limitations in design that can affect the generalization of the findings. Valid critiques of the research include difficulties often seen in studies with this population: small sample sizes, varying grade and ability levels of subjects, variation in diagnosis and criteria for inclusion of subjects, recruitment of subjects by convenience, lack of control groups, etc.

- At the same time, some important information was learned in these studies, and the interventions may, in fact, be effective.
- This section summarizes the research, highlights important findings, and suggests practical ways to translate the research into practice.

Research Summary 6.5 describes an intervention that used both direct instruction and peer partners.

Research Summary 6.5
Effects of a Reciprocal Questioning Intervention on the Question Generation and Responding of Children with Autism Spectrum Disorder   **Kelly J. Whalon and Mary Frances Hanline 2008**
This study focused on direct instruction of the reciprocal questioning reading comprehension strategy for elementary school students with autism and peer partners.
Participants
Three male students with autism, ages seven and eight had identified reading comprehension issues. Their cognitive functioning scores (IQs) ranged from 92 to 112.   • Austin received reading instruction in his self-contained classroom.   • Barry and Chris received reading instruction in both a self-contained classroom and a general education setting.   Nine typically developing peers from the mainstream classroom were randomly paired with each of the three students for different sessions in the intervention.

Research Summary 6.5

Materials

The SCORE curriculum, used for direct instruction of cooperative behavior (Vernon and colleagues 1996).

Storybooks from the Marc Brown author series

Researcher-created materials, which included:
- Visual story cards that used words and images to describe story elements of setting, characters, events, the problem, and the solution
- Laminated question word cards that included words and images representing Who? What? When? Where? Why? and How?
- Written examples of generic and specific questions related to each story element
- A self-monitoring checklist with cues, words, and visuals for asking questions before, during, and after reading

What the Researchers and Students Did

Seven school days before baseline, the researcher provided two small group sessions of direct instruction to help the students and peers understand the story elements of setting, characters, events, problems, and solutions. Familiar stories of "Goldilocks and the Three Bears" and "Cloudy with a Chance of Meatballs" were used.

One of the researchers facilitated the small-group sessions in a familiar, small room in the school. In two pre-baseline sessions of 20 minutes each, the study subjects and one of nine peers were prompted to ask one another questions while they took turns reading a grade-level storybook aloud. No other guidance was given.

Next, direct instruction using the SCORE social skills curriculum was provided daily for about thirty minutes, for one week, to teach students and peers cooperative behaviors. Small groups consisted of one student with autism and three typical peers.
- SCORE stands for **S**hare ideas, **C**ompliment, **O**ffer help or encouragement, **R**ecommend changes nicely, and **E**xercise self-control.
- Students learned about the skills and could define them, generate examples, and do role-play.
- During intervention, students received stickers on a chart when they demonstrated SCORE behaviors.

Ten to twelve reading intervention sessions with cooperative pairs used a structured, scripted, repetitive format. Sessions were held four days a week for approximately 40 minutes each.

Research Summary 6.5

In the first session, the researcher used a "think aloud" procedure to teach the question generation strategy.

- She began by verbally walking the students through the mental processes involved in constructing a question while reading.
- The researcher and participants took turns generating questions and responding to them.
- In the following session, participants generated questions without assistance.

In subsequent sessions, students used a visual checklist and an interactive, visual storyboard to monitor their participation. The researcher praised successful question generation and responses.

- Verbal prompts, corrective feedback, and modeling were offered when participants had difficulty forming or answering questions.
- When offering corrective feedback, the researcher also explained why a question or response was not on target.
- She then modeled an appropriate, clear question or response.

The intervention was implemented as intended according to measures of treatment fidelity. Please refer to the study for details and samples of the visual tools.

Results

All three autistic children asked more unprompted questions and answered more questions once the intervention began. Gains were immediate for two of the participants. One participant's performance was more variable.

- The intervention was **highly effective** for two students and **moderately effective** for one student.
- All three students made significant gains in unprompted question generation, with PND scores of 85, 91, and 100%.
- All three students made significant gains responding to peer questions, with PND scores of 100%.

Both participants with autism and their general education peers required more prompting to answer inferential questions about information that was not explicitly stated.

Students and parents were pleased with the intervention. Typical peers also benefited from the instruction. The students with autism and the peers got to know one another better. Some negative peer perceptions of the students with autism changed as a result.

There are mixed reviews of this study, mostly positive.

- Accardo's analysis (2015) found it **effective** because all three students learned to ask unprompted questions, with an average gain of 31% over baseline.
- El Zein and colleagues (2013) called the study "suggestive," because the results were mixed and the gains were medium in size.
- The researchers reported that despite the positive results, their study didn't include a generalization measure. Therefore, it's unclear whether student gains would carry over to curriculum-based assessment, such as weekly reading tests or story retell after reading.

Despite research design issues, this study is like a master class on how to adapt a strategy to benefit learners with autism. An excellent level of detail about the intervention is provided in the journal article to enable anyone to follow the method. More information about how to structure instruction is also discussed at the end of the chapter.

When using a cooperative learning model with peers, it's essential to teach everyone in the group social skills before starting. Peers should be enlisted carefully and given information in advance about the students with whom they will work.

6.6 Multiple, Thematic Exposure (Related Narrative Stories)

This quasi-experimental study aimed to establish a cause-and-effect relationship between an intervention and an outcome in a naturalistic setting, such as a classroom. Coalescent and Griffith (1998) demonstrated that repeated exposure to the language and concepts in a series of stories, or *thematic stories,* could improve recall and comprehension. Using three related narrative stories about rabbits, students were prompted to **relate** information from one rabbit story to another.

- As a result, they were more successful with recall and oral retelling, two indicators of improved comprehension.
- Drawing and writing about the stories improved retelling even more.
- Research Summary 6.6 provides details about the research.

Research Summary 6.6
Multiple, Thematic Exposure: Related Narrative Stories

Autism and Literacy: Looking into the Classroom with Rabbit Stories.
Rita Colasent and Penny L. Griffith 1998

This limited study focused on providing a series of *related narrative stories* about rabbits, based on the hypothesis that repeated exposure to the language and concepts in a series of stories would improve recall and comprehension.

Participants

This intervention was used in a middle-school special education classroom. The seven students ranged in age from 12 to 15 years old. Their developmental levels ranged from 5 to 8 years. The intervention was focused on three students with autism, 14-year-old girl, a 13-year-old boy, and a 14-year-old bilingual boy (Spanish-English). The classroom teacher, who was also a literacy specialist, delivered the intervention.

Materials

Three books of about 20 to 25 pages each were selected and read aloud to the students. Each book was read over a period of three days.
- *Who's in Rabbit's House?* by Verna Aardema (1977)
- *Foolish Rabbit's Big Mistake* by Rafe Martin and Ed Young (1985)
- *The Velveteen Rabbit* by Margery Williams (1971)

What the Researchers Did

Pre-teaching of basic factual concepts about rabbits was done before the first story was read. Students were guided to predict events during reading.
- Questions were asked and students were interviewed to measure comprehension after each of the three stories.
- Students were asked to retell favorite parts of each story through writing and drawing.

Results

The students were able to relate information from one rabbit story to another.
- They had more correct responses to questions after stories two and three, supporting recall and comprehension.
- Drawing and writing about the stories improved retelling even more, because the students linked information from all three stories into the pictures.

Research Summary 6.6
Multiple, Thematic Exposure: Related Narrative Stories

- Students wrote more sentences and longer sentences after the third story.
- They also used more sophisticated vocabulary and multi-syllable words when retelling.
- Students were observed to be more engaged with thematic stories compared to the daily stories that were unconnected.

While more research is needed, the authors suggest that understanding narrative is not beyond the ability of readers with autism. Thematic stories, multiple exposures, and reading aloud may particularly benefit individuals with autism and poor verbal skills or weak auditory comprehension.

This intervention had an **impact** but doesn't qualify as evidence-based using today's standards. Still, there are two reasons that this technique makes a lot of sense and seems like a good fit for readers with hyperlexia.

First, the study participants were more severely impacted by features of their autism than a typical reader with hyperlexia. However, the students made excellent gains in comprehension using this method. These encouraging results make it worth trying with readers with hyperlexia and/ or autism without hyperlexia.

Second, many readers with autism **give themselves multiple thematic exposures** in their areas of interest. They **want** to read multiple materials to learn more.

- As a result, readers with autism typically develop extensive vocabulary and advanced factual knowledge about the topics that fascinate them.
- What they learn from one source supports their understanding of the next.
- This method may help students learn school subjects and material.

Teachers and parents who wish to use this method can:

1. Use related narratives to create a solid fact base that helps students make text-to-text connections to improve understanding.

2. Choose at least one selection to serve as a **primer passage**, basic and easy for the reader to understand, at the student's independent reading level. The other selections can be curricular material that the student needs to understand.

3. Ask students to draw pictures or write about each story after it is read. They may be able to make connections between the texts, the images, and their own writing.

6.7 Computer-Based Instruction

In addition to conducting a well-designed individual study, there is another way to establish a practice as evidence-based. It involves reviewing and combining multiple studies that measure the same intervention, in a similar way, with a similar population.

Research Summary 6.7 explains how Root and colleagues used this process to establish computer-based instruction (CAI) as an evidence-based practice for students with autism (2017). Discussion follows the summary.

Research Summary 6.7
Computer-Assisted Instruction (CAI)

Establishing Computer-Assisted Instruction to Teach Academics
to Students with Autism as an Evidence-Based Practice
Jenny Root, Bradley Stevenson, Luann Ley Davis,
Jennifer Geddes-Hall, and David Test 2017

This research team analyzed 14 to 15 recent research studies to determine if there was enough collective evidence to support evidence-based status for CAI to teach academic skills to students with autism spectrum disorder. The authors define *computer-assisted instruction* as "any instruction in which a computer is the central feature of an intervention that supports learning, presents learning materials, or checks a learner's knowledge" (p. 276).

Method

The research article describes how the research team identified single-case studies to include or exclude from analysis. They describe the process of analysis in detail.

Single-case research usually follows how one to three participants fare with a specific intervention, in a limited timeframe.

Research Summary 6.7
Computer-Assisted Instruction (CAI)

The study used criteria from NTACT, the National Technical Assistance Center on Transition, to determine whether a practice can be considered an *evidence-based practice* (EBP 2015). The NTACT formula for single-case research studies is 5-3-20.

This means gathering collective evidence from different sources as follows:
- From at least **five** high-quality or acceptable-quality studies
- That used rigorous research designs
- Conducted by **three** independent research teams
- With **at least 20 participants** across studies
- That demonstrates a functional relationship between the intervention and outcome
- That calculates the effect size (the impact) or reports data that allows for calculation.

If there is any evidence from group or single case designs that demonstrates negative effects, the practice cannot be considered evidence-based.

Results

CAI was established as an Evidence Based Practice (EBP) to teach academics to students with autism through analysis of ten studies of high or acceptable quality, done by seven research groups that included 30 participants with autism. No negative evidence was found.

One concern about this analysis is the broad definition of the three essential terms of the analysis: **autism**, **computer-assisted instruction,** and **academics**.

- There is tremendous variability among individuals with a diagnosis of autism. This analysis includes individuals of diverse abilities, ages, and backgrounds, who were essentially lumped into one group.
- Two studies by Spooner and colleagues addressed reading comprehension (2014, 2015). Each study had only a single participant. It was not clear whether the participants were good decoders with relatively poorer comprehension.

When it comes to the definition of computer-assisted instruction, CAI can take many forms and use different methods. It can include simply taking a quiz on a computer or tablet (Khowaja & Salim 2013).

- Formats can include tablets, desktop computers, laptops, websites, and software.
- Materials can range from commercial programs, to software, to teacher-designed materials, etc.
- There is also variability in the delivery of instruction, including the amount of time the student participates, the level of independence or support, etc.
- With this broad range of options, CAI can be a good fit for autistic learners, especially for those with a high interest in computers and tablets.

The authors defined Academics as "skills related to literacy, mathematics, science, or social studies" (p. 281).

- Only two of the twelve single-case studies addressed reading and comprehension.
- Other literacy-based studies focused on basic skills, map reading, symbol identification, grammar, spelling, writing, and vocabulary.

CAI was also established as an EBP to teach academics (skills related to literacy, mathematics, science, or social studies) to students with autism, based on the analysis of two high-quality group-design studies that met NTACT criteria for EBP (Travers et al. 2011; Whalen et al. 2010). This is good news.

- However, as with the Root research, *academics* is a very general term.
- Teaching addition skills and teaching comprehension skills are very different aspects of academics.
- Additional robust evidence, particularly in the area of comprehension instruction, would be valuable to confirm the declaration of evidence-based status for CAI to specifically improve reading comprehension for students with autism.

Choosing and Using EBPs

The studies presented in this chapter provide direction and guidance for using the methods described by the researchers.

- Several of the original research articles include teaching materials, examples or other helpful information to help you implement the practice yourself.
- Remember, there's nothing to lose and everything to gain by trying the promising evidence-based practices described in this chapter, based on the individual needs of the readers you wish to help.

CHAPTER 7

Effective Methods from Single-Case Research

This chapter identifies numerous interventions that may improve comprehension for readers with autism, based on more than two dozen small studies. The chapter:

- Briefly describes single-case research design.
- Explains how research studies were identified for inclusion in this chapter.
- Describes four types of effective practices and summarizes key points from thirteen studies that demonstrated their effectiveness.
- Revisits the recommendations of the National Reading Panel (NICHD 2000) for comprehension interventions, analyzing how they may be used for readers with autism and comprehension difficulties.

Putting New Information to Good Use

This chapter credits those who are out there leading the way and doing the work, even on a small scale.

- It presents reliable information from current research about comprehension interventions for readers with autism that may be suitable for use before, during, and/or after reading.
- The majority of the study participants had the hyperlexic profile of grade-level decoding skills with comparatively lower comprehension.

What Is Single-Case Research Design?

This research method focuses on studying a single participant or small group over time. Most single-case studies have only one to three participants.

- Investigators are often classroom teachers, facilitating the intervention in the classroom or resource room during the normal school day.

- Intervention sessions are usually short (15 to 30 minutes each), carried out over a limited time period, such as a few weeks.

In single-case research, the researcher takes data before, during, and after the intervention to measure progress and determine if the intervention is effective. Each participant's progress is compared to their own starting baseline data as a measure of effectiveness. Remember:

- Results from small single-case studies cannot be generalized to hold true for a larger group.
- Positive results from one single-case research study *cannot* confer evidence-based status to an intervention.
- Only research studies that have an experimental design and a well-matched control (comparison) group can conclude that an intervention is evidenced-based.

Single-case studies are sometimes criticized as being open to researcher bias. The researcher who facilitates the intervention really wants it to work, and may find it hard to be objective about progress. So why does anyone bother to conduct single-case studies?

- A single-case study is like a test to understand the use of an instructional approach and determine if it works for a small group of participants.
- This research method usually has **strong internal validity**. This means that the results can be tied directly to the intervention being studied, rather than to other variables.
- The interventions usually take place in a naturalistic setting (school) and are easy to implement.
- Results can be used to refine the intervention and build support for future research.
- Promising single-case studies are sometimes expanded to a more robust experimental method with more participants.

Why Are Single-Case Studies Important?

The short answer: to make the most of the information that's available! Now, more than ever, we need as much reliable information as possible.

- The "best-evidence synthesis" encourages the consideration of all pertinent studies, including those with limitations in study design or small numbers of participants (Slavin 1995).
- The most relevant factor is the **impact** of the intervention.

This chapter aims to **bridge the gap between research and practice** by providing concise summaries of high-impact, effective interventions. Several different researchers reviewed and analyzed recent single-case studies on autism and reading comprehension published between 2007 and 2020 (Accardo 2015; El Zein et al. 2013; Fernandes et al. 2016; Finnegan & Mazin 2016; Singh et al. 2020; Tárraga-Mínguez, Gómez-Marí & Sanz-Cervera 2020; Whalon et al. 2009).

- I read the seven reviews mentioned above, paying attention to the analysis of study design, effectiveness of the intervention, and the reviewers' confidence in the results.
- Next, I read more than 45 individual journal articles describing specific studies.

Thirteen studies were selected for this chapter because they:

- Target comprehension skills (vs. decoding skills or recall of facts).
- Include more than one student with autism in the study.
- Focus primarily on participants who fit the reading profile of poor comprehension compared to decoding skills.
- Had positive results for almost all participants, with medium to high impact.
- Were recent (less than 20 years old).

I created a summary for **each** of the included studies.

- The summaries provide a clear picture of the ages of the participants, how the interventions were implemented, and the results.

- The most important information in the summaries, in my view, is **how the researchers structured the interventions, tailoring them to meet the anticipated needs of learners with autism**. I believe that is the key to effectiveness.

How the Summaries are Organized

While several studies could fit in multiple categories, the research findings for effective practices are organized into the four categories shown here. The categories are highlighted with letters and color coding in the chapter to help you find information.

A.	Direct, Explicit Instruction
B.	Direct Instruction Using Commercial Programs
C.	Graphic Organizers
D.	Metacognitive Strategies

You can skim through the summary graphics to find the interventions that are most relevant to the students you teach, and the specific skills you need to teach them.

- You may consider trying some of the procedures and strategies in the research.
- The original articles provide extensive information about the interventions, including details about the materials and procedures.
- Remember to refer back to the Primer Passage in Chapter 6 for help with some of the research terms and jargon, such as PND and PEM.

A. Direct, Explicit Instruction

Based on all of the research articles reviewed for this book, there is some consensus about what works! The first area of agreement among researchers and reviewers alike is that autistic **readers with comprehension deficits need direct, explicit instruction to learn comprehension skills and strategies**. No matter what skill is being targeted, direct, explicit instruction was the preferred method for teaching students with autism of all ages in numerous studies.

- Five single-case studies based on direct, explicit instruction were shown to be effective in improving reading comprehension.
- This section begins with an explanation of direct, explicit instruction, and continues with summaries of the first three studies.

Research Studies Using Direct, Explicit Instruction

Effective Practices: Direct, Explicit Instruction	
A1	Teacher-led shared reading
A2	Question development
A3	Anaphoric cueing

What Is Direct, Explicit Instruction?

As described in Chapter 6, this method emphasizes direct teaching, explicit explanations, and immediate feedback.

- Teachers provide clear learning objectives, modeling, and step-by-step guidance.
- Teaching is often scripted for consistency.
- Students are highly engaged and have multiple opportunities for guided practice and teacher feedback.

The second area of agreement among researchers and reviewers is that **readers with autism need direct, explicit instruction delivered as one-to-one teaching or in small-group instruction**. All of the researchers used these instructional settings. To get the same results as the researchers did, the same delivery model should be followed.

Individual and small-group instruction makes sense for this population, especially because their comprehension issues often interfere with understanding the teacher's explanations during whole-class activities. Recognized benefits of small group instruction include that **teachers** can:

- Provide intensive instruction to target specific skills and learning needs.
- Address individual gaps in knowledge more effectively.
- Monitor students' progress and adjust instruction accordingly.

Benefits of small-group instruction for students with autism include that **students** can:

- Feel more comfortable being part of a smaller group.
- Let the teacher know when they are lost or not understanding something.
- Learn social skills like teamwork, communication, and problem-solving in a safe, adult-mediated situation.
- Monitor and manage their own attention and behavior, and respond to teacher expectations.

Research Summaries

The graphic that follows is a detailed example of one research study that used direct, explicit instruction. This detailed information provides a window into the intervention, including materials and procedures.

A Prime Example of Direct, Explicit Instruction: Teacher-Led Shared Reading

The children in this study are not described as having stronger word recognition than decoding per se, but the intervention was successful, and the summary may provide useful information.

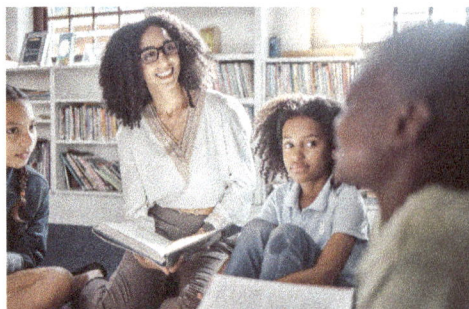

Research Summary A1: *Direct, Explicit Instruction*

Teacher-Led Shared Reading
The Effects of a Shared Reading Intervention on Narrative Story Comprehension and Task Engagement of Students with Autism Spectrum Disorder
So Yeon Kim, Mandy Rispoli, Catherine Lori,
Emily Gregori and Matthew Brodhead 2018

This research studied the effects of a shared reading intervention using before-during-and-after strategies on narrative story comprehension and task engagement of elementary-aged students with autism.

Participants

The children were three boys with autism, ages six, seven, and eight, who received behavioral services in an autism clinic. All three communicated verbally. Ryan, age seven, and Noah, age six, could read sentences of three to five words aloud. David could read short sentences aloud if they contained familiar sight words.

Materials

The researchers used *Nate the Great Talks Turkey* (Sharmat & Sharmat 2007), which has a reading level of J (appropriate ages: six to eight), and Lexile® of 520L (appropriate ages: six to nine).

This grade-level narrative storybook:
- Included an age- and gender-matched main character (not an animal or an imaginary character).
- Was written in diary or essay format.
- Was set in an environment of daily living (e.g., school, home).
- Could be divided into shorter chapters.
- Included pictures.

The story was adapted to create "chapters" of four paragraphs with three pictures from the original book. Two types of visual cues were added to the adapted chapters:
- At the end of each paragraph, a stop sign was inserted to encourage the participant to stop reading and think about the contents of the paragraph.
- Second, keywords were highlighted in yellow to help participants notice important information and find answers from relevant text.

Research Summary A1: *Direct, Explicit Instruction*

What the Researchers Did

Intervention sessions were delivered one-to-one for each participant by the first study author, once a day, three times per week, in an autism behavioral clinic. A new chapter was introduced for each session.

Baseline sessions lasted approximately nine minutes per session. Intervention sessions lasted 25 to 40 minutes. Maintenance sessions were about ten minutes long.

The Fidelity Checklist in the published study *outlines every step to be followed during the intervention.*

The shared story reading intervention included three stages of strategies: (1) before reading, (b) during reading, and (c) after reading, as illustrated by the study authors. Figure used with permission.

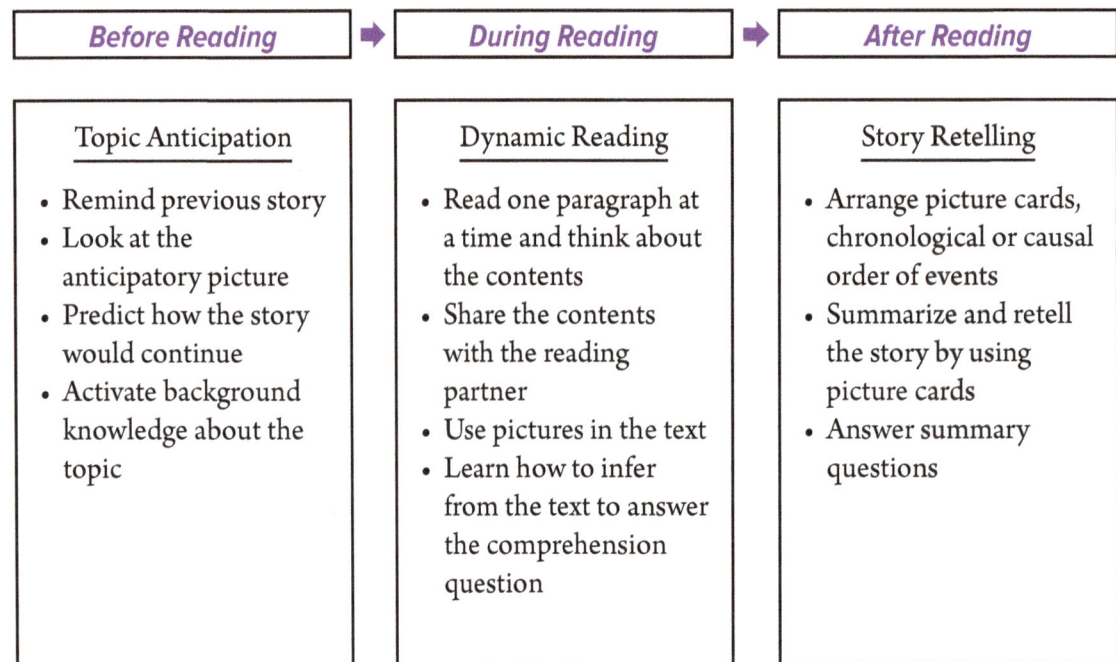

Before Reading ➡	*During Reading* ➡	*After Reading*
Topic Anticipation	Dynamic Reading	Story Retelling
• Remind previous story • Look at the anticipatory picture • Predict how the story would continue • Activate background knowledge about the topic	• Read one paragraph at a time and think about the contents • Share the contents with the reading partner • Use pictures in the text • Learn how to infer from the text to answer the comprehension question	• Arrange picture cards, chronological or causal order of events • Summarize and retell the story by using picture cards • Answer summary questions

---

Research Summary A1: *Direct, Explicit Instruction*

Results

All participants demonstrated improvements in reading comprehension. The improvements endured during the monitoring phase. The improvement was small for two subjects and medium for the third.

Engagement in reading improved for all three students during the intervention.
- The researchers consider the intervention to be cost-effective, easy to implement, and socially valid.
- Reading improvements resulted from the whole reading intervention package as it was delivered; the authors are uncertain if deviations from their method would have positive outcomes.

The graphics that follow provide relevant information from two more studies categorized as *direct, explicit instruction*. Please refer to the original articles for complete information.

Research Summary A2: Direct, Explicit Instruction

Question Development
Reading Comprehension Interventions for Students with Autism Spectrum Disorders:
An Alternating Treatments Comparison
Michael Solis, Farah El Zein, Sharon Vaughn,
Lisa V. McCulley, and Terry S. Falcomata 2014

The researchers conducted two studies on two different reading comprehension interventions, with and without applied behavioral analysis (ABA) techniques.
The first study compared the effectiveness of literal question development with and without ABA.

Study 1, Question Development, Participants

Two fifth-grade boys participated: Kevin, age 13, and Sean, age 12. Both boys had an autism diagnosis and a speech impairment diagnosis (SI).
- Kevin also had an attention deficit hyperactivity disorder diagnosis (ADHD).
- Both boys received special education services in special ed and general education settings, with behavioral supports.

Research Summary A2: Direct, Explicit Instruction

- Kevin's basic reading score on the Woodcock-Johnson III test was 70, or two standard deviations below the average score of 100 (statistically significant).
- His comprehension score was 75, 5 points higher than his basic reading.
- Sean could read 140 words per minute. His reading level was 4th grade.

The instructor for the intervention was a graduate student with three years of teaching experience with autistic students and extensive experience using ABA techniques.

Materials

The intervention package included:

- **A structured lesson plan** that detailed the instructional routine, including direct instruction, modeling, guided practice, and independent practice.
- **Graphic organizers** to provide students with a structured, visual framework for relating prior knowledge to new information.
- **ABA techniques** that were integrated into the intervention to proactively address off-task behavior. These included positive reinforcement with a token economy, and a checklist (visual support) to self-monitor use of the steps in the strategy.
- **Adapted text** based on the students' favorite interests. The narrative and expository texts were at a third to fifth-grade level.
- **Passages** that ranged from single paragraphs of 60 words to multiple paragraphs of 150 words or more. Text had three levels of difficulty: "single paragraph-easy," "multi-paragraph-medium," and "single paragraph-hard."
- **Curriculum-based measures** (CBM) were used to measure comprehension outcome.

What the Researchers and Students Did

The intervention was delivered one-to-one in a quiet area away from other students. Alternating treatments were randomly delivered in 30-minute sessions, four to five times per week, for two weeks.

The question development (QD) intervention was modified from the Question-Answer Relationships strategy, called QAR for short (Raphael 1982).

Following the structured lesson plan, the student read the text aloud. The interventionist provided question stems, or question-starters, (who, what, where, and when). She asked the student to use those words to develop a literal question, using information that was "right there" in the text. The interventionist scaffolded support as needed.

In the QD + ABA condition, ABA elements of a graphic organizer, a token economy, an image that clarified meaning, and readings based on preferred interests were added to the regular teaching procedure.

Research Summary A2: Direct, Explicit Instruction

Results

To support on-task behavior and improvement in comprehension, the addition of ABA techniques better supported the behavioral and instructional needs of the students (compared to the same interventions without ABA techniques).

- Sean's scores on curriculum-based measures (CBM) reading probes were higher during the question development + ABA treatment (M = 74%) compared to scores (M = 47%) w/o ABA.
- Sean's PND score on CBM reading probes and on-task behavior were both 100% in favor of question development + ABA. The intervention was highly effective for him.
- Kevin's scores on CBM reading probes were higher during the question development + ABA treatment (M = 73%) compared to scores (M = 48%) w/o ABA.
- Kevin's PND for on-task behavior was 75% in favor of question development + ABA.
- These scores indicate that the intervention was moderately effective in improving on-task behavior for Kevin. There was a problem with Kevin's PND data for question development.

Research Summary A3: Direct, Explicit Instruction

Anaphoric Cueing
Reading Comprehension Interventions for Students with Autism Spectrum Disorders An Alternating Treatments Comparison
Michael Solis, Farah El Zein, Sharon Vaughn,
Lisa V. McCulley, and Terry S. Falcomata 2014

The researchers conducted two studies on two different reading comprehension interventions, with and without applied behavioral analysis (ABA) techniques. The second study compared the effectiveness of an anaphoric cuing intervention with and without ABA techniques.

Participant Study 2, Anaphoric Cueing

Two third-grade boys participated: Tom and Gary, both age ten. Both boys had an autism spectrum diagnosis and a speech impairment diagnosis (SI).
- Both boys received special education services in special ed and general education settings, with behavioral supports. Reading scores were not available.
- The instructor was the same person who facilitated the Question Development intervention.

Research Summary A3: Direct, Explicit Instruction

Materials

The same materials were used as described in Summary A2.

What the Researchers and Students Did

The intervention was delivered one-on-one in a quiet area away from other students. Alternating treatments were randomly delivered in 30-minute sessions, four to five times per week, for two weeks.

Anaphoric cueing is a form of questioning that clarifies the referent of a pronoun. An example of a sentence presented in the research is, "Gregory bundled up in **his** warmest clothes before **he** went outside to play."
- The pronouns were in boldface type and underlined, as visual cues.
- The student was asked to identify the person the pronouns represented.

The interventionist followed the structured lesson plan that detailed the instructional routine. This included direct instruction on anaphoric cueing, modeling, guided practice, and independent practice.

In the QD + ABA condition, ABA elements of a graphic organizer, a token economy, an image that clarified meaning, and readings based on preferred interests were added to the regular teaching procedure.

Results

To support on-task behavior and improvement in comprehension, the addition of ABA techniques better supported the behavioral and instructional needs of the students (compared to the same interventions without ABA techniques).
- Tom's scores on CBM reading probes were higher during the question development + ABA treatment (M = 76%) compared to scores (M = 48%) w/o ABA.
- Tom's PND score on CBM reading probes was 75% in favor of anaphoric cueing + ABA. The intervention was moderately effective for him.
- Tom's PND for on-task behavior was 100% in favor of anaphoric cueing + ABA, indicating that the intervention was highly effective for this.
- Gary's scores on CBM reading probes were higher during the question development + ABA treatment (M = 83%) compared to scores (M = 65%) w/o ABA.
- Gary's PND score on CBM reading probes was 50% in favor of anaphoric cueing + ABA. The intervention was minimally effective for him.
- Gary's PND for on-task behavior was 100 % in favor of anaphoric cueing + ABA, indicating that the intervention was highly effective for him.

B. Direct, Explicit Instruction Using Commercial Programs

Direct, explicit instruction has been explained in depth. This section includes two studies that used commercial programs with explicit instruction. The section begins by describing commercial reading programs in general, and the specific program used by the researchers.

Effective Practices: Direct Instruction Using Commercial Programs	
B1	Corrective Reading Thinking Basic: Comprehension Level A Focused on statement inferences, using facts, and analogies
B2	Corrective Reading Thinking Basic: Comprehension Level A Focused on picture analogies, deductions, inductions, and opposites

What Are Commercial Programs?

Commercial programs are packaged programs developed by an educational company and sold to schools.

- They're designed to provide struggling readers with focused, intensive intervention in areas such as decoding, comprehension, and fluency.
- Commercial programs usually include curriculum materials, teacher scripts, and assessments.

What Is the Corrective Reading Program?

The Corrective Reading program, also known as SRA Corrective Reading, is an example of a specialized commercial remediation program. It includes:

- Testing materials to screen and identify reading problems, including comprehension issues (Engelmann and colleagues 1989).
- Placement tests that determine the student's current level of skills and needs. This provides a specific starting level for direct instruction.
- Lessons to help students progress from their initial level through the complete program.

The Corrective Reading program addresses multiple comprehension skills that researchers have identified as problem areas for students with autism. Skills range from vocabulary and applying prior knowledge to higher-order thinking skills, such as making inferences and analyzing evidence.

- Oral language comprehension is enhanced through thinking operations such as creating analogies and providing evidence for beliefs or conclusions.
- Program "strands" can help students develop skills in classification, deduction, description, induction, meaning of opposite and the same, statement inference, and understanding true and false.
- The program also includes useful information to broaden students' background knowledge.

Testing continues throughout the program to determine mastery of skills after direct instruction, before moving on to the next level.

- SRA program materials also include a curriculum called Reading for Understanding (Thurstone 2003) that is designed to improve overall reading comprehension and strengthen inferential, critical thinking, and reasoning skills.
- Anecdotally, Corrective Reading was used very successfully with students with hyperlexia in our local school district. One student I know made years of progress during each intensive summer program he participated in. (Your results may vary!)

Research Summaries

The graphics that follow provide a brief summary of two studies by the same authors that used direct instruction with SRA Corrective Reading. Please refer to the original articles for complete information.

Research Summary B1: Direct Instruction with a Commercial Program

Effectiveness of Direct Instruction for Teaching Statement Inference, Use of Facts, and Analogies to Students With Developmental Disabilities and Reading Delays
Margaret Munro Flores & Jennifer B. Ganz 2007

This study tested the effectiveness of a direct instruction reading program to improve inference skills, the use of facts, and the understanding of analogies for elementary school students.

Participants

Four total students. Two of them were autistic: one female, age eleven, in grade five, and one male, age fourteen, in grade six

Materials

The researchers used the direct instruction program *Corrective Reading Thinking Basics: Comprehension Level A* (Engelmann and colleagues 2002).

The program is divided into strands of developing skills, and each lesson includes instruction in several strands. The researchers chose three strands for this study: statement inference, using facts, and analogies.

What the Researchers and Students Did

Intervention sessions were delivered in a small group by the researchers, five days a week for 20 minutes, during regular instructional time. One author carried out instruction three to four times per week, and the other instructed one to two times per week.

The researchers followed the procedures and instructor behaviors as directed in the program manual. They (a) followed the given script, (b) prompted choral student responses (where students answer aloud together), (c) used a clear signal to elicit student responses, (d) corrected errors with immediate modeling for incorrect responses or responses that were not in unison, (e) led students by responding with them, and (f) asked students to respond independently. In some cases, individual students were asked questions, and the researchers followed the scripted procedures.

Research Summary B1: Direct Instruction with a Commercial Program

Results

This intervention is considered **highly effective** (El Zein and colleagues 2013).

- All four students experienced success with the program, meeting the criterion across the inference, using facts and analogies strands.
- There was an immediate, marked change in student performance between the baseline and treatment conditions.
- Both students with autism had a PND score of 100% on statement inference and using facts.
- One student with autism had a PND score of 100% on analogies, and the other scored 88%.
- All students maintained their performance after reaching the criterion and following the end of instruction.
- All students maintained performance one month after instruction ended.

Other Considerations

- Only three strands of the Corrective Reading program were used in the research.
- It is difficult to generalize the findings of this small study. The authors suggest that to bridge the gap between research and practice, teachers who have been trained to use the SRA program should implement the same research procedures in a typical classroom.
- Research is also needed to determine what modifications or accommodations may be needed for other students with autism to participate in the program.

Research Summary B2: Direct Instruction with a Commercial Program

Effects of Direct Instruction on the Reading Comprehension of Students with Autism and Developmental Disabilities
Margaret Munro Flores & Jennifer B. Ganz 2007

This study tested the effectiveness of a direct instruction reading program to improve induction and deduction skills and the understanding of analogies for elementary school students with autism.

Participants

Four total students, two with autism: one female, age twelve, in grade five, and one male, age fourteen, in grade six. The two students with autism are probably the same individuals who participated in the first Flores and Ganz study, based on test scores.

Research Summary B2: Direct Instruction with a Commercial Program

Materials

The researchers extended their previous study by using the *Direct Instruction program Corrective Reading Thinking Basics: Comprehension Level A* (Engelmann and colleagues 2002).

The program is divided into strands of developing skills, and each lesson includes instruction in several strands. The researchers chose three strands for this study: picture analogies, inductions, and deductions. The opposites strand was added based on student progress.

- In **picture analogies**, students completed an analogy by selecting a picture.
- In **deductions**, students used a descriptive statement and a series of pictures to evaluate whether an event was true or false, or maybe happened.
- In **inductions**, students were given a series of facts about a phenomenon and then generated rules about it.
- In **opposites**, students listened to a statement and then restated it by using the opposite of one word of the original.

What the Researchers and Students Did

Intervention sessions were delivered in a small group by the researchers, five days a week for 20 minutes, during regular instructional time. One author carried out instruction three to four times per week, and the other instructed one to two times per week.

The researchers followed the procedures and instructor behaviors as directed in the program manual. They (a) followed the given script, (b) prompted choral student responses, (c) used a clear signal to elicit student responses, (d) corrected errors with immediate modeling for incorrect responses or responses that were not in unison, (e) led students by responding *with* them, and (f) asked students to respond independently.

In some cases, individual students were asked questions, and the researchers followed the scripted procedures.

Results

This intervention is considered **highly effective** with certainty of evidence (El Zein and colleagues 2013).

- There was an immediate, marked change in student performance between the baseline and treatment conditions.
- PND scores for the students with autism were 100% for analogies, deductions, and inductions.

Research Summary B2: Direct Instruction with a Commercial Program

- All students made marked progress as measured by the program placement test, each placing into the next level of the program.
- All students maintained their performance after reaching criterion and following the end of instruction.
- Six weeks after instruction ended, two students maintained their performance in all four conditions at 100%.One student had a decrease from 100% to 83% in one strand. The fourth student had decreases in all four strands, but was well above baseline performance.

Other Considerations

- It's difficult to generalize the findings of this small study. The authors suggest that to bridge the gap between research and practice, teachers who have been trained to use the SRA program should implement the same research procedures in a typical classroom.
- Research is also needed to determine what modifications or accommodations may be needed for other students with autism to participate in the program.

C. Graphic Organizers

What Is a Graphic Organizer?

A *graphic organizer* is a visual tool used to organize information and show the relationship between words and concepts. A graphic organizer is usually a diagram or layout with blanks to be filled in by a student to represent thoughts and ideas.

- Graphic organizers come in many formats to structure the organization of ideas.
- Examples include diagrams, webs, graphs, charts, mind maps and outlines.
- Graphic organizers are also called *concept maps*.

Graphic organizers are designed for specific purposes, such as to compare and contrast, or to sequence events. When using graphic organizers, the student is taught to fill in specific information in a specific manner.

- You may have noticed a variety of graphic organizers used (intentionally) throughout this book, such as charts.

- Graphic organizers are recommended by the National Reading Panel (NRP) (NICHD 2000) as an effective way to improve comprehension for the average reader.

When I first published *Drawing a Blank* in 2011, there was no research available about the use of graphic organizers to improve comprehension for autistic readers. I suggested that graphic organizers were "promising" because several features of the tool make them a great fit for readers with hyperlexia. Now, multiple studies confirm this idea.

- The meta-analysis by Singh and colleagues (2020) concluded that visually cued instruction using tools including graphic organizers is a **highly effective approach** for improving reading comprehension in students with autism.
- The meta-analysis by Finnegan and Mazin (2016) confirms that **research supports the use of graphic organizers to support comprehension in students with autism**.
- Five studies in this section describe how graphic organizers improved the performance of students with autism on measures of reading comprehension.

Advantages for Readers with Autism

Because graphic organizers are visual, spatial, concrete, and structured, they are well matched to the strengths of readers with autism. Students can be taught to routinely use different types of graphic organizers before, during, and after reading.

- Graphic organizers can help readers make sense of text, organize ideas, and remember.
- These tools organize information in a clear way. They can make difficult text more accessible and meaningful to the reader (El Zein and colleagues 2013).

Graphic organizers can also help overcome some of the known difficulties that readers with autism may experience.

- For example, the use of visual tools can assist with executive functioning by developing organizational skills to manage information that may seem overwhelming and incomprehensible.

- Graphic organizers are useful to illustrate and emphasize relationships between different elements in the material.
- Graphic organizers can help autistic readers learn to perceive connections and similarities. Noticing similarities is often more difficult for autistic readers compared to the usual strong ability to notice differences (Floyd, Jeppson & Goldberg 2020).
- Graphic organizers are recommended by O'Connor and Klein (2004) as a structured way to stimulate relevant prior knowledge. This idea was suggested after using questions to generate prior knowledge **backfired** in their intervention study (See Chapter 6).

The visual representation of the relationships among ideas may be ideal for learning concepts (Erhen 2005; Gately 2008). This is especially helpful for students with autism who have difficulty understanding relationships between concepts, categories, and ideas.

- Graphic organizers can help with the understanding of stories by organizing information about the characters, plots, and relationships in narratives.
- Completed graphic organizers can be used as a foundation for generating written descriptions, sentences, or summaries.

Research Using Graphic Organizers

Five specific types of graphic organizers have been demonstrated as effective in improving reading comprehension for readers with autism in research studies.

Effective Practices: Graphic Organizers	
C1	Venn Diagram for Compare and Contrast
C2	Story Structure or Story Maps
C3	Character Event Map
C4	Organizer for Text Structures
C5	Organizer to Sort Wh- Questions

Here are descriptions of these five types of organizers.

<table>
<tr><td colspan="2">Five Formats of Graphic Organizers Used in Research with Students with Autism</td></tr>
<tr>
<td>C1</td>
<td>Venn Diagram for Compare and Contrast
Most people are familiar with two overlapping circles used to visualize differences and comparisons between two ideas.
<ul>
<li>The area of overlap is the area of commonality.</li>
<li>The outer circles indicate unique characteristics.</li>
</ul>
</td>
</tr>
<tr>
<td>C2</td>
<td>Story Structure Map or Story Maps
This visual tool is used to identify, organize, and understand key components of a story (or narrative). Story maps use formats such as flowcharts or diagrams to show story elements, including the plot, characters, setting, perspectives, and the sequence of events. Story maps can be used to:
<ul>
<li>Track story elements while reading</li>
<li>Draw attention to relevant features of the story.</li>
<li>Create a causal chain of events for the plot, conflict, and resolution.</li>
<li>Analyze a completed story.</li>
<li>Help remember information and answer questions.</li>
<li>Plan a story before writing.</li>
</ul>
</td>
</tr>
<tr>
<td>C3</td>
<td>Character Event Map
This visual tool helps students understand a character's journey in a story and how they are impacted by events in the narrative.
<ul>
<li>The map can be used during and after reading to understand and analyze the character's thoughts, feelings, motivations, desires, and actions.</li>
<li>Character maps require the use of inference skills to notice clues about information that is not explicitly stated in the story.</li>
</ul>
</td>
</tr>
<tr>
<td>C4</td>
<td>Organizer for Text Structures
A variety of graphic organizers can be used to help readers organize ideas in stories (narrative text) or expository material, such as academic content in textbooks. The strategy focuses on identifying how the author organizes the text and how important information is highlighted.
<ul>
<li>Organizers for narrative text structure include sequencing events in a story and describing a character.</li>
<li>Organizers for expository text include description, sequence, compare-contrast, cause and effect, and problem and solution.</li>
</ul>
</td>
</tr>
<tr>
<td>C5</td>
<td>Organizer to Sort Wh- Questions
Wh- questions are also known as the 5W's: Who? What? Where? When? and Why? Graphic organizers help students find and organize answers to these questions during or after reading.
<ul>
<li>Sorting activities with words, pictures, and sentence strips are often used with this organizer to help students identify and respond to different types of questions.</li>
<li>"Why?" is the most difficult category of questions to master because the answer is not always explicitly stated in the text, and the answer may involve inference.</li>
<li>The completed visual is useful after reading to help remember information and for retelling.</li>
</ul>
</td>
</tr>
</table>

Research Summaries

A Prime Example: Research with a Compare-Contrast Graphic Organizer

The summary below (formatted as a graphic organizer) explains in detail how a teacher successfully used a compare-and-contrast organizer with explicit instruction to improve the comprehension of academic concepts for middle school students.

Graphic Organizers Research Summary C1:
Venn Diagram for Compare and Contrast

Does Compare-Contrast Text Structure Help Students
with Autism Spectrum Disorder Comprehend Science Text?
Christina R. Carnahan & Pamela S. Williamson 2013

This study measured the effects of using a Venn diagram type of graphic organizer to improve understanding of science passages for middle school students.

Participants

Three male middle school students with high-functioning autism and their teacher, who was a certified reading specialist. Everett and Michael were thirteen years old and in seventh grade. Kevin was thirteen years old and in eighth grade. All three students decoded below grade level, and their comprehension was even lower.

Materials

The researchers developed three-paragraph expository passages about grade-level science concepts.
- The passages clearly highlighted the compare-contrast text structure and included **bold text** for key words.
- The wording of the passages was matched to the instructional reading level of the participants.
- A different passage was used for each intervention session.

The paragraphs in the passages were three sentences long and followed a formula:
- The first paragraph introduced two concepts (such as plants and animals) and spelled out specific ways that the two concepts were alike and different.
- The second and third paragraphs expanded on these ideas.

Graphic Organizers Research Summary C1:
Venn Diagram for Compare and Contrast

Ten comprehension questions were developed for each passage. Five questions included "right there" information, or facts explicitly stated in the text.

- Five questions were inferential, using sentence starters such as "Why does ... ?" or "What would happen if ... ?"
- Another type of inferential question asked students to connect something from the passage to their prior knowledge.

The compare-contrast intervention package also included a handout of signal words for compare and contrast.

- *Same* signal words included both, alike, can, and same.
- *Different* signal words included two kinds, different, cannot, and do not.

Students were each given a Venn diagram to complete independently at the end of the session. Examples of the materials and the exact procedure followed during implementation of the intervention are included in the published study.

What the Researchers and Students Did

Intervention sessions were conducted by the teacher during the regular classroom group reading time for 10 sessions. The researchers do not explicitly state the length of the sessions. There were a total of eight intervention sessions and two maintenance sessions.

1. The teacher asked students to read the title of the passage.
2. The teacher reviewed the compare and contrast signal words with students, reading each word aloud and describing it briefly.
3. The teacher asked the students to summarize the compare and contrast concept.
4. The teacher reviewed the Venn diagram, reminding students about the spaces that represented "different" and the space that represented "same."
5. Students took turns reading each paragraph, one at a time.
   a. After reading, the teacher asked students to identify the key words in the paragraph.
   b. Then, they were asked to summarize the paragraph, using compare and contrast language.
   c. The teacher asked three guiding questions:
      What are the two ideas? How are they the same? How are they different?
6. After summarizing, students were asked to complete their Venn diagram.
7. Once the Venn diagram was completed, the teacher read the ten comprehension questions aloud, one question at a time, separately to each student (so that they could not hear their peers' responses).
   a. Students could look back at the text to find answers and correct errors in responses.
   b. They could answer verbally or write their answers on the organizer.

**Graphic Organizers Research Summary C1:
Venn Diagram for Compare and Contrast**

Results

- All three students averaged 95–100% accuracy on comprehension questions during and after the intervention, a substantial increase compared to baseline.
- The intervention was **highly effective** for one student and **effective** for two.
- When students completed the Venn diagrams, they rephrased and wrote their own thoughts, rather than copying from the text.
- The researchers reported that it appeared the students had learned the thinking process to comprehend compare-contrast text, and no longer needed to rely on the use of Venn diagrams after the intervention was complete.
- As a result of the intervention, students were able to access challenging academic content that otherwise would have been beyond their reading (and comprehension) levels.

This high-impact intervention appears easy to implement according to the researchers' model. The teacher implemented it with 100% fidelity.

- The study supports the idea that embedding explicit instruction of text structure into academic content can improve learning.
- The successful use of the *visual* structure of the Venn diagram reminds us of the learning strength of many people with autism: understanding visual input.
- Note that the participants had below-grade-level decoding *and* comprehension. It is reasonable to infer that the intervention would be helpful to readers with hyperlexia.

Other Research Using Graphic Organizers

The summaries that follow provide the characteristics of participants in four additional studies that used graphic organizers.

- Pertinent information about implementation can guide you in using these options.
- Please refer to the original articles for complete information.

Graphic Organizers Research Summary C2: Story Maps

Effects of a Story Map on Accelerated Reader Postreading Test Scores in Students with High-Functioning Autism
Suzanne Griggs Stringfield, Deanna Luscre and David L. Gast 2011

This study investigated the effects of a story map graphic organizer on the reading comprehension of elementary students with autism.

Participants

Three boys with high-functioning autism, ranged in age from eight to eleven. They received most of their academic instruction in the same self-contained classroom. The interventionist was the boys' classroom teacher.
- One student had cognitive abilities (IQs) in the average range, and two were just slightly above the cutoff for average.
- They could decode words, but each boy tested one to three years behind grade level in reading.
- All three boys had at least one goal to improve comprehension.

Materials

The reading materials were short Accelerate Reader (AR) books (maximum ten pages) with pictures. Reading AR books on a computer and answering literal multiple-choice questions was part of the students' regular language arts routine. A quiz score of 85% indicated successful reading (meaning that the reader could recognize the correct answer).

What the Researchers and Students Did

The intervention was delivered one-to-one in 42 sessions of 15 minutes each. During the baseline phase, each participant individually read a story that they had not read before from the Accelerated Reader program.
- The quiz format was adapted, and the questions were orally presented to the participants.
- Each student had to provide a short answer without looking back at the story.

To begin the intervention phase, after reading their book, the children were taught to use a story map as a post-reading organizing tool. This known as the story map condition of the research. The teacher:
- Explained the purpose of using the organizer, that it could help the students get correct answers on AR quizzes.
- Explained the meaning of each item on the specific organizer: the setting (characters, time, and place) and basic plot (beginning, middle, and end).

Graphic Organizers Research Summary C2: Story Maps

- Provided an example and a non-example for each setting element, and asked students to contribute an idea about the story sequence.
- Related the different elements to other familiar stories.

The teacher answered questions and showed students where to write the information.
- She directed students to use the organizer to fill in the answers for the story they had just read, pointing to different sections.
- Students were allowed to use the completed story map during the quiz.
- During the choice condition, when participants can choose the options they prefer, they could choose which story they wanted to read and choose to use the story map, or not.

Results

All participants met the criterion (i.e., three consecutive days of 80% independent story map completion and 100% on AR quizzes during story map condition, and maintained this level of performance during choice and maintenance conditions. All were literal questions.
- Positive effects on recall of the story were quick and maintained during the study.
- All three students had made significant gains in unprompted question generation, with PND scores of 85, 88, and 100%.
- Based on data scores for correct responses on the multiple-choice AR quizzes, the intervention was found to be **moderately effective** for two students and **highly effective** for one.
- This study met the criteria set for certainty of evidence and was found to be conclusive.

Students learned to use the graphic organizers independently. Once the method was learned, some students chose not to use it, possibly indicating that they had internalized the process and no longer needed the graphic organizer.

Graphic Organizers Research Summary C3: Character Event Map

Improving Comprehension of Narrative Using Character Event Maps
for High School Students with Autism Spectrum Disorder
Pamela S. Williamson, Christina R. Carnahan,
Nicole Birri and Christopher Swoboda 2015

This study examined the effectiveness of an intervention that taught high school students how to complete character event maps for book chapters. The maps were then used to predict events in coming chapters.

Participants

Three males with autism, ages 16 to 17. One student, York, had lower comprehension compared to his sixth-grade decoding ability (the profile of hyperlexia). The other two had better comprehension abilities than decoding skills (but all were well below grade level). All three students were verbal but had low standardized language scores.

Materials

- *The Hunger Games* (Collins 2010) text and unabridged audio version
- Key literacy terms with definitions
- Character-specific character event maps with three columns for "Who is involved?" "What happened? and, "What it means," with five to seven events per chapter
- A visual aid with headers of four literary terms: idiom, metaphor, foreshadowing, and irony, and lines for text examples
- A table to apply the literary terms to characters and events in each chapter

What the Teacher and Students Did

The three students' special education teacher delivered the intervention package in small-group weekly sessions of 30 minutes each, for 22 weeks.
- In each session, the students read along silently while an unabridged audio version of a book chapter was played.
- The teacher, who was very familiar with *The Hunger Games* series of books, assisted students in completing the character map and the literary terms for each chapter, modeling the procedure using the "think-aloud" technique.
- In the following session, the map was reviewed, and students tried to predict what would happen in the chapter for that day. Then they listened and followed along to a new chapter, and repeated the routine, completing the character maps.

Graphic Organizers Research Summary C3: Character Event Map

Explicit instruction included explaining the purpose and value of the character event maps.

- The teacher identified three parts of an event: What happened, who was involved, and what it means, or the importance to the story.
- She verbally discussed the three events of the character map to help students fill it in.
- A student summarized the information in their own words.
- Another student was asked about the importance of the events.
- Students verbally reviewed the literary terms and chapter examples.

Evaluation

- Next, students responded to ten specially prepared explicit and inferential questions to assess their understanding of the chapter.
- Students were allowed to look back in the text for any questions they answered incorrectly.
- Trends in the student responses were evaluated using visual analysis.

Results

The intervention was highly effective.

- During intervention and follow-up, there was immediate improvement in comprehension for all three students, with all three having PND scores of 100%
- Baseline scores with traditional classroom comprehension supports were 60% and 58% for two students, and 35% for York.
- Two of the students answered 95% and 95% of the questions correctly; York averaged 79% correct.
- The students appeared to pay attention to meaning as they read and learned to think more systematically about text.
- The students learned to complete the character maps independently.
- The students were very interested in the novel and were eager to read and discuss it each week while completing their character maps.
- All three students reported that the intervention strategies helped them improve their comprehension.

Graphic Organizer Research Summary C4: Expository Text Structures

Increasing Comprehension of Expository Science Text for
Students with Autism Spectrum Disorder
Christina R. Carnahan, Pamela Williamson, Nicole Birri,
Christopher Swoboda & K.K. Snyder 2015

This study evaluated the effects of a text pattern intervention package on the ability of students with autism to comprehend traditional science texts.
- Students received direct instruction in types of text structures such as description, compare-contrast, cause and effect, and sequence.
- They learned to use a text structure organization sheet before reading.
- They completed an analysis and summary sheet while reading and after reading.

Participants

Three male high school students with high-functioning autism, ages 15 to 16. One student, Ryan, age 15, matched the reading profile of hyperlexia. He decoded at the upper middle school level, with comprehension at the fifth-grade level. He was diagnosed with autism in fourth grade.
- The other two students were diagnosed around age four.
- Their decoding was below grade level, but their comprehension was not lower than their decoding.

Materials

Science passages for each session were three to four pages in length, including figures and tables. They contained a maximum of four different text patterns.

The passages were matched to students' independent reading level.
- Ryan and Andy read at a fifth-grade level. Their intervention material was late sixth grade. They received intervention together.
- Sam comprehended at an upper-middle school level, and read from a grade-level science text. He received one-to-one intervention.

Ten comprehension questions were developed for each passage.
- Five literal questions included two definitions. The other three related to literal information in the text patterns, such as comparing two concepts.
- Five inferential questions included stating the main idea, drawing conclusions, and applying the information.

The researchers also created a **text pattern organization guide** for four text structures: description, compare-contrast, cause and effect, and sequence. The guide described the use, purpose, and signal words (such as "both" or "as a result").

Graphic Organizer Research Summary C4: Expository Text Structures

A **text analysis and summary sheet** was created to draw students' attention to the text pattern and to the important content in the passage.
- The first question was a prediction.
- Three questions related to the author's purpose and the related text pattern.
- The final item required students to refer to their text pattern graphic organizers to write or draw a summary of the passage.

What the Researchers and Students Did

The intervention was delivered by a teacher in pull-out sessions in a resource room during language arts. The length of each session was not stated in the journal article. It appears there were 16 total sessions, including baseline, intervention, and maintenance.

The teacher used systematic instruction with a structured teaching routine that included:
- Discussing the purpose and benefit of understanding text patterns.
- Previewing and reviewing the text pattern sheet.
- Having students read the text aloud (taking turns or solo).
- Reviewing signal words.
- Completing items on the text structure form about the text pattern and signal words.
- Completing a graphic organizer together for each section of the text.
- Prompting corrections if needed.
- Reviewing the graphic organizers, with students providing a verbal summary of each.
- Completing comprehension questions.

Students were allowed to look back in the text to correct any wrong answers on their comprehension questions and improve their scores (to compensate for memory issues vs. comprehension issues).

Results

Data was collected using checklists at baseline, during intervention, and at maintenance two weeks after the final intervention session.
- The instruction was **highly effective** during the intervention and maintenance phases for all three participants.
- Ryan, the student who fit the hyperlexic reading pattern, averaged 54% correct at baseline. His scores improved to an average of 90% correct responses during intervention. He scored 95% during follow-up.
- Participants reported that the intervention was helpful for reading science texts. This is a positive result because science content can be complex and abstract.

Graphic Organizer Research Summary C5: Organizer to Sort Wh- Questions

Effects of Wh- Question Graphic Organizers on Reading Comprehension Skills of Students with Autism Spectrum Disorder
Keri S. Bethune & Charles L. Wood 2013

This study measured the effects of teaching elementary grade students how to use a graphic organizer to answer literal Wh- questions.

Participant Characteristics:

Three male autistic students, age ten. Two students had cognitive abilities in the average range, and one tested slightly below the cutoff for average. All three fit the hyperlexic profile of stronger word-reading scores compared to comprehension scores.

Materials

The graphic organizer used for the study had four columns, each with a literal question header at the top: who, what, where, and what doing. These categories correspond to person, thing, place, and event. (Inferential questions such as Why? or When? were not included).

Texts at the students' reading level were selected from a Direct Instruction program. Students read a new story of two to four pages in each session.

What the Researchers and Students Did

Students were explicitly taught to sort eight words on the graphic organizer, with two words per question category.
- Individual intervention sessions lasted about ten minutes each and were conducted in the classroom at the student's desk during regular instruction time.
- A total of 30 sessions were conducted for the baseline, intervention, and maintenance phases.
- After the student completed each organizer, the researcher checked for literal comprehension with an additional eight factual recall questions, two questions from each category.

Results

- Student 1's responses to the eight questions were at 0% correct at baseline and improved to 100% with intervention. The intervention was **highly effective**.
- Student 2's responses were 33% correct at baseline and 75% after intervention.
- Student 3's responses were 40% correct at baseline and 100% during the maintenance phase.
- Mean scores on questions increased by 96%. Significant improvement in accuracy scores for all three students generalized to their classroom reading worksheets post-intervention.
- The study establishes preliminary evidence of the effectiveness of this intervention for students with autism.
- The students reported that the graphic organizers were helpful.

Make the Most of Graphic Organizers

In addition to the types of graphic organizers highlighted in this chapter, many other formats are well-matched to the areas of need of hyperlexic readers, including those used for the following purposes:

Describe (features or characteristics)	Separate relevant from irrelevant ideas	Sequence events in a story or process (retell)
Categorize or classify objects	Show cause and effect	Draw conclusions
Predict	Relate concepts	Problem-solve

Ready-made graphic organizers are usually part of the curriculum used in schools and in commercial reading programs. Graphic organizers can also be created using computer graphics or word-processing programs.

- For example, the PowerPoint® program in the Microsoft Office Suite includes graphic organizers to organize ideas such as sequences, processes, and cycles.
- The program can be used to create PowerPoint slides, and wording can be easily inserted into the figures.

Tips for teaching students to use graphic organizers are found in Appendix D. This appendix also includes extensive information to teach a related skill, using **text structure** to improve comprehension.

D. Metacognitive Strategies

What Is a Metacognitive Strategy?

Metacognitive strategies can be described as the process of "thinking about thinking," or "learning about learning." They are also called **SRSD techniques**, for self-regulated strategy development.

- These methods help learners become more aware of their own behavior, monitor their performance, reflect on difficulties, and fix breakdowns in understanding.
- Using metacognitive strategies can help readers feel more confident, empowered, and in control of their learning.

Three research studies focused on teaching specific **ways of thinking while reading**. All of them were shown to be **effective** or **highly effective** in improving reading comprehension for students with autism (Singh and colleagues 2020).

- This section begins with an explanation of two metacognitive strategies that have not yet been discussed. (QAR, or Question-Answer Relationships has been described).
- The section concludes with summaries of the research.

Effective Practices: Metacognitive Strategies	
D1	TWA Strategy: Think Before-While-After Reading
D2	Self-Directed Question-and-Answer Relationships
D3	Collaborative Strategic Reading-High School

What Is the TWA Strategy?

This reading comprehension strategy helps students actively engage with text and monitor their understanding while reading. It is particularly useful for informational or expository text. The strategy includes three things to think about before, during, and after reading (Mason 2013):

- **Think before reading (T)** = The author's purpose, what you know, and what you want to know.
- **While reading (W)** = Your reading speed, connections to what you know, and reread to understand when needed.
- **After reading (A)** = Identify the main idea, summarize details, and state what you learned.

What Is Collaborative Strategic Reading?

Collaborative Strategic Reading, or CSR, is a form of collaborative learning. Students work together to support their understanding of text, especially expository or informational text.

- First, students are taught to use specific reading comprehension strategies, including predicting, questioning, clarifying, and summarizing.
- Next, they preview the text to notice text structure, such as headings, diagrams, and other visual cues.
- As they read, students monitor their comprehension, stopping to ask themselves whether or not they are understanding the material. (This is similar to the final strategy described in Chapter 9, called "Clink or Clunk").
- Students collaborate to identify main ideas and summarize.
- They discuss and look for answers about anything that is unclear.

Outside of autism research, CSR is a fully developed, evidence-based instructional approach to improve reading comprehension (Reutebuch and colleagues 2015).

- It's been evaluated through numerous quasi-experimental and experimental studies, and two recent randomized controlled trials.
- Results demonstrated improved reading outcomes for students with learning disabilities and for students at risk for reading difficulties, including English learners.
- CSR may be promising for students with autism, but it hasn't been widely researched for this population.

Research Summaries

The graphics that follow provide a brief summary of three studies that used metacognitive strategies. Please refer to the original articles for complete information.

Research Summary D1 Metacognitive Strategies

Effects of the TWA Strategy on Expository Reading of Students with Autism
Sarah Howorth, Christopher Lopata,
Marcus Thomeer and Jonathan Rodgers 2016

This research studied the effects of explicit instruction in the TWA metacognitive strategy with the reading comprehension of students with autism.

- The TWA approach prompts readers to focus on elements of a text before, during, and after reading.
- TWA has been validated for students with learning disabilities through more than 25 years of research.
- This small study is the first to test the effectiveness of TWA for students with autism.

Participants

Four male students with autism, aged ten to eleven, from three school districts.

- Their cognitive ability was greater than 90 (average IQ or higher).
- All four boys had a discrepancy between their own decoding scores and comprehension scores, consistent with the profile of hyperlexia.
- Their internal gaps ranged from 1 to 4.5 standard deviations (SDs). A SD is 15 points. A gap of 20 points or greater is cause for concern.
- Simon had an internal gap of 18 points between his ability to decode and his comprehension score. Marks's gap was 23 points.
- Oliver had an internal gap of 46 points.
- Paul had a gap of 67 points between his strong ability to decode and his highly impaired ability to comprehend what he read.

Materials

The materials were not described in the research article, except to say it was expository text.

What the Researchers and Students Did

The intervention was conducted individually with each student by a researcher in a resource room during English language arts instruction time. After baseline data was gathered, the researcher delivered nine highly-structured intervention sessions of 45 minutes each with positive behavioral reinforcement.

Research Summary D1 Metacognitive Strategies

Explicit instruction included modeling with "think aloud" for two sessions, supported practice for two sessions, and independent practice of the TWA strategies for two sessions. The content included three things to think about before, during, and after reading.

- **Think before reading (T)**
- **While reading (W)**
- **After reading (A)**

Each student created their own checklist to follow based on the TWA strategy. The students referred to their customized visual cues throughout the intervention.

Students were also taught highlighting skills. They were asked to come up with a mnemonic to help them remember the colors. One student invented this pun-based memory tool:

- The main ideas in pink using the mnemonic, "I pink this is the main idea."
- Details in green using the mnemonic, "Do you a-green this is an important detail?"
- Rhetorical information in orange using the mnemonic prompt, "Orange you glad this isn't important?"

Assessment

Two measures were used to assess reading comprehension at baseline, during intervention, and in the maintenance phase.

Oral retelling. After reading, students were asked to orally retell everything they remembered. This method was used to measure participants' comprehension of text passages. A rubric was used to rate the accuracy, sequence, main ideas, and details retold. The rubric also noted the level of prompting needed to support a student's response.

Questions. Students were asked to independently read and answer ten comprehension questions during baseline, intervention, and maintenance sessions.

- The questions were matched to their instructional reading level and were generated at a free website, https://www.readworks.org/.
- The ten questions corresponded to the student's understanding of text structure, explicit information, inference, identifying the main idea, vocabulary, and sentence-level syntax.

Research Summary D1 Metacognitive Strategies

Results

The mastery criterion was set at independent use of eight of the nine steps in the TWA strategy. All three students met this criterion after only six intervention sessions.

Data from the oral retelling and comprehension questions was analyzed.

Scores over 90% indicated that the intervention was **very effective**, 89 to 70% indicated **effective**, 69 to 50% indicated **questionable**, and below 50% indicated **ineffective**.

- **The intervention phase was *very effective* for Simon, Paul, and Mark in both retell and comprehension questions. It was effective for Oliver in both areas. Gains were sustained at maintenance.**
- **A more stringent PND analysis of data showed the intervention was *very effective* for Simon and *effective* for Mark in both areas.**

The students and their parents reported satisfaction with the intervention and mentioned specific ways that it helped the students improve their comprehension.

Metacognitive Strategies Research Summary D2
Self-Directed Question-and-Answer Relationships (QAR)

Discourse Comprehension Intervention for High-Functioning Students with Autism Spectrum Disorders: Preliminary Findings from a School-Based Study
Jakob Åsberg and Annika Dahlgren Sandberg 2010

This Swedish study involved a classroom-based intervention to support comprehension of narrative text by using question-and-answer relationships (QAR), an explicit, structured cognitive framework. The intervention begins with explicit instruction, teacher modeling, and scaffolding. Responsibility to use the strategy is gradually released to students.

Participants

Twelve students with high-functioning autism, aged ten to fifteen. All had vocabulary and decoding skills in the average range with poor comprehension, fitting the profile of hyperlexia. Cognitive ability scores (IQ) ranged from 83 to 125.

- The students attended special school units in a school outside Stockholm.
- Five teachers implemented the interventions in their classrooms.
- Peers in each classroom also received the intervention.
- Sixteen typically developing children made up the comparison group.

Metacognitive Strategies Research Summary D2
Self-Directed Question-and-Answer Relationships (QAR)

Materials

- A training booklet containing 13 stories of increasing length from Franzén (1997) was edited by the study authors and provided to the teachers and children.
- At the end of each story, students responded to questions about the story.
- In addition, students needed to identify the type of question and where the answer could be found (Raphael, Highfield & Au 2006) as follows:

Right there: Information is directly mentioned in one sentence in the text.
Reflect and search: Information must be inferred by integrating different sentence or text passages and using text-connecting inferences.
On my own: Information has to be inferred using world knowledge.

What the Researchers and Students Did

The intervention focused on building meaning through these four active processes:
- Locating information
- Integrating information within the story
- Integrating story information with prior knowledge
- Meta-comprehension, noticing when your own comprehension fails and repairing it.

The researchers provided an informational lecture for teachers, speech and language therapists, and assistants at the school to explain the cognitive and linguistic roots of comprehension difficulties. Instruction to improve comprehension was discussed.

One of the goals of the QAR technique is to equip teachers with "an explicit set of concepts for talking and thinking about the activity of comprehension" (p. 93).

Teachers who planned to implement the intervention attended seminars to review, test, and discuss the training materials.

Training sessions were held two to three days a week, for 20 to 30 minutes, for four weeks. Intervention for younger students was adapted to a total of ten to twelve shorter sessions.
- The students read parts of the text independently or the teacher read aloud.
- The teachers provided direct explanations and definitions. They identified the three different information sources and modeled strategies to answer questions.
- This was followed by guided practice and closely monitored scaffolded practice.
- When possible, small group discussions were encouraged, so students could compare their answers and learn from one another.

Metacognitive Strategies Research Summary D2
Self-Directed Question-and-Answer Relationships (QAR)

Before and after the intervention, narrative listening comprehension was measured using four texts each from the standardized Discourse Comprehension Test (DCT) (Brookshire and Nicholas 1993).

- Students were asked to give yes/no answers.
- Children were asked to explain the thinking behind their correct "no" answers.
- Most children explained spontaneously.

Teachers were also asked to rate whether they thought the intervention was good for the comprehension development of the target students.

- They gave feedback on the question, "In what way did it work or not work?"
- Another question asked whether teachers would continue using a similar comprehension approach for each student in the future.

Results

- Comparison of the pre- and post-intervention scores on the DCT revealed significant improvement in comprehension for the children with autism.
- The intervention had a medium effect size of 0.35.
- The mean teacher rating of improved comprehension ability after training was 3.66, with 1 meaning "no improvement" and 5 meaning "very much better."
- Teachers reported that they would use this or a similar intervention again for eleven of the twelve students.
- Eleven of the twelve students were mostly positive about the training.

Metacognitive Strategies Research Summary D3
Collaborative Strategic Reading

Investigating a Reading Comprehension Intervention for High School
Children with Autism Spectrum Disorder: A Pilot Study
Colleen K. Reutebuch, Farah El Zein, MK Kim, Aron N. Weinberg and S. Vaughn 2015

This research studied the use of an adapted version of the Collaborative Strategic Reading–High School (CSR–HS) intervention and measured the effects on the reading comprehension of three high school students with autism.

Participants

A total of six students participated in the CSR–HS intervention. Three students had autism. Three academically advanced, typically developing peers were their reading partners.

The three students with autism in the study were considered high-functioning, with cognitive abilities in the average range or greater.

They spent the majority of their school day mainstreamed and were expected to be successful with an academic curriculum.

All three had limited social interactions with peers and adults.

Some had behavior that interfered with learning and task completion, including being off-task, non-compliant, or sensory-seeking.

All three could read with some understanding but struggled with comprehension, as follows:

Hector, age fifteen, in ninth grade, read at a third-grade instructional level and scored at grade two for passage comprehension.

Brian, age sixteen, in tenth grade read at a second-grade instructional level and scored at kindergarten, month eight, for passage comprehension.

Sofia, age seventeen, in eleventh grade, read at a fifth-grade instructional level and scored a grade equivalent of 4.8 on passage comprehension.

Materials

The intervention was based on the Collaborative Strategic Reading metacognitive reading program (CSR).

The researchers wanted to tailor CSR to the needs of autistic learners.

They wanted to adapt CSR so it could be used across reading topics and classes.

Metacognitive Strategies Research Summary D3
Collaborative Strategic Reading

They wanted the intervention to appeal to students and educators.

With these goals in mind, specific adaptations were made, including to:

Incorporate specific evidence-based practices used with autistic students, such as priming, prompting, and self-monitoring. An example of priming is pre-teaching relevant information about the topic, concepts, and vocabulary.

Structure the delivery of the intervention, including a detailed, repetitive lesson plan for interventionists to use before, during, and after reading.

Provide prompts for monitoring and questioning during reading.

Provide a graphic organizer to help with summarizing (a visual support).

The adapted version became the CSR–High School Intervention, or CSR–HS.

Instructional grade-level texts of three to four paragraphs each and corresponding comprehension questions were selected from *Read Naturally* passages.

High-interest topics in the expository text were included, such as animals and mysterious events.

Comprehension probes were limited to four multiple-choice questions about facts from the text.

What the Researchers and Students Did

Participants with autism were paired with a typically developing reading partner to learn and use reading strategies with informational text. Students were carefully paired with appropriate role models with whom they had interacted successfully prior to the intervention.

A total of 41 intervention sessions were conducted by two trained graduate students. Sessions were held two to three times per week for 30 minutes each over 16 weeks. Comprehension checks were collected at each session.

The students also received a 50-minute tutorial session weekly with interventionists.

These sessions included reviewing a previous intervention and CSR–HS strategies, or preparing for the next session (priming).

Social coaching for interacting with peer partners was also provided.

Metacognitive Strategies Research Summary D3
Collaborative Strategic Reading

Researchers tracked positive social interactions and the number of challenging behaviors observed during the intervention.

Individualized modifications to the program were introduced for Brian when he had difficulty working with the peer partner, which resulted in improvement.

Results

The intervention was **effective** based on a PEM score of 0.83. Students maintained gains during the maintenance phase.

Accuracy on reading comprehension tasks increased for all three participants.

Scores on multiple-choice comprehension questions increased by 14%.

Increases in social interactions were documented. Challenging behaviors decreased.

The small study demonstrates that CSR–HS can be an effective tool for high school students with autism, resulting in academic, social, and behavioral progress.

Summary

Hopefully you're inspired by the information in this chapter! It's encouraging to get some guidance from individual studies about what's **effective**, even if the studies are small.

- The interventions were not difficult to carry out.
- Gains were made for individuals with autism of all ages.
- There was a high degree of satisfaction among teachers, students, and parents.

Some of these options may be beneficial for the student(s) you work with. To individualize instruction to a particular person with autism and hyperlexia, here are five considerations to keep in mind:

1. The significant variation among individuals with autism affects the effectiveness of a particular strategy or teaching method in research and practice.
2. Methods that work for some students with autism may not work for others.

3. Strategies used with students with autism must take into account both the person's general cognitive profile and individual variations in strengths and needs (O'Connor & Klein 2004).

4. Methods helpful to students with other learning differences *may be* appropriate for some students with autism, particularly with modification or adaptation.

5. Some methods that work for students with other learning differences *are not* effective for those with autism, particularly without tailor-made modifications.

Making Connections: Revisiting Recommendations of the NRP

One of the questions that drives research in the field of special education is whether teaching strategies and methods that are effective for typical learners will help atypical learners. This idea connects back to the recommendations made by the National Reading Panel for typically developing children (NICHD 2000, Shanahan 2017).

- Very little is known about the use of NRP comprehension strategies for children with autism (Chiang & Lin 2007).
- In their meta-analysis of interventions for comprehension, El Zein et al. (2013) concluded that "**modifying** instructional interventions associated with improved comprehension for students with reading difficulties **may** improve reading comprehension in students with autism."
- The next logical question is *how* teaching method needs to be modified for learners with a particular diagnosis or learning profile.
- The studies in this chapter provide insights to help answer this question.

Based on the research presented and everything that has been discussed to this point about autism and hyperlexia, we can review the NRP's recommendations to consider which might be effective for this population *if modified or adapted*.

Figure 7.1 represents my analysis.

Figure 7.1

16 Strategies to Improve Reading Comprehension
from the National Reading Panel Report
Color-Coded Tailored to Learners with Hyperlexia
https://www.nichd.nih.gov/sites/default/files/publications/pubs/nrp/documents/report.pdf

Green: A **good fit** with the strengths of readers with autism and hyperlexia or a good idea in general.

Yellow: Yes, please, but **teach prerequisite skills first, including social skills**.

- **Add structure, routines, or visual supports** to these processes, such as graphic organizers, as much as possible.
- **Avoid** methods that backfired in studies, such as pre-reading questions to activate prior knowledge.

Blue: A **challenging fit** to the learning profile of students with hyperlexia, in this author's opinion. Students are asked to learn something that is not well aligned with their cognitive profile. Teaching these methods would involve significantly tailored individualization, structure, and support.

Graphic and semantic organizers
Visual tools, like story maps, help readers organize and remember information from text.

Story structure
Students learn how the structure of a story (e.g., characters, plot, setting) influences comprehension and memory.

Vocabulary instruction
Teaching specific vocabulary words, either in context or through separate lessons, can significantly impact comprehension.

Teacher preparation
Providing teachers with training and resources to effectively implement comprehension strategies.

Prior knowledge
Activating and using students' existing knowledge and experiences to connect with the text (with appropriate methods as discussed in this book).

Active reading
Engaging in activities that encourage focused attention and interaction with the text.

Listening actively
Engaging in active listening skills during reading and discussion.

Question generation
Students generate their own questions about the text, promoting active reading and deeper understanding.

Question answering
Readers answer questions posed by the teacher or peers, receiving immediate feedback.

Comprehension monitoring
Readers become aware of their own understanding and identify areas where they need to clarify or revisit material.

Summarization
Readers identify the main ideas and supporting details of a text, often in their own words.

Cooperative learning
Students work together in small groups to practice reading strategies and support each other's comprehension.

Psycholinguistics
Understanding the language structure and processes involved in comprehension.

Mental imagery
Creating visual images in the mind while reading to enhance comprehension.

Inferencing
Making logical conclusions based on text information and background knowledge.

Multiple strategy teaching
Combining different strategies for a more comprehensive approach to reading.

Guidance for Teaching

The NRP identified question generation as the single most effective reading comprehension strategy.

- Question generation can be particularly difficult for autistic individuals, as seen with difficulties with conversation skills.
- Responding to questions can be equally difficult, as evidenced by the number of students whose IEP goals include answering basic Wh- questions from preschool age onward.

Clearly, this is a key strategy, but how can it be effectively taught to readers with autism? Whalon and colleagues (2009) suggested how to modify the instruction of an active reading questioning strategy by teaching the child to generate questions using a visual cue card paired with a script and self-monitoring checklist.

- As progress is made, support is faded to a visual cue paired with a signal word.
- Then a visual cue is used alone, until the student can generate questions independently.
- For independent use of the strategy, teachers create and teach the student to use a self-monitoring checklist that prompts the student **when** to stop and ask questions while reading.

These suggestions can be a useful template for modifying instruction for other NRP recommendations. With these insights as inspiration, I've systematized the recommendations of Whalon's team and provided additional relevant steps and details. These ideas are shown in Figure 7.2.

Figure 7.2

	Suggestions for Teaching NRP Skills to Readers with Autism
1	**Think through the steps used in the strategy from the perspective of the hyperlexic reader. What will be difficult for them?** • How can you break the process down into steps that simplify it? • How can you add structure and provide visual supports to clarify the process? • What kind of prompts will students need to learn and use the strategy? • When and how should these be provided?
2	**Plan the structural supports and visual cues to help students understand and use the strategy.** Create and provide written instructions, visual cue cards, scripts, signal words, images, graphic organizers, self-monitoring checklists, etc.
3	**Teach essential pre-requisite skills first.** For example, you can't teach someone to summarize if s/he can't separate relevant from irrelevant ideas.
4	**Use direct, explicit instruction to teach the strategy. Small group instruction is preferred for these learners.** Explain the purpose of the strategy. Model using the visual materials and prompts while "thinking through" the process aloud.
5	**Provide support (scaffolding) for interactive student practice** with teacher feedback until mastery is achieved.
6	**Use positive reinforcement** for attempts and success throughout the process.
7	**Fade support** as students show mastery.
8	**Transfer responsibility** to the student to use the strategy with any self-monitoring tools.
9	**Monitor student use and success** with the strategy and provide correction as needed.
10	**Check for generalization and application of strategy use** in different areas of the curriculum, projects, etc.

What's Next?

The chapters that follow present information about promising practices that hopefully someday will be converted to research-based or evidence-based practices as reading comprehension interventions for students with autism are studied further. In the meantime, you may find these ideas helpful for engaging struggling students.

- Chapter 8 presents strategies to improve vocabulary.
- Chapter 9 presents creative and innovative ideas to improve comprehension.

Building Vocabulary—Practical Strategies to Improve Comprehension

Vocabulary, or word meaning, is a recognized key to comprehension. This chapter explores promising practices to build vocabulary and help hyperlexic readers understand word meaning. The chapter offers:

- Tips for deciding what words to teach to hyperlexic readers.
- Ten options for improving vocabulary, including the potential benefits of each idea.

How Do Children Learn What Words Mean?

As we've discussed, readers with hyperlexia can quickly identify or decode words, without understanding what those words mean.

- For this reason, hyperlexia is sometimes called *word calling*. This term suggests that the reader is *not* interacting with, relating to, and holding onto the meaning of the words being read (Truch 2004).
- **As a result**, readers with hyperlexia do not add new words to their personal vocabulary through reading as other readers do.
- They don't *store* new word meanings in memory to draw upon later.

Children also need exposure to **rich oral language experiences** to develop vocabulary (Diamond & Gutlohn 2006; NICHY 2000).

- Chapter 2 discussed that limited socialization and communication skills can also limit exposure to oral language experiences.
- Due to restricted and repetitive interests, readers with autism often have a vocabulary that is narrow and deep, rather than wide and diverse.
- The more the person engages in their favorite interests (usually alone), the more they want to do so. This can make it more difficult to interest them in other children and activities.

Most children learn vocabulary through **incidental learning**, or picking up new word meanings through everyday exposure. This source is not likely to be sufficient to produce the amount of vocabulary growth that readers with autism need to keep pace with classroom instruction and manage the wide variety of materials they will need to read.

How Do Readers Grow Their Vocabulary?

Research in vocabulary instruction indicates that explicit instruction of **unfamiliar or key words** should take place before reading.

- This leads to a greater understanding of the whole text.
- For readers on the spectrum, preparing to read **in a way that works for them** can be one of the most important steps of the reading process.

Readers also need ways to **figure out the meaning** of unknown words they come across while reading.

- This includes learning to understand the meaning of words and phrases **from context** and through **word analysis** (Diamond & Gutlohn 2006; NICHY 2000).
- Figure 8.1 shows an example of expected vocabulary development for eighth grade, from the Common Core Content Standards. Students are responsible for **discovering meaning** in multiple ways.

Figure 8.1

Common Core English Language Standards Grade 8

1	Determine or clarify the meaning of unknown and multiple-meaning words or phrases based on *grade 8 reading and content*, choosing flexibly from a range of strategies.
	   a. **Use context** (e.g., the overall meaning of a sentence or paragraph; a word's position or function in a sentence) as a clue to the meaning of a word or phrase.
	   b. **Use common, grade-appropriate Greek or Latin affixes and roots** as clues to the meaning of a word (e.g., precede, recede, secede).
	   c. **Consult general and specialized reference materials** (e.g., dictionaries, glossaries, thesauruses), both print and digital, to find the pronunciation of a word or determine or clarify its precise meaning or its part of speech.
	   d. **Verify the preliminary determination of the meaning of a word or phrase** (e.g., by checking the inferred meaning in context or in a dictionary).

2	Demonstrate understanding of figurative language, word relationships, and nuances in word meanings.
	   a. **Interpret figures of speech** (e.g., verbal irony, puns) in context.
	   b. **Use the relationship between particular words** to better understand each of the words.
	   c. **Distinguish among the connotations** (associations) of words with similar denotations (definitions) (e.g., bullheaded, willful, firm, persistent, resolute).

3	**Acquire and use accurately grade-appropriate general academic and domain-specific words and phrases; gather vocabulary knowledge when considering a word or phrase important to comprehension or expression.**

These active, constructive processes require flexibility in thinking, the ability to make multiple connections, and a wide vocabulary of synonyms. As students advance in school, academic tasks and vocabulary become more complex and abstract.

- As a result, it's not surprising that the demands of the curriculum are often a mismatch with the skill sets of readers with autism.
- This makes it clear why vocabulary instruction and preparation for reading must be **direct**, **strategic**, and **effective** to help students with autism grow their vocabulary and understanding of word meanings.

Research on Vocabulary and Readers with Autism

There's not enough time to teach someone *all* the words s/he needs to know in a lifetime.

- Unfortunately, there's very little research on what works to build vocabulary for readers with autism, which should not be surprising at this point!
- Fortunately, many excellent materials are available to help expand vocabulary and teach word-learning strategies.

Everyone with autism is different, and there is no "one-size-fits-all" or single answer to the question of *how* to teach specific vocabulary skills, or *what* interventions or resources to use. The guidelines shown in Figure 8.2, tailored to the strengths of readers with autism, may be helpful in intentional efforts to teach vocabulary, expand word meaning, and meet the needs of a particular individual.

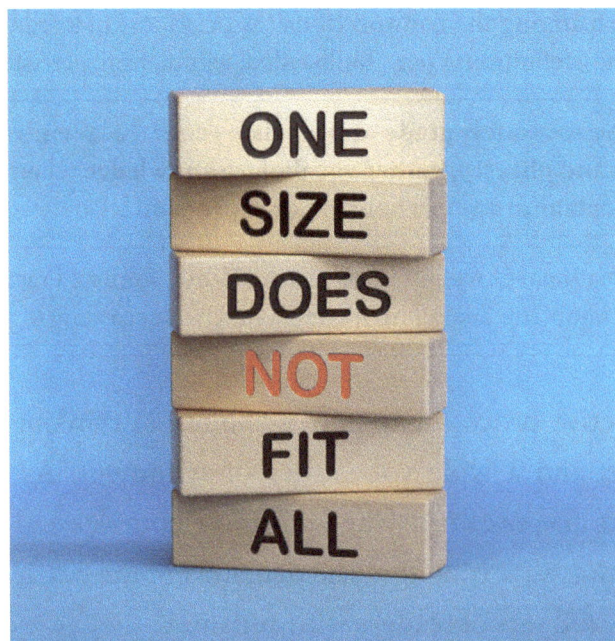

Figure 8.2

Tips for Teaching Vocabulary	
Make It Relevant	
Choose keywords that are important to understanding content material.	Teach useful words that are encountered often (high-frequency words).
Teach words in meaningful contexts and groupings, rather than in isolation.	
Tailor to Visual and Concrete Strengths	
Show, rather than tell, whenever possible.	Provide sentences to demonstrate the correct usage of the word, and have students follow the model to come up with their own sentences.
Use Systematic Strengths	
Teach rote, concrete ways to dissect words, such as breaking them into roots, prefixes and suffixes.	Work from the known to the unknown (e.g., connect meaning through synonyms).
Teach homographs: Words that look alike but aren't pronounced alike (*tear*, as in rip, and crying a *tear*)	Focus on words with multiple meanings.
Engage and Motivate	
Use motivating materials when presenting techniques or strategies, including text from students' favorite interest or area of expertise.	Demonstrate the power of discovering meaning: Show the cause-and-effect relationship between finding meaning and the value to the individual (such as following instructions to build a model)
Provide ways for the student to come across the same word for multiple exposures and active encounters (such as reading, writing, hearing, classifying, etc.).	Teach the connotation of words to help infer meaning and take perspective, enriching the reading experience.

Activities to Expand Vocabulary

This chapter presents a variety of ideas to expand vocabulary and ways to help readers figure out the meaning of new words (and phrases) they come across while reading.

- Several activities are specially designed for this book.
- Other methods were included if they're likely to be a good match to the learning needs, strengths, and interests of many students with autism.

The options listed below are explained in detail in this chapter. The headings are lettered and highlighted in green to help you spot them.

A. Turn on the closed captions on television or video screens.

B. Teach vocabulary through synonyms—electronic texts and e-readers

C. Electronic dictionaries

D. Use objects to pre-teach vocabulary

E. Visual dictionaries

F. Connotation: Shades of meaning and "What to say?"

G. Word elements: Root meanings and affixes

H. The DISSECT mnemonic

I. Homographs

J. Explicit instruction of idioms

The section for these suggestions may include:

- A description of the strategy or idea.
- The "fit" for readers with hyperlexia.
- Steps, examples, or materials for teaching.
- Ideas for generalization or application.

A. Turn on the Closed Captions

A *closed caption* is text that appears on a TV or other screen for television programs, movies, or DVDs. The words match the dialogue of the narrator or character who is speaking.

- Originally designed for people who are deaf or hard of hearing, captions have benefits for other viewers, including viewers with autism.

- In addition to words, captions also provide other information that is relevant to the story, like the mood or the name of the music being played.

The closed caption feature is found on most televisions under "settings," "sound options," or "accessibility."

- DVDs or Blu-ray discs usually have a caption option on the main menu.
- There is no need to ask the person with autism to read the captions. It can become an automatic process!
- Figure 8.3 describes ten benefits of displaying captions, showing just how helpful this no-cost option can be.

Figure 8.3

	Ten Advantages of Using Closed Captions for Readers with Autism
1	Captions map speech onto print, connecting the spoken word and the written word.
2	Objects and concepts are presented in context, with oral and written language to reinforce meaning.
3	Captions are a multimodal way to simultaneously improve understanding of spoken and written language.
4	Seeing captions while the person on screen talks helps the reader understand that text is what a person says, written down (as in story books and narratives).
5	For those with auditory processing issues, captions can fill in gaps of words that were missed, with a potential reaction of, "Oh, *that's* what they're saying!"
6	Some autistic people have difficulty distinguishing the separation between spoken words and hear "strings of sounds" (e.g., "hamburgerandfries"). The viewer can begin to recognize discrete words when they appear on the screen.
7	The person with autism may be motivated to read captions when watching preferred, familiar shows and videos. Decoding and fluency may also improve as a result.
8	When captions are used during videos that are replayed frequently, the reader will have multiple or repeated exposures to vocabulary words and ideas.
9	Captions can also help improve self-monitoring skills. When following along, the reader may start to notice when a mistake is made or a word is left out.
10	An unexpected benefit is expanding knowledge in music. Captions often include the name of the piece and the artist. This can be a good topic of conversation.

B. Enhancing Vocabulary Through Synonyms—Electronic Texts and e-Readers

Research supports learning synonyms **in context** as an effective way to grow vocabulary (Kluth & Chandler-Olcott 2008; Texas Reading Initiative 2002). Using a **synonym strategy** is a quick-and-easy way to clarify the meanings of unfamiliar words in context.

- One of the best options to do this is using electronic textbooks or e-readers such as a Kindle® or iPad® (Urrea and colleagues 2024).
- Students can learn to use the synonym feature, and numerous other comprehension supports that the technology offers.

Assistive technology (AT) can be defined as "electronic or digital devices, 'apps,' or software used to improve specific skills" (Syriopoulou-Delli & Gkiolnta 2020).

- Both electronic textbooks and e-readers are assistive technology.
- Electronic textbooks often offer features to help readers actively overcome obstacles in the text in real time. In addition to definitions, synonyms, and additional images to help with the visualization of a word or concept, readers can hear the particular words or the whole text spoken aloud.
- There's clear educational benefit to providing electronic textbooks to readers with autism who need them.

Please note: Any AT needs must be considered for every student with an individualized education program (IEP).

- An IEP meeting is the perfect time to bring up the option of using electronic textbooks or e-readers at school and at home.
- This option is especially appropriate for students with goals in their IEP to improve comprehension or vocabulary.

A low-tech **alternative synonym strategy** is to type text into a word-processing program on a computer (such as Microsoft Word). This keeps the word in context while deciding which synonym fits best in a sentence. Figure 8.4 describes the process.

Figure 8.4

	How to Use the Synonym Strategy on a Computer
	Type text into a word-processing document. Then right-click on any word to see a list of synonyms. Choose one and click on it, and the synonym will be substituted into the text automatically.
1	You can create your own sentences to teach the technique, or use the sample shown below. Then choose authentic text from grade-level materials for guided practice and generalization of the skill.
2	Text example: The boys were ==uncertain== about what to do next. They had never seen a ==cadaver==, much less had one blocking their ==egress==.
3	Ask the student to pre-read the text and use the word processor's highlighting tool to identify any words s/he does not know: The boys were uncertain about what to do next. They had never seen a cadaver, much less had one blocking their egress.
4	For each highlighted word, right-click with the mouse to bring up the synonym menu. Discuss the meaning of the options. Click on one that seems most appropriate. It will be inserted automatically into the text.
5	
6	Here's what the example text looks like with the synonym substitution for all of the unknown words: The boys were ==unsure== about what to do next. They had never seen a ==dead body==, much less had one blocking their ==way out==.

227

How to Use the Synonym Strategy on a Computer

7	Have the student read the text with the substituted, familiar words in place of the unfamiliar words. Decide if the selected substitute words make sense by looking for clues in the text that "prove" whether the student picked a good synonym. Point out any clues that indicate a mistake was made. • Check for understanding of the passage with the synonyms in place. • Finally, ask the reader to re-read the original text and check for understanding.
8	If the student does not know the meaning of any synonyms on the list, many times an antonym (a word that means the opposite) is included that will clarify meaning. The Thesaurus feature is another option.

Whether using electronic text or a computer, this simple technique has several advantages over other methods of "finding the meaning of the word." Figure 8.5 suggests why it may be a good fit.

Figure 8.5

Advantages/Fit of the Synonym Strategy for Readers with Hyperlexia

1	Research suggests that computer-based instruction (CBI) or computer-assisted instruction (CAI) has good potential for learners on the spectrum (see Research Summary 6.7) . Computer-based activities may engage the learner and encourage them to read more, particularly if computers are an area of strength or high interest.
2	The technique can help the reader maintain the train of thought without being distracted by a dictionary, and can be a useful tool for lifelong reading.
3	The activity builds on "the known" to connect and create meaning of the unknown.
4	The method addresses pre-reading, vocabulary, self-monitoring skills, and the use of context.
5	Many individuals with autism prefer word processing over handwriting due to fine-motor issues that can make handwriting difficult. They can practice the synonym strategy when learning keyboarding skills.
6	The technique may help with executive function, language processing, and problem-solving skills.

Generalization and Other Applications

The synonym strategy is a clear opportunity for vocabulary growth. Here are some ideas:

- Students can keep lists of the words they've looked up and what they mean right on the computer, create personal dictionaries, keep track of all the synonyms they know for a particular word, find visual images or clip art to go with their dictionaries, and so on.
- The strategy can be used in reverse to help students expand their vocabulary when writing. They can type in their own original writing, highlight "ordinary" words, and click to select a more powerful or precise synonym.

C. Electronic Dictionaries

An electronic dictionary is a small handheld device that's integrated with reference materials. It can provide almost instant clarification when a reader is unsure of the meaning of the word.

- Most people find an electronic dictionary quicker and easier to use than a traditional dictionary.
- There are now dictionary phone or tablet apps that make electronic lookup even more convenient.
    - An example is the free Dictionary.com app, the 2009 winner of "Best App Ever Award for Primary and Middle School Kids." It includes almost one million words and definitions plus 90,000 synonyms and antonyms.
    - No Internet connection is needed to use the app, which also includes audio pronunciations and similarly spelled words.
    - This type of app may be ideal for students who already have a tablet or personal computer.

My son Tom first used an electronic dictionary at the age of 24. It was the first time he had used an assistive technology device to support comprehension. He used it in a formal testing situation with good results.

- He could answer more test items when he was able to clarify the meaning of particular words in the questions.

- This made me realize how wise it would have been to teach Tom to use the device from the start of his reading career.

Advantages/Fit for Readers with Hyperlexia

Figure 8.6 describes potential benefits of using electronic dictionaries or apps and why they may be a good fit for readers with hyperlexia.

Figure 8.6

	Advantages of Using Electronic Dictionaries or Dictionary Apps
1	They're small, portable, and user-friendly.
2	They can provide almost instant clarification when a reader is unsure of a word.
3	They are easier and less disruptive to use than a traditional dictionary, and might be used more often, in a variety of situations, with positive results.
4	They can also be used quietly to clarify the meaning of spoken words during class lectures or presentations to help the person keep pace with instruction (rather than feeling lost due to missing a key word).
5	These lifelong tools can transition along with the student for community instruction, the workplace, or other environments.
6	Bilingual dictionaries for bilingual students or those learning a second language can help the person expand their vocabulary in both languages.
7	Once the need for this type of device is established and related to the student's language disability, an electronic dictionary may be allowed for formal testing, including college testing or state board examinations. In most cases, the device is provided by the testing organization, so it is wise to find out the brand and model that will be provided so the person has time to practice using it and getting comfortable with it.

D. Using Objects to Pre-Teach Vocabulary

This is an idea that fits in the category of "Don't tell them, show them!" Before presenting literature or content with unfamiliar vocabulary, parents, students and teachers can **gather a collection of thematic objects** related to the story.

- This method provides an experiential, hands-on learning opportunity to create meaning and grow vocabulary.
- Students can touch and explore the items to gain first-hand knowledge.
- The technique is especially helpful if the objects are unusual, unfamiliar, or not commonly used.

Advantages for Readers with Hyperlexia

Figure 8.7 describes several advantages of using objects to teach vocabulary,. This is followed by Figure 8.8, Steps for Teaching.

Figure 8.7

Advantages of Using Objects to Pre-Teach Vocabulary	
1	This is a concrete and visual way to grow a vocabulary of nouns, adjectives, and verbs that can be used in reading, speaking, and writing.
2	While viewing, experiencing, or handling the object, the student can learn and apply new vocabulary about the item's characteristics and attributes in context.
3	Students can be taught to describe features, characteristics, and details of the item based on what they see, hear, smell, touch, or taste (if applicable).
4	Individuals with autism tend to be visual and concrete thinkers *and* learners, and often have a very strong natural focus on objects. Therefore, this method may draw their attention, sustain engagement, and be motivating.
5	Experiencing real objects can help create a visual memory that can be drawn upon while reading to help with visualization. This visual/nonverbal image is called an *imogen*, and is part of the dual-coding system described in Chapter 2.

Figure 8.8

	Steps for Using Objects to Pre-Teach Vocabulary
1	Preview the story or other curricular material.
2	Identify important objects or items in the story that are likely to be unfamiliar. An example is a thimble from a story about pioneer days when women and girls embroidered samplers.
3	Try to obtain as many of the key items as you can. To do this, you may consider: • Sending home a request to borrow items that families may have. • Inviting a local historical society to showcase particular items. • Checking out garage sales and thrift stores. • Using models or toy versions to represent larger items.
4	Display the items and give students a chance to experience and explore them. Students should have a chance to touch, hold, and feel the objects as long as it is safe to do so (or not, for example, if the item is a *saber*). Encourage students to use all of their senses to experience each object and generate words to describe it.
5	Explain what each item is called and its purpose. Answer questions that students may have. (This can also be done as a game with multiple-choice answers).
6	After this preparation, present the story or material. When the now-familiar objects and vocabulary are referenced, the reader will no longer face the obstacle of the "unknown." This leaves more energy to devote to understanding elements of the plot, characters, or content.

E. Image Search and Visual Dictionaries

Readers with autism have a hard time visualizing, creating visual images in response to spoken or written words (Truch 2004).

- They often can't imagine what something would look like from reading a description.
- Such readers need help to learn to visualize.

Albert Einstein famously said, "If I *can't* picture it, I *can't* understand it."

- Einstein is thought to have had Asperger's syndrome (James 2003). What better voice to emphasize the importance of needing to visualize to understand?
- Remember the saying, "A picture is worth a thousand words!"

Many readers with autism are not familiar with items they have not personally seen before. Some are less familiar with common items than one might suspect.

- After practicing with objects to expand vocabulary and stimulate interest, it is logical (and easier!) to shift the focus from objects to pictures.
- Sometimes it's not possible to gather the needed objects, especially from another historical period, so using realistic images is the next best thing.

Photographs, clip art, drawings, and other images are useful to enhance comprehension. The Internet and word-processing programs are two good sources of images. Selected images can be used to create a personal glossary or dictionary to reinforce word meanings related to story and academic reading.

> **Note**: Some images have copyright protection, which would limit the reproduction of images for publications such as this book, but should not affect personal or educational use. Be sure to cite the sources of images when needed. Also, especially at home, always provide adequate supervision and monitoring of students for these and any other educational experiences using the Internet.

Figure 8.9 details some of the advantages of using images as a pre-reading strategy.

Figure 8.9

	Advantages of Using Visual Images for Readers with Hyperlexia
1	It's estimated that a student needs 12 meaningful exposures to a word to be able to understand it. Pre-reading activities that include searching for images or sorting carefully selected visuals provided by the teacher or parent provide multiple exposures.
2	Activities using computer searches (on the Internet or in a word-processing program) for images can be visual, concrete, and motivating. Once particular words are no longer an obstacle, fluency of thought may improve, and text will be less difficult or frustrating.
3	The use of images gives students a chance to explore and understand the attributes and features of the objects. Looking at images can help the reader understand their use or purpose. This can also improve word knowledge *and* relevant world knowledge needed to understand new material and concepts.
4	The use of images can help create the connection between descriptions in text and real objects and can help learners with autism begin to pay attention to descriptive details to create their own mental visual images while reading (*imagining* or *visualizing*).
5	The reader can be taught to use language to describe the item or object based on multiple attributes. The student will be able to literally see more features, details, and significant information to retell, discuss, or describe. This strategy can build a wider vocabulary of nouns, adjectives, and verbs, which can have a positive effect on retelling the story and writing.
6	Activities that ask students to select from different options in a set of images provided by a teacher or parent can help them learn to pay attention to important details that best match a specific description.
7	After viewing and describing images as a pre-reading activity, learners are much more likely to understand the related word in the context of a story or passage when it is read.

An Example Using Internet Images

There a many online sources for images. Google Images describes itself as "the most comprehensive image search on the web." My grandfather was a bricklayer's assistant and carried a *hod* up a ladder. Google Images helped me understand what this means, as shown in Figure 8.10. Now I know why grandpa's arms were so strong and why his back hurt all the time.

Figure 8.10

Public Works Administration: New Jersey "Hod carriers move bricks up for the construction of the Tea Neck High School."

This photo is part of an extensive collection of historical images from the FDR presidency. It is in the public domain, copyright-free, and found at http://www.fdrlibrary.marist.edu/archives/collections.html.

Using images of key vocabulary provides excellent visual cues and enhances understanding. A photo like this one can show historical context and add depth of meaning to the understanding of a word.

Ideas for Use

Figure 8.11 shows three images for the word *bridge*. All of them fit the *Encarta Dictionary* definition, "a structure that is built above and across a river, road, or other obstacle to allow people or vehicles to cross it." Yet only one of the images will be the best match to a description from a particular story.

Figure 8.11. Clip art images of bridges from Microsoft Word 2007.

A set of images like this can be used to create a **Word Detective** Game worksheet for key vocabulary words. Hear are simple steps to do this:

1. Create a vocabulary list for a lesson, a story to be read, or a content theme.
2. Pre-search and select one image that matches each word and two images that don't.
3. Use the format of a riddle to write descriptive clues about the word, including the important features and significance of the item.
4. Have students pick the correct image from a field of three visual choices (one correct and two incorrect) and label it with the key word.

For example, a Word Detective riddle for the word *meter* is, "Use me when you need to know how many stamps to put on a letter." Image choices could include a water, postage, and parking meter.

- This activity can teach the student to pay attention to relevant details in both the descriptions and the corresponding images.

- Once familiar with these types of activities, students can find their own images for key vocabulary words and create their own descriptions based on the images.
- Students can create Word Detective clues matched to images to "play the game" with one another.

Many teachers pre-teach vocabulary from stories on a whiteboard. Another option is to have students create PowerPoint™ presentations of vocabulary from text (from literature or core curriculum such as science or social studies).

- Teams of students can work together to create one slide for each key word. Each slide should present the word in context, quoted from the sentence in the story or text.
- Students can review, choose, and insert an image from clip art or an image library on the slide that best illustrates the meaning as described in the story.
- The class can merge all the slides to create a single presentation. They can review it before and after reading the selection, and use it to study for tests.

F. Connotation: Shades of Meaning

Readers with ASD may struggle to understand inference at the word level, or *connotation*. This includes understanding that authors purposefully select particular words to convey specific meaning.

- Words that appear to be synonyms often have subtle, implied meaning that can be invisible or confusing to readers with hyperlexia.
- They must be explicitly taught to look for unstated meaning and the emotion behind words.

Exploring connotation is another opportunity to expand vocabulary through synonyms. Analyzing specific words selected by an author provides clues to the author's intent and perspective, including attitudes and judgments s/he wishes to convey about characters or objects being described. When Temple Grandin reviewed my first edition of *Drawing a Blank*, she was enthusiastic about this idea!

Examples are synonyms for hungry: *peckish, ravenous,* and *famished.* Clearly, the author's word choice in a description reflects his or her perspective about the person's level of hunger, perhaps related to the context described. Figure 8.12 describes the Shades of Meaning Activity to explore hidden meaning and "rank" synonyms.

Figure 8.12

<table>
<tr><td colspan="2">Introduction to Teaching Shades of Meaning
This activity helps connect the concrete and visual concept of shades of color
to the abstract concept of shades of meaning.</td></tr>
<tr><td>1</td><td>A way to make the concept of connotation visual and concrete is to use paint chips to illustrate the "shades of meaning."
• Paint chips are small cards with samples of paint colors.
• They usually have three-to-five shades of a color on each sample, from light to dark.
• You can find these in the paint department at a home improvement store.
• The examples in this section use paint chips with four shades per card.</td></tr>
<tr><td>2</td><td>Start with a very familiar word, such as *fun,* and four synonyms for fun: *enjoyable, exciting, awesome,* and *amusing.* Explain that these words all mean the same thing, they are synonyms, but that there is a hidden meaning behind the words.</td></tr>
<tr><td>3</td><td>Point out that the synonyms for *fun* range from words used to describe something that is a little bit fun to words that mean something is really, really fun.
• Ask students to think about something they like and relate to personally, such as a video game or an amusement park.
• Talk about which words students would choose to talk about something that is "kind of fun" and words to describe something that is "really, really fun."
• With the consensus of the adult and students, demonstrate how to rank the words in order, from a little fun to the most fun.</td></tr>
<tr><td>4</td><td>Write the words in order on a paint chip according to their "intensity" of meaning, from "lightest to darkest" or "weakest to strongest."
• Write the word with the "lightest" (least emotional or least strong) shade of meaning on the palest color stripe.
• Write the words with more "intense" connotation on the darker stripes.
• An example is shown in Figure 8.13.</td></tr>
</table>

Figure 8.13 presents visual examples of paint chips with synonyms. These examples use a commercial paint chip from a paint or home improvement store.

- If four-part chips are not available, you or your students can create graduated color chips using a word processor.
- Students can also use art supplies to match colors to the intensity of the word meanings.

Figure 8.13. Paint chip examples.

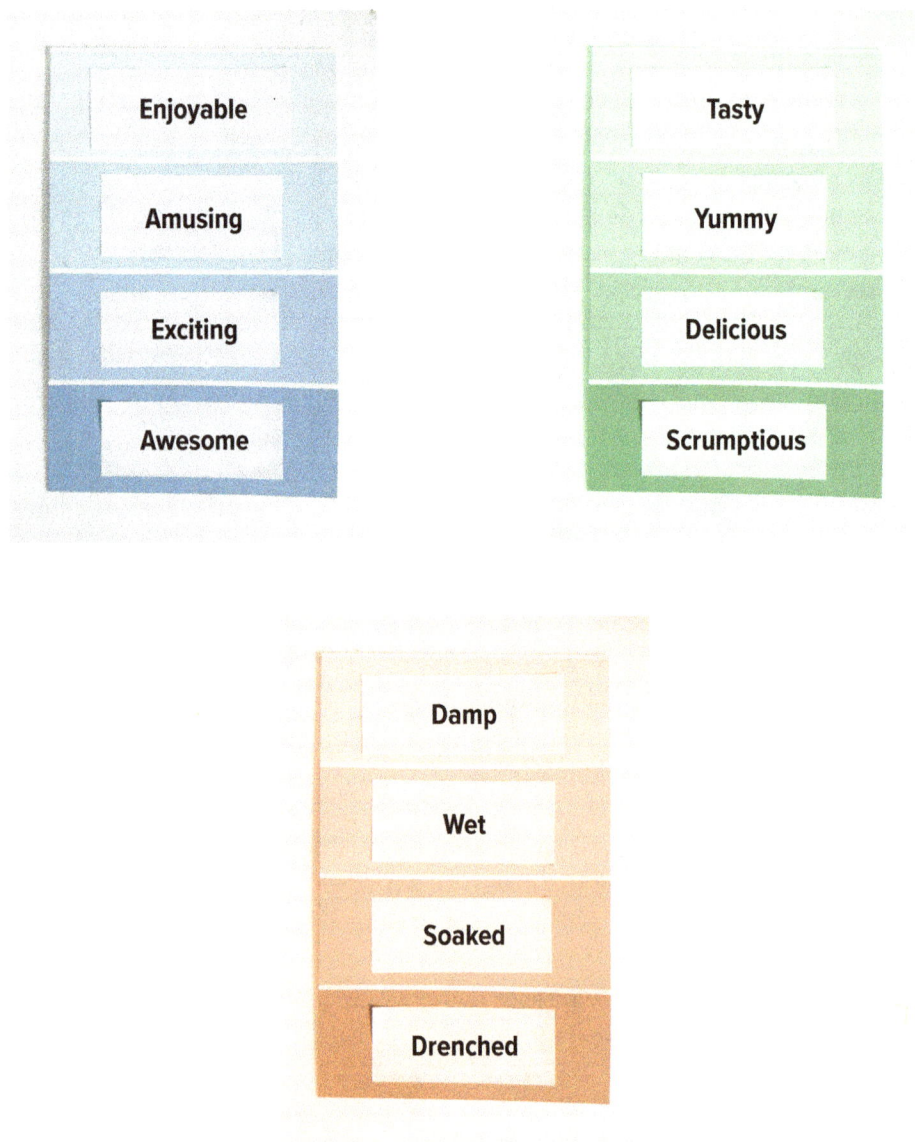

| Enjoyable |
| Amusing |
| Exciting |
| Awesome |

| Tasty |
| Yummy |
| Delicious |
| Scrumptious |

| Damp |
| Wet |
| Soaked |
| Drenched |

Figure 8.14 provides teaching tips for Shades of Meaning.

Figure 8.14

	Teaching Shades of Meaning
1	Explain that *connotation* refers to the undertone or feeling behind the words, like **a secret or implied meaning**. • Show how the class ranked the words in order from the weakest to the strongest connotation, or feeling. • Make sure students understand this before continuing.
2	Select a few more key words and their synonyms from areas of high interest, such as favorite foods or television shows, for group practice. Then provide words and paint chips to groups of students for independent practice.
3	Once the concept has been established using high-interest topics, select other connotative synonyms to teach from appropriate grade or reading-level material. • Synonyms for these words may be found quickly using the word/thesaurus feature of any word-processing program or an electronic dictionary/app. • Include synonyms that are *laden* with implied meaning whenever possible.
4	Students can also be taught to judge whether a word conveys a positive, negative, or neutral meaning before ranking words. • This helps in ranking words with the least amount of emotion and the most emotion behind them. • Words can be strongly positive or strongly negative, and the strongest word, whether positive or negative, belongs on the darkest shade of the paint chip.

Figure 8.15 offers more examples for teaching students to rate words as positive, negative, or neutral, then rank according to the intensity of implied emotion. This is followed by Figure 8.16, Key Points about Connotation.

Figure 8.15

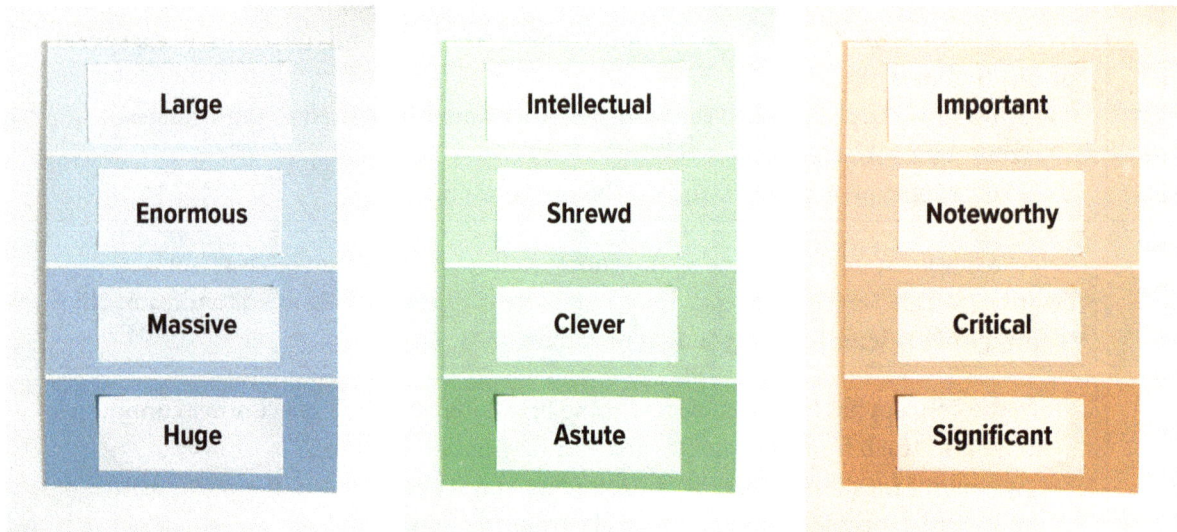

Figure 8.16

	Key Points about Connotation
	Help students understand these important ideas.
1	Intentionally choosing words with particular connotations can communicate both meaning *and* feeling.
2	An author's word choice reflects his or her perspective and is intended to be positive, negative, or neutral.
3	The connotation of synonyms is *subjective*. Different people can have different feelings or reactions to the implied meanings.
4	It's OK for people to have different opinions about the subtle or hidden meanings of words. Depending on their experience and perspective, people may rank the intensity of the words differently.
5	People also choose words with connotation when speaking, like in the dialogue of characters in a book or in real life, to add/infer special meaning.

Activities that teach the connotation of words and the thoughts and feelings behind them can contribute to gains in several areas at once. Benefits may transfer to reading, writing, and speaking. Figure 8.17 describes the fit of connotation activities for autistic readers.

Figure 8.17

	Advantages of Using the Shades of Meaning Activity
1	Learning about word choice and connotation is a concrete way to teach the concepts of implied meaning and inference at the word level. This may help develop awareness of other types of inference, and the ability to "read between the lines."
2	Recognizing connotation may help the reader perceive the subtle views of one character in a story about another, depending on how the character describes someone else in dialogue.
3	This is an opportunity for the reader to build theory of mind (ToM). Understanding the thoughts and intentions of others includes recognizing the author's purpose when selecting particular words.
4	Many people with autism like to make lists and may enjoy keeping lists of synonyms or creating personal dictionaries of new words. They can learn to rate words as positive, negative, or neutral, to further improve understanding when reading.
5	Expanding vocabulary through connotation can help students with autism vary their word choices and select precise meanings when **writing**, selecting a synonym that best represents both meaning *and* feeling.
6	In **speaking**, the learner with autism may learn to choose words with sensitivity to the feelings of the listener.

Application of Connotation: What to Say?

What to Say? is an activity that was inspired by Shades of Meaning. Once the concept of connotation is understood, What to Say? adds a personal and social dimension to the idea of word choice.

- An example is how to answer Grandma when she asks how you like her cooking.
- Synonyms to the rescue!

Besides building vocabulary through synonyms, "What to Say?" can help build social understanding and conversation skills.

- "What to Say?" teaches that depending on what people are thinking and feeling, the speaker can select certain words with hidden meaning.
- This activity can help the person with autism understand that word choice can be (and often *should* be) guided by sensitivity to others and taking the perspective of the social partner (theory of mind).
- Materials and a description of the activity are found in Appendix D.

Other Applications

"Shades of Meaning" and "What to Say?" may inspire you to create other activities to explore connotation.

- One idea is to help students recognize the types of words that are used in persuasion, such as advertising, to convince shoppers how great a product is.
- Students can select connotative words to argue for or against a particular product, activity, or point of view.

G. Word Elements: Root Meanings and Affixes

Learning word parts can grow vocabulary and help all readers determine the meaning of words they come across while reading (Armbruster et al. 2003; Gillett 2010; Texas Reading Initiative [TRI] 2002).

- Calhoon (2001) studied the word recognition skills of ten children with autism.
- He found that their understanding of word parts, grapheme-phonemes, and recognition of high-frequency words was **intact**.
- The children also understood onsets and rime. For example in the word "cat," the sound of the letter "c" is the onset, and the sounds of the vowels or consonants that follow are the rime (at). They could switch out the onset or initial sound of a word like *cat* to make words that rhyme with it, such as *bat, mat* and *sat*.
- To build on these strengths, Calhoon recommends teaching **word families**, **root meaning** (word parts), and **structural analysis** (suffixes and prefixes) to grow vocabulary.

Using this concrete method, readers are first taught the meaning of common word elements or word parts. This includes prefixes that are found at the start of words, and suffixes found at the end of words (together they are called affixes).

- Examples include prefixes such as *re-, dis-,* or *un-* and suffixes such as *-ment* and *-tion.*
- Readers then break individual words into parts, identify the meaning of each part, and recombine the parts to find the meaning of the whole word.
- Words like *unkind, beautiful,* and *slowly* can be more easily understood by breaking them apart, once the meanings of the individual parts are known.

The word parts that are important to know have been identified through research.

- Figure 8.18 summarizes the most popular affixes based on this research.
- This is an excellent starting point for selecting the most strategic word parts to teach.

Figure 8.18

The Most Popular Prefixes and Suffixes to Teach	
What	**Why**
Prefixes un-, re-, dis-, and these forms of "not:" im-/in-/il-/ir	These are the top prefixes attached to nouns, used in 97% of words in printed English at school.
Suffixes -s/-es,-ed, -ing, and -ly	These are the top four suffixes attached to nouns, used in 97% of words in printed English at school.
Prefixes un-, re-, dis-, over-, mis-, and out-	These are the prefixes most commonly used to form new verbs.
Suffixes -ise, -en, -ate, -(i)fy	These are the most common suffixes for verbs. -ise is the most common affix in academic English.
Adapted from Promoting Vocabulary Development: Components of Effective Vocabulary Instruction 2002 Online Revised Edition (Texas Reading Initiative) and White, Sowell, and Yanagihara 1989.	

To enhance understanding in specific subject areas, like science or mathematics, it is helpful to teach the meaning of Greek and Latin root words that are commonly used, such as *meter*, meaning "measure," and *dict*, meaning "tell."

- Recognizing the meaning of word parts enables the reader to break down longer and more complex words into parts and identify root meanings.
- Examples are thermometer, metric, predict, and dictionary.

A specialized list of words to teach can be made for each subject area.

- A list for social studies, for example, could include roots like *phon* (sound), *port* (carry), and *scrib/script* (write).
- More lists of key word parts and their meaning, including common root words, are found in Appendix E.

Advantages for Readers with Hyperlexia

Of all the methods our team used, my son, Tom, reported that learning the meaning of prefixes, suffixes, and root words was *the* vocabulary breakthrough for him. He made use of it whenever possible. Teachers and parents can begin to teach the meaning of word parts to readers from an early age.

Prefix + Root + Suffix = Discover Word Meaning

Figure 8.19 explains why understanding word parts is a good fit with the learning profile of many autistic students.

Figure 8.19

	Advantages of Word Parts for Readers with Autism
1	The meaning of the roots and affixes is clear, concrete, and predictable.
2	Using word elements can capitalize on skills in rote memorization and repetition.
3	Students may find it easy to memorize the meaning of many the roots and affixes listed in entire charts when visually presented (see charts in Appendix E).
4	The word parts strategy is like turning reading into math. • The process of adding the parts to make a whole, or breaking the whole into its parts, is like following a mathematical formula. • This can tap into concrete logic and mathematical strengths often seen in students with autism and hyperlexia.
5	Many students with autism like to make lists. They may enjoy keeping lists of word parts, categorizing them to reinforce the meaning, or creating personal dictionaries of new words.
6	Having a good vocabulary in a specific area can provide a useful, personal link to many word parts, which can help in learning and remembering.
7	When relating word parts to known words, students with autism may have a surprisingly sophisticated, specific vocabulary to draw upon, based on reading in their area of special interest.

Steps for Teaching

Figure 8.20 summarizes a sequence of steps for teaching nine key prefixes that are a good starting point for teaching at about the fourth or fifth-grade level.

Figure 8.20

	Teaching Nine Key Prefixes

1	Start by explicitly defining and teaching the concept of a prefix, focusing on the three key features that all must be present together:
	1. It's a group of letters that go in front of a word,
	2. It changes the meaning, and
	3. When you take a prefix away, a word is left.
	   a. Give words as examples, like *unkind*. Show how the un- in *unkind* adheres to all three rules of a prefix.
	   b. Then provide nonexamples, words such as *uncle* and *unit*. They don't have a prefix, although they look like they do.

2	In the next lesson, focus on the negative meanings of *un-* and *dis-*, which mean "not." Start with the meaning of a known word, like *obey*, then add the prefix *dis-* so students see how the meaning of the word is changed.
3	Introduce four more prefixes that mean "not:" *in-*, *im-*, *ir-*, and *non-*. Show how these prefixes change the meaning of known words.
4	Introduce two different meanings of the prefix *re-*, *back* and *again*. Revisit other meanings of *un-* and *dis-* (do the *opposite*), as well as *in-* and *im-* (*in* or *into*).
5	Finally, introduce these useful prefixes: *en-*, *em-*, *over-*, and *mis-*.
	Inspired by White, Sowell & Yanagihara 1989

Figure 8.21 provides suggestions for tailoring teaching based on the strengths and needs often seen in autistic readers.

Figure 8.21

Tailor the Teaching of Word Parts To engage the **interest**, **attention**, **motivation**, and **memory** of the learner	
1	Once the concept of using word parts has been introduced, the steps have been reviewed, and meanings have been introduced, practice the skill by breaking down words selected from the student's area of special interest, whether it is *Star Wars*, dinosaurs, the weather, or other favorite interests.
2	While many charts and materials give example words to show what a word part means, it can be especially helpful to personalize the connection for readers with autism by linking the meaning to the student's personal interest or experience (Brown and Lee 2025). • The charts of key prefixes, root words, and suffixes provided in Appendix E have been adapted to include a **personal example** column. • This may create a stronger link to the concepts by improving interest or motivation.
3	Many types of graphic organizers have been used successfully with autistic students, providing a clear, repetitive template. One example of a Graphic Organizer for **structured word inquiry** is the Frayer model. Students explore the root, definition, characteristics, examples, and non-examples of a word.
4	One creative educator teaches Latin root words by linking them to Harry Potter magic spells (a high-interest subject for many!). Some fun ideas for teaching Greek and Latin roots are available at The Classroom's website, https://www.theclassroom.com/fun-games-teach-greek-latin-roots-12149112.html.
	Please refer to Appendix E for additional teaching materials

Use Favorite Objects

Another idea tailored to learners with autism is to use **objects** of high interest, such as toy cars, toy trains, blocks, or Lego® bricks, as manipulatives to teach word parts. This idea taps into the benefits of multimodal teaching and the potential positive effects of experiential learning on memory (TRI 2002). Using objects that the student likes can engage their interest and attention.

Figure 8.22 shows how train cars can be used to teach word parts.

Figure 8.22

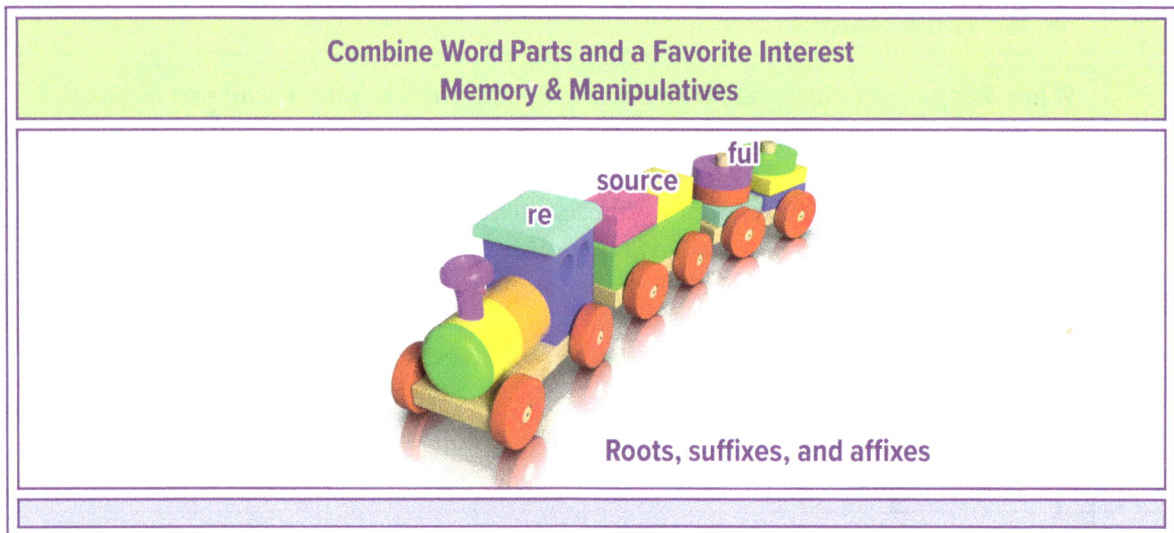

Combine Word Parts and a Favorite Interest
Memory & Manipulatives

Roots, suffixes, and affixes

To follow this model, you can use removable labels or sticky notes to temporarily transform ordinary items into teaching tools.

- Using the objects, word parts can be joined together and taken apart to try new combinations.
- Start with two word parts and build to longer words.
- Change out prefixes and suffixes to create new words using the same root.

This option may be particularly appropriate for younger learners. If the objects that an older learner prefers are considered juvenile they can be used during private instruction to avoid stigma.

H. The DISSECT Mnemonic

The idea of teaching roots and affixes fits beautifully with the DISSECT **mnemonic**, a letter-strategy tool that readers can use to remember the steps to take when they come across a new multisyllabic word (Lenz & Hughes 1990).

- One step of a process is linked to each letter in the word.
- The reader simply spells the word to remember how to step himself through an active process, shown in Figure 8.23.

Figure 8.23

The DISSECT mnemonic
The steps to D-I-S-S-E-C-T are as follows: • **D** Discover the word's context. • **I** Isolate the prefix. • **S** Separate the suffix. • **S** Say the stem or root word. • **E** Examine the stem or root word. • **C** Check with someone. • **T** Try the dictionary (or, per this text, dictionary alternatives)
Adapted from Lenz & Hughes 1990

dis·sec·tion

dis = apart, *section* = to cut

Research shows that mnemonics can be effective as memory-enhancing tools for readers with learning disabilities, particularly because they rely on areas of strength such as memory for pictures and *acoustic memory*, for sound (Fasih, Izadpanah & Shanahvaz 2018; Scruggs & Mastropieri 2000). Potential benefits for readers with autism are shown in Figure 8.24.

Figure 8.24

	Advantages of Mnemonics for Readers with Autism
1	Using a mnemonic such as DISSECT can support the type of active, dynamic thinking practiced by good readers (Shanahan 2006). The technique gives students clear steps to follow to actively engage with text and clarify meaning while reading.
2	Successfully identifying the meaning of an unknown word using the mnemonic can help unlock the meaning of an entire sentence or paragraph. This can improve access to the curriculum and be particularly useful in subjects like science or social studies that include longer and more complex words.
3	Readers with hyperlexia who have a strong rote memory may benefit from the structure provided by memory tools to understand words in reading assignments and expand their vocabulary.

I. Teaching Homographs

Homographs are words that are spelled the same but have different meanings. Examples of homographs are **contract** and **does.** Analyzing the parts of the word "homograph" helps to remember the meaning:

> *homo* = same; *graph* = write
> Homographs are *written* the *same*.

The meaning of each homograph changes significantly, depending on how the word is pronounced. The pronunciation depends on the **context** in which the word is found, and the **meaning that is appropriate to that context**.

- The difference in pronunciation is sometimes created by accenting or emphasizing a different syllable, as in <u>con</u>test and con<u>test.</u>
- The different meanings are usually two different parts of speech, such as a noun and a verb, as in *contrast*.
- The two different meanings of the same word are often unrelated, as in *tear* (water in the eye and a rip in fabric).

Some single-syllable words are homographs. These words are also spelled the same, but pronounced differently. An example is *dove* (a bird) and *dove* (past tense of *dive*). Here's a sentence using these words: The *dove* circled the water and then *dove* into the pool.

- In this case, the different pronunciation has nothing to do with accentuation.
- As with multi-syllable homographs, the difference in pronunciation changes the meaning, often dramatically, and depends on the context where the word is found.

What Research Reveals

The **need** to teach homographs **is based on research** indicating that readers with autism typically use **a word-by-word** reading strategy rather than integrating the words into whole thoughts and ideas as they read (Hoy and colleagues 2004). For this reason, students with autism often struggle with the following skills when reading:

- Reading homographs.
- Using context.
- Monitoring their own understanding as they read.
- Stopping and clarifying when things do not make sense (Brock, Norbury, Einav & Nation 2008; Happé 1997; Nation & Norbury 2005; Wahlberg 2001a).

The way readers with autism deal with homographs **while reading aloud** is a clear indicator of their difficulty using context and self-monitoring (Holman 2004).

- Typically, they do not change pronunciation to distinguish different meanings of the same word based on context clues.

- Readers with hyperlexia appear not to **listen to themselves** and self-correct when they choose the wrong pronunciation.
- For example, when reading this sentence aloud: "The *dove* circled the water and then *dove* into the pool," the reader would pick one pronunciation of dove, use it in both instances, and continue reading, unaware of the breakdown in meaning.

The *DOVE* circled the water...   **...and then *DOVE* into the pool.**

Advantages for Readers with Hyperlexia

Teaching readers with hyperlexia about homographs may result in gains in *resolving ambiguity*, using context to figure out the meaning of a word (O'Connor & Klein 2004). Figure 8.25 lists several other benefits that may be gained through instruction in homographs. These include the potential to generalize different skills once key concepts are understood.

Figure 8.25

	Advantages of Learning about Homographs for Readers with Hyperlexia
1	**Motivation and interest.** The idea of homographs may be interesting to readers with hyperlexia. They may remember the homographs listed in homograph charts, or want to create their own word lists. They may be interested in reading sentences that contain homographs. This heightened interest may increase vigilance and attention to context while reading.
2	**Self-monitoring.** The homograph strategy can also help build self-awareness and self-monitoring of comprehension. Learning how to "manage" homographs may help readers learn to pause and clarify meaning, rather than just reading on without stopping to repair an error. • Readers may begin listening to themselves and correcting themselves while reading aloud. • When students learn to stop, clarify, and self-correct before moving on, they may be able to apply these skills to other situations, for example, when coming across pronouns (anaphoric cueing).
3	**Context clues.** To read a homograph correctly, the reader has to pay attention to context and look for clues. Homograph activities can increase awareness and provide practice on using context clues.
4	**Generalization.** Additional support may help students generalize their skill with homographs. They may improve attention to context clues for big-picture purposes beyond the word level. This includes recognizing cause and effect in a plot, noticing elements of foreshadowing to predict the plot of a story, or inferring the thoughts of a character by noticing connotative word choices in story dialogue.
5	**Cohesion.** Learning to pay attention to homographs may help the reader to begin making sense of words as integrated parts of a sentence that contribute to the whole meaning, rather than using a word-by-word reading technique.
6	**Vocabulary development.** By learning the strategy using specific, familiar words, students can relate to the concept of "one word, different meanings."

Please refer to **Appendix D** for more materials and instructions to teach homographs.

J. Explicit Instruction of Idioms

An *idiom* is a phrase or expression that does not mean what it literally says, such as, "It's raining cats and dogs." The real meaning of an idiom is usually quite different from the literal or word-for-word interpretation.

Idioms are specific to every culture and do not translate well from one language to another.

- The figurative meaning of idioms often has a historical context or geographic connection. An example is "spill the beans" that refers to the Greek voting system of using colored beans to make decisions.
- There are about 25,000 idioms in English. Many American idioms are related to animals and body parts.

Not knowing the history, origin, or meaning of different idioms can make them difficult to understand. Typical children learn idioms gradually, over a lifetime.

- Increased exposure improves learning.
- Using context clues is integral to understanding idioms.

Some idioms may also be understood by analyzing the individual words. An example is "bury the hatchet," that signifies making peace. Understanding each word, that a weapon will be buried and no longer used, gives good clues to the meaning of the idiom.

Idioms may also be learned as a "chunk" of language. This means learning the meaning of the entire phrase as a unit of meaning. An example is learning that "beat around the bush" means not getting to the point.

When coming across an idiom, the reader needs to **"read" the author's intention** and ask him or herself: "Am I supposed to take these words literally, or not?"

- A reader with autism is likely to interpret idioms literally because s/he may miss clues in the text that hint at the author's intended meaning.
- Therefore, explicit instruction and repeated exposure are needed (Norbury 2004).

In *transparent idioms*, like "skate on thin ice," the meaning is close to the actual interpretation of the words. Transparent idioms are easier to learn because the reader is likely to associate the literal meaning with the intended meaning.

In contrast, the words in *opaque idioms*, like "kick the bucket," don't have much to do with the actual meaning. It's possible that opaque idioms are harder to learn because the reader is **not** likely to associate the literal meaning with the intended meaning (Norbury 2004). Figure 8.26 presents tips for teaching idioms.

Figure 8.26

	Suggestions for Teaching Idioms to Readers with Autism
1	Select idioms that are common (frequently used in speech or writing) and relevant (found in the curriculum and selected readings).
2	Use materials that compare both the literal and the figurative meanings of an idiom. Materials with illustrations are a plus because they are visual and concrete.
3	When reading text, model the opportunity to guess the meaning of an idiom by looking for context clues before looking for the real answer. Provide guided practice to help students learn the technique.
4	Consider using materials designed for English language learners, as these may help students on the spectrum.
5	Make a distinction between idioms that are outdated and more current idioms. • It may be helpful to categorize "old idioms" and "new idioms." • It doesn't help when teenagers with autism tell classmates that something "cool" is the "bee's knees" because they learned the idiom and want to use it. • Consider teaching slang idioms that are not objectionable. Check with classmates to identify common current idioms that may apply to young adult fiction.

Materials for Teaching

Materials and curricula for teaching idioms are widely available, including these:

- *What Did You Say? What Do You Mean?: An Illustrated Guide to Understanding Metaphors* by Jude Welton and Jane Telford (Author, Illustrator). Jessica Kingsley Publishers 2004.
- *In a Pickle and Other Funny Idioms* (2007), *Mad as a Wet Hen* (2007), and *It Figures! Fun Figures of Speech* (1993), by Marvin Terban and Guilio Maestro (Author, Illustrator). San Anselmo, CA: Sandpiper Press.
- *One and Only Sam: A Story Explaining Idioms for Children with Asperger Syndrome and Other Communication Difficulties* by Aileen Stalker. Jessica Kingsley Publishers 2009.
- Many teachers like Amelia Bedelia books, in which Amelia misinterprets idioms.
- Images for the literal interpretations of many idioms may be found online using major search engines.

Conclusion

This chapter presented ten ideas to help readers with autism grow vocabulary and understand the meaning of words or phrases they come across while reading.

- The ideas and activities have additional benefits, including increasing self-awareness, self-monitoring, and social understanding, and becoming actively involved in the construction of meaning.
- Using techniques to understand what words mean also helps build prerequisite skills and can help improve understanding in larger reading tasks, at the sentence, paragraph, chapter, or whole-text level.

The next chapter explores creative and entertaining ways to enhance understanding of text.

CHAPTER 9

Innovative and Creative Ways to Teach Comprehension Skills

This chapter presents engaging teaching ideas using media, visual strategies, and manipulatives. The aim is to teach a specific skill or breakthrough concept that can have positive ripple effects on reading comprehension from that point on.

Excellent materials are available online, in educational catalogs, and in other sources to teach many of the comprehension skills that readers with hyperlexia need to learn.

- The facts and insights shared in this book can help parents and professionals **be selective** when considering what materials, techniques and tools to use.
- You can determine which other methods, materials, and activities may be helpful based on your understanding of hyperlexia and the needs of a particular individual.

The six teaching suggestions presented here are likely to be a good match to the needs, strengths, interests, and sensory preferences of many students with autism. A description, advantages, examples, steps, and resources are provided for each option. They're also highlighted in blue to help you find them.

The strategies are:
- **A.** Pre-viewing a film before reading
- **B.** Reading scripts of plays and films
- **C.** Finding the main idea
- **D.** Marking text to summarize
- **E.** Previewing text
- **F.** Audio books
- **G.** Clink *or* Clunk? for comprehension monitoring.

A. Previewing a Film Before Reading

Many teachers show a film of a story or literary work before reading the corresponding book. This practice can be a good fit for students with autism, starting with short movies and books that are closely matched in content.

- With an understanding of how people with autism tend to think and learn, it's a good idea to pick a film and book about a preferred topic or favorite interest to help make the connection between film and written stories.
- Remember to **turn on the captions** while watching!
- Figure 9.1 explains five advantages of pre-viewing films with readers with autism.

Figure 9.1

	Advantages of Film to Improve Comprehension for Readers with Autism
1	Things that are familiar are easier to understand than the unfamiliar. Viewing a film creates specific, concrete background knowledge for reading.
2	Much of the information about a topic, character, historical period, setting, etc. is presented visually, and can be understood without also having to process language.
3	The elements of the film, such as plot, characters, and themes, can be analyzed after viewing, before looking at the same elements in text.
4	New vocabulary is introduced with visual context to clarify meaning. This exposure can help the reader understand novel objects, descriptions, and concepts in the text.
5	Seeing films before reading may engage a learner's interest and attention in a way that a book alone may not.

Films Can Support Visualization During Reading

Relating films to books can be an excellent way to teach visualization skills. Because of their difficulties with visualization and limited world knowledge, it is helpful for readers with autism to have something concrete to visualize while reading.

- Until they are adept at creating visual images on their own, students can *borrow* visual images from the filmmaker.

- When reading the corresponding text later, the reader can connect the words with the images and information stored in memory.
- The connection between words and images can be reinforced by showing examples of how words in the text are converted to a visual image, and how visual images in the film are translated into words.

Social Benefits

A final benefit of this method is a social one. Becoming adept at and enjoying analyzing books and films together provides expanded opportunities for socialization.

- Most people form friendships through shared interests.
- Most communities have book clubs and groups that like to see movies together.

Steps for Teaching Visualization Through Film

Parents as well as professionals can use the ideas that follow to create the link between books, films and visualization. It is easier than ever to locate movies through streaming formats or other online options, matching films to the literature that will be used in school.

Figure 9.2 provides an example of how to use a film as a pre-reading activity for the book *Beethoven* (1992).

- The reading level is around fourth grade, which may be close to the independent reading level of many readers with autism, even those who are in the upper grades.
- Several versions of the book contain photographs from the movie to reinforce the visual images.
- It may have a special appeal to students who love dogs or animals.
- The same model can be adapted for any book and film, for readers of all ages.

Figure 9.2

	Example: Teaching Visualization with Film and Book Beethoven
1	Preview the entire film and read the book. Plan to show portions of the film and discuss matching text with students, one section at a time. • For example, show one scene and read the corresponding chapter, then the next scene and chapter, and so on. • This "chunking" tends to work well within the timeframe of a class period or remediation session.
2	After viewing a scene from the film, point out specific descriptions in the book. Compare them to the corresponding scenes from the film. Discuss how the filmmaker translated the author's words into images.
3	When comparing passages of text to specific scenes, "think aloud" to discuss what (if any) images you envisioned for various scenes from the text that were different from the actual ones in the film. • For example, you might say, "I pictured Beethoven wearing a black keg barrel on his collar, and the filmmaker chose a brown one." • Then, select other descriptive text and ask the student to make a similar comparison of what s/he expected from the text description and what s/he saw.
4	According to research with students with autism, talking, writing, and drawing about stories can reinforce comprehension (Colasent & Griffith 1998). Students can also draw a scene from the film that they liked.
5	Another option is to ask students to draw two pictures that compare a description from the book to the matching scene in the film. • Ask students to explain their drawings to an adult or peer. • Ask students to listen to a partner talk about their images.
6	Connect to the idea that **the student can create images while reading like the movie maker did.** Ask the student to remember to **create their own mental pictures while reading,** as if s/he is going to make a movie of what s/he is reading about.

	Example: Teaching Visualization with Film and Book Beethoven
7	Lead a discussion about the difference between the student's own mental images and the filmmaker's. • This is an opportunity to discuss and learn about **perspective taking**, theory of mind ToM), and the intention of the author. • It also teaches **cognitive flexibility** (accepting a different point of view, or the fact that there are multiple points of view).
8	In a more advanced lesson, discuss the differences between the book and the film to teach about *artistic license* in filmmaking and the filmmaker's perspective. • Why does the screenwriter change the ending? What does s/he know about the audience? • What is a possible reason or motivation to change the story?

A useful resource for linking film and literature is the website **Teach with Movies**, at https://teachwithmovies.org/. This free site was established in 1998 to review and select movies to supplement school curriculum and support social-emotional learning.

- An estimated 80% of site visitors are educators, including homeschooling parents.
- The site offers 450 free learning guides, lesson plans, and worksheets for a variety of films that are appropriate for different grade levels.

Note: Not All Images Have Equal Impact

It's important to note that showing drawings or photographs of a complex scene before reading may not be as effective as viewing a film.

- Individuals with autism are reported to miss the gist or point of photographs, or focus on the wrong details (Brock and colleagues 2009; Norbury and colleagues 2009).
- Perhaps it is the dimensionality or realism of films that makes them more appealing and more effective as a way to connect descriptions in text with visual images.

B. Reading Scripts of Plays and Films

Reading a script is a pre-reading strategy for a text can be active and engaging. This suggestion comes from a friend named Merritt, who had tremendous breakthroughs with comprehension when he discovered this strategy on his own during high school.

The Internet Movie Script Database touts itself as being the "biggest collection of movie scripts available anywhere on the web." The IMSDb promises, "Our site lets you read or download movie scripts for free."

Figure 9.3 provides a snippet of the script from the film *Into the Wild* quoted from http://www.imsdb.com/.

Figure 9.3

BILLIE
I'm so glad you're getting out of that place you're living. It was so much nicer when you lived on campus.

WALT
You'll come to Annandale before you disappear on us, won't you?

CHRIS
(reluctantly)
Sure, I will.

Carine's not so sure.

BILLIE
You promise?

CHRIS
(whining)
Mom.

Figure 9.4 explains potential advantages of reading scripts before reading books.

Figure 9.4

	Advantages of Reading Scripts for Readers with Hyperlexia
1	Choosing a story and script of interest to the reader with autism as a starting point for teaching may be a great way to engage and motivate a reluctant reader, as well as build confidence.
2	The script reveals the thoughts and feelings of the characters. • To guide the actors in creating the visual scenes, the scriptwriter provides precise details about the actions and motivations of the characters and the specific emotions attached to the dialogue. • Readers can learn to watch for words that indicate the level or intensity of emotion in a certain scene or the perspectives of the characters.
3	The screenwriter overtly states the reactions of the characters to one another so that the actors can create the desired effect by translating the written directions into their acting. This can help with understanding cause and effect.
4	Nonverbal cues, physical actions, and the demeanor of the actors are clearly spelled out in the script. These overt specifics may help the reader with autism make the connection between the "direction" written in the script and the behaviors seen on film or stage.
5	Because drama is often dramatic (pun intended), the verbal and nonverbal expressions of emotions may be easier for the person to perceive, with a context for understanding the cause and effect of those emotions. This will have a positive effect on communication skills.

It's a good idea to start small and be selective.
- Choose a script or part of a script that will enhance understanding of the book.
- Focus on verbal and nonverbal cues, the perspectives of the characters, cause and effect, descriptors used to indicate the level of emotion needed in delivering a particular line of dialogue, or any other nuance you wish to emphasize to enhance meaning.

Cooperative activities such as taking turns reading dialogue aloud or even acting out parts of a script can be engaging for all students.

- Teach them to notice and follow **overt direction and cues** when delivering their lines.
- This is also an excellent opportunity to help students see the **purpose** and **meaning** behind the actions that the scriptwriter plans.
- The interactive social experience is an added benefit.

Emerging research shows that drama can be an excellent way to help individuals with autism experience interacting with characters, actions, and plots (Wilkinson & Semrud-Clikeman 2008).

- This can be particularly beneficial if the learner had limited dramatic play during childhood.
- Reading and acting out scripts may lead to an interest in drama for students with autism, which is emerging as a therapeutic tool to build social competence and problem-solving skills (Drill & Bellini 2022; Guli and colleagues 2008; Peter 2009).
- It may be a time to shine for the student with autism, who may be able to memorize lines and remember their cues.

The ultimate connection is to go full circle, from script, to film, to examining the original literature that is the foundation for the entire scene. This will help the reader understand how the author's meaning and intention have been interpreted by the screenwriter and by the actors.

Scripts for Teaching

Scripts offer a variety of teaching opportunities. They're particularly valuable for bringing emotions and thoughts to life. Figure 9.5 offers suggestions for using scripts.

Figure 9.5

	Teaching with Scripts
1	Follow the steps described earlier in this chapter for comparing a movie and a book as a way to compare a play and a book. • Have students compare a chapter in the book to a scene in the play, looking for similarities and differences. • Students can compare what was *kept* in the script and what was *cut* compared to the book. This activity requires rereading and provides extra practice and exposure to the story. • Students can discuss why a playwright might deviate from the book and why they agree or disagree with the playwright's decision.
2	To explore emotions and perspective taking, select scenes from the play that describe a clear emotional component. For example, using the scene from *Into the Wild*, students can take turns acting out Carine's silent doubt and Chris's whiny, "Mom."
3	Teach the concept of degrees of emotion by having different groups of students re-enact the same lines of dialogue. • Assign a degree of emotion (intensity) ranging from "a little emotion" to "a lot of emotion" to each group. • This is similar to the Shades of Meaning activity in Chapter 8, because you and the students can use precise synonyms to describe different levels of intensity in a similar feeling (upset, mad, enraged, furious, or down, sad, glum, miserable, depressed, etc.). • Help students pay attention to cues and clues from the scriptwriter to show this range. • Encourage students to use facial expressions and body language to express emotion and intensity. • When the scene is read in the book, readers can match clues in the text to cues in the script about the emotions or behaviors of the characters.

Reader's Theatre

Reader's Theatre is a free online resource that provides scripts and plays adapted from literature (Prescott 2003).

- Readers take different parts in the script and have fun dramatizing the story (without memorization or props).
- A variety of well-known children's stories have been converted for Reader's Theatre, such as *The Very Hungry Caterpillar*, *Where the Wild Things Are*, and *Casey at the Bat*.
- More information and scripts are available at www.teachingheart.net/readerstheater.htm.

Tip

Silent reading is often a problem for readers with hyperlexia (Myles and colleagues 2002). Many families and educators report that books on tape, another media tool, have helped students improve their reading skills and comprehension.

Listening while reading silently supports the processing of print and auditory language and oral language comprehension, which all support reading comprehension.

Using the read-aloud feature of electronic textbooks and e-books can help accomplish the same important goals.

C. Finding the Main Idea

Finding the main idea is a critical skill to support understanding at the paragraph or text level.

- Identifying the main idea helps readers remember and organize ideas from a paragraph.
- Readers continuously link one main idea to the next.

- As simple as it sounds, many readers with autism struggle with this.

Some readers with autism explain that all the sentences in a paragraph appear **equally important** to them.
- One woman told me that for her, reading is like highlighting all the sentences in a paragraph in the color gray. Nothing stands out.
- As a result, these readers can't see that one idea is **more important** than another.
- They cannot **judge** which idea is **the most important**.

When the main idea is *not* identified:
- There is **no cohesion** to the group of sentences. Understanding is compromised.
- The reader may over-focus on an unimportant detail or remember nothing at all about what was read.
- This can build until the reader feels completely lost.

Missing the point and not remembering the main ideas can also make writing or retelling almost impossible. Research shows that:
- The retelling of students on the spectrum (orally or in writing) is noticeably different from that of students with similar levels of intelligence who do not have autism (Holman 2004).
- The responses of students on the spectrum tend to be superficial and lack the relevant main points and important details (Loveland and colleagues 1990).
- Individuals with autism **miss the gist** or the big ideas (Wahlberg 2001a).

Benefits of Explicit Instruction for Readers with Hyperlexia
It's probably not an exaggeration that every teacher in every elementary classroom discusses the importance of finding the main idea.
- Still, many students with autism don't benefit from typical instruction to learn the skill. Sometimes "instruction" is being asked to find the main idea, without help to make the judgments involved in the process.

- Therefore, students with hyperlexia need to be explicitly taught to identify the main idea, starting at the paragraph level.

Figure 9.6 explains the benefits of mastering this **essential** skill, using whatever materials and methods are most appropriate.

Figure 9.6

	Benefits of Explicit Instruction to Identify the Main Idea
1	Learning to find the main idea creates a foundation of concepts and knowledge that is the real purpose behind reading, with all the benefits and connections that result.
2	Identifying the main idea enhances the meaning of all sentences in a paragraph. • Students learn that different sentences in a paragraph have different purposes. • These include providing support for the main idea, an example, or clarification. • When the main idea is identified, the reader can see how the sentences relate to one another as a cohesive whole.
3	Finding the main idea helps with organizing ideas and related skills such as summarizing, taking notes, and studying.
4	Getting the point and internalizing the meaning allows a reader to explain their understanding to others (retell) or write about what was read in an organized way.

A Hands-On Activity for Students to Identify the Main Idea

One activity to teach the skill of identifying the main idea consists of writing the sentences of a paragraph on sentence strips, putting them in the correct order, and deciding **by process of elimination** which of the sentences is the main idea.

- The physical aspect of sentence strips and the students' ability to manipulate them match well with two skills that many students with autism have: understanding concrete objects and arranging objects.

- Figure 9.7 describes how to find the main idea using sentence strips.

Figure 9.7

	Find the Main Idea by Process of Elimination
1	Prime instruction by explaining what a main idea is, along with the purpose and benefits of learning to find the main idea. Give examples or analogies that the student can relate to.
2	Choose high-interest material at the student's independent reading level.
3	Select one paragraph that has a clear main idea. Write each sentence from the paragraph on a separate sentence strip.
4	Arrange the strips in the correct order so that the sentences flow and make sense.
5	Ask the student to remove the first strip and read the paragraph. Ask the student to judge if the remaining sentences still make sense. Replace the sentence.
6	Continue removing sentences one at a time and rereading. This process will help the student identify **the one sentence that needs to be there to glue the paragraph together** (provide cohesion and meaning). Share your thoughts and prompt as needed.
7	Rearrange the strips to put the main idea first, and have the student read. Rearrange the strips to put the main idea last, and have the student read. Point out that these are the most common places that writers put the main idea, so they are good places to start when looking for it.
8	Guided practice: Practice the same procedure with a few more paragraphs until the student can demonstrate the skill independently. Provide strips from another paragraph for the student to repeat the procedure with you or a peer. Finally, practice the skill using grade-level narrative and expository text. Remove the support of sentence strips when the student shows they understand the concept.
9	Monitor and support the student's independent use of the strategy across the curriculum.

The same exercise can be carried out in a word-processing document.

1. Using a paragraph written in a word-processing document, have the student highlight and cut one sentence at a time. After reading the remaining sentences, have them paste the cut sentence back in.

2. Ask the student to judge the sense of the whole paragraph based on the absence or presence of one of the sentences to decide which sentence is central to the meaning.

D. Mark Text to Show the Main Idea and Summarize

Good readers mark text to highlight main ideas while reading to help with understanding and memory. Once a student knows how to find the main idea, s/he can practice marking it. Here are some options for marking text:

- **Underline main ideas with a pencil.** One advantage of this low-tech method is that it is erasable—especially important for students who are still learning and may make mistakes, or would be very stressed if they made a mistake and would want to fix it. Another option is to copy text onto paper or print it from a computer, and use highlighters. The reader can color-code the text, highlighting the main idea in one color and supporting details in another.

- **Color-code ideas using a computer.** Type text into a word-processing document. Use the highlight tool to highlight the main idea of each paragraph. Use another color for supporting ideas or examples.

- **In a multi-paragraph text, ask the student to highlight the main idea in each paragraph.** The highlighted ideas can be copied to create an outline or summary. The last step to create a summary would be to rephrase the list of main ideas, creating a summary in the student's own words.

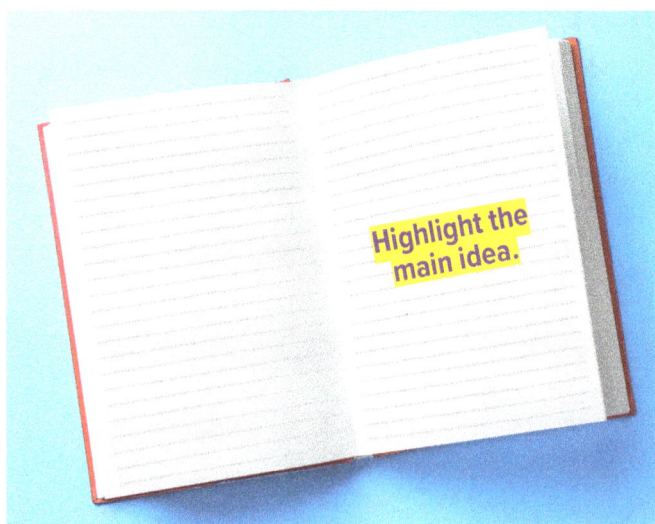

Highlight the main idea.

A Few More Bright Ideas

Revisit the tremendous potential benefit of using **electronic texts** to help identify and mark main ideas to facilitate comprehension of grade-level material that otherwise would be at the student's frustration level.

More research is being done on using technology such as computers and tablets for this type of task. I predict it will be evidence-based before long.

A tip for college-level readers who could use some help recognizing the main idea is to **buy used textbooks** that have already been highlighted. Be sure to check a few passages to be sure that the previous owner got it right! Once Tom and I figured this out, we never bought new textbooks again!

Removable highlighter tape can be used in textbooks, in storybooks, or on worksheets when learning to highlight. Educational supply stores sell it.

E. Previewing Text

Previewing text involves looking at the material to be read before reading. This can be done with expository (academic) texts or narratives. The steps and benefits of previewing expository are described in in Chapters 6 and 7. Previewing narrative material is sometimes called doing a "book walk" or a "picture walk."

- The purpose of this pre-reading activity is to familiarize the reader with the structure of the material and provide a brief overview of the content by focusing on the visual cues.
- Previewing is closely tied to the organization of text.
- Previewing stories may engage the reader's interest and clarify the big picture.

Previewing can help students who have a hard time with prediction perceive the order and sequence of events.

- Then, when they read in detail, the whole story may seem more integrated and cohesive.
- This may be especially useful to connect two versions of media when using a movie and a book together.

Figure 9.8 explains eight steps that are the foundation of a lesson plan to teach the skill of previewing text. This can be done by educational professionals, homeschooling parents, and parents or caregivers at home.

Figure 9.8

	Eight Steps for Previewing Narrative Text
1	Explain why we preview (to see what the material is about and how it's organized).
2	Explain what previewing is (a strategy to improve understanding and prepare to read by first looking at the material to get a general idea).
3	Relate previewing to something known. For example, a movie trailer is a short segment to get our interest. A movie preview allows us to grasp the main idea, theme, and type of movie it will be (e.g., comedy, thriller, drama, sci-fi, fantasy). Story previews can also provide hints about the book.
4	Model previewing by doing a book walk or picture walk with a well-structured, easy story. Think aloud to ask questions or make comments such as, "I think this picture is a clue to the action in the story," and "What will this story be about?" For books without pictures, review text organization and layout. Look at headings and chapter titles to find clues to the main ideas.
5	Check for understanding. Ask what material will be covered in a specific section based on a heading, a word in bold print, etc.
6	Conduct guided practice. Think aloud as you guide students through a chapter or other material they will be assigned. Ask students to tell you about what is important based on the clues they see (headings, bolded words).
7	Support independent practice. • Start with a short book that the student prefers (due to familiarity, the content or the theme). • Ask the student to demonstrate the skill using the preferred material. • Practice: Move to an unknown text on a similar theme to keep interest.
8	Support generalization. Move to unfamiliar material at an easy reading level, and then to more difficult material after easier material is mastered.

F. Audio Books

Many autistic individuals have strong visual skills, and others prefer to learn by listening. These students may benefit from using **audio books**. A huge library of textbooks, fiction and non-fiction books in audio format are available at no charge from The National Library Service (NLS) for the Blind and Print Disabled (formerly called Talking Books).

- The NLS program is not just for people who are visually impaired.
- It is available to others who can benefit from it.

Participants receive a special audio player that can change the tone, volume and speed of the audio book.

- Books can be downloaded from the NLS website onto a USB drive and inserted into the player.
- Books can also be ordered online. They're sent and returned through the mail at no charge.

For those who learn well by listening there are several advantages to using the specialized NLS audio player and audio books.

- Slowing down the speed at which the book is read can create a good match to the processing speed of the learner.
- A real person narrates the audio tape, not a computer. This may make the recording more appealing and interesting to the listener.
- If the student also has their own physical copy of the text, s/he can read along with the audio book at an appropriate speed.
  - Seeing and hearing simultaneously may help the student understand better.
  - This is similar to the idea of turning on captions on videos or televisions, with the benefit of seeing and hearing the same information at the same time.

You can apply for the nationwide, free program at the NLS website or at your local public library. To learn more, visit:

https://www.loc.gov/programs/national-library-service-for-the-blind-and-print-disabled/about-this-service/

G. Clink or Clunk?

This fun and easy method is the fastest way I know of to teach a reader to self-monitor their comprehension, sentence by sentence.

- One of the young readers with autism that I worked with in a literacy clinic was enthusiastic about this technique because he loved hearing the sounds involved.
- The activity helped him understand the idea of self-monitoring very quickly!
- Figure 9.9 explains how Clink or Clunk? works.

Figure 9.9

	Clink or Clunk? The Sound of Self-Monitoring
1	Gather materials: • A small glass bottle with a wide neck, such as a bottle for a coffee drink. • Five or six metal nuts and five or six small metal bolts or screws (items used to fix things). • Several paragraphs of high-interest material at the student's independent *and* instructional reading level.
2	Test the objects to be sure that when you drop one item into the bottle, it makes a *clink* sound, and when you drop the other, it makes a *clunk* sound. Switch the materials up until you find the right mix.
3	Explain what comprehension monitoring is and why it's helpful (i.e., to notice if you understand what you're reading, to stop and figure something out).
4	Relate monitoring to something that the student knows about. An example is GPS in a car that helps you know if you're on track and going in the right direction. Car GPS tells you when you get off track and "recalculates" to get you back on track.
5	Introduce the materials. Let the student have fun dropping the objects into the bottle and distinguishing the clink and clunk sounds. • Explain that while reading each sentence with you, s/he will drop in a nut to *clink* when s/he understands. • S/he will drop in a bolt to *clunk* when s/he does not understand.
6	Model the strategy by reading the first paragraph aloud. Stop after each sentence and ask the student if s/he understands it, or not. Prompt the student to drop the appropriate object into the bottle.

	Clink or Clunk? The Sound of Self-Monitoring
7	Verify understanding by asking the student to explain the meaning of the sentence in their own words. If the student did *not* understand, explain that it's time to stop and "repair" or fix up the breakdown in understanding. Take the lead to help them "fix up" the meaning. They can re-read the sentence and drop in a "clink" nut.
8	Continue guided practice. Have the student monitor their comprehension sentence by sentence. Progress from independent level materials to instructional level materials. When they don't understand, help them identify *what* they don't understand. Work together on "fix-ups," or comprehension repairs.
9	Continue until the student can independently monitor their comprehension.
10	The student can use the materials to monitor their comprehension and generalize the skill to curriculum materials or homework (depending on the setting).
11	Gradually reduce the physical materials and substitute a sentence-by-sentence technique **the student likes**, such as making a check mark in pencil for sentences that were understood, and an *X* for sentences that were not. They can still imagine the clink or clunk sounds if they want to.
12	This introductory lesson on self-monitoring should be followed up by teaching the student strategies for repairing meaning (anaphoric cueing, using context, etc.).

More Ideas and Resources for Teaching

One thing I've learned is that people always want more ideas for teaching. I know I do. One source that's popular with general education teachers is *The Reading Strategies Book* by literacy specialist Jennifer Serravallo (Heineman 2015).

- More than 200 pages of the book address comprehension skills. Strategies are well described and include custom graphic organizers or visuals.
- Suggested language is provided for explaining the concept and teaching the steps.
- While the information is not autism-specific, some of the ideas may be a good match for students with hyperlexia.

Another source from the same *New York Times* best-selling author is *Understanding Texts & Readers* (Heineman 2018).

- This book suggests stories and texts matched to a wide range of reading levels.
- Ideas are provided to help students systematically interpret narrative (story) elements and analyze expository (academic) material.
- You can search online for helpful resources from a variety of sources.

You, the Researcher!

When you want even **more** answers about what works, you can do your own research! For classroom teachers and other educators:

- One option is to select a particular method or strategy and track progress, focusing on the progress made by the student with autism compared to classroom peers with similar language and cognitive abilities.
- Or, work with another teacher to compare the effectiveness of two different methods with similar groups of students.
- Do pre-testing and post-testing of comprehension before and after instruction or strategy use.
- Let parents know what you are researching. Parents can be a very important source of information, with insights to share. They are often willing partners in the effort to improve comprehension.

A Final Thought

The individualized nature of the help needed by readers with autism suggests the need for individualized approaches, including special education services and educational therapy.

- Because of the diversity among those on the autism spectrum, the evidence shows that one-to-one or small group explicit instruction and individualized remediation programs are most effective.
- Hans Asperger (the person for whom Asperger's syndrome is named) also recognized the need for individual attention, especially because of difficulties that the students may have working in groups or getting lost during regular classroom instruction (Frith 2004).

Whatever approach you choose, start by building on strengths and interests. Asperger advocated building on strengths, circumventing weaknesses, and using special interests to guide learning (Frith 2004).

- Teach concepts using materials that are concrete and visual.
- Spark interest by using preferred topics and interests to demonstrate new ideas.
- A solid foundation based on familiar, stimulating subjects can lead to success with abstraction, generalization, and greater understanding.

Conclusion

To assist parents and educational professionals working with the growing and diverse population of individuals with autism, we've examined the *observable* and *invisible* features of autism. We've discussed *how* and *why* these characteristics affect literacy development and reading comprehension.

- The demands of comprehension at the word, sentence, and text level and key research findings about comprehension issues in autism give direction for using effective interventions.

- Strategies, activities, and resources to improve comprehension were suggested that are either supported by research or appear to be a good match to the needs and learning style of students on the spectrum.

- These ideas can help educational professionals and parents teach readers with autism how to gain meaning from the richness of the written word.

There's much to be learned and much more to be done to help readers with hyperlexia realize their potential. I'm here with you in the trenches! I know that many people living and working on a daily basis with someone with hyperlexia have wonderful insights, experience, and resources to share. Please visit my website, www.readingautism.com, to continue the discussion and share ideas about **what works.**

REFERENCES

Accardo, A. L. (2015). Research synthesis: Effective practices for improving the reading comprehension of students with autism spectrum disorder. *DADD Online Journal 2*(1), 7–20. https://rdw.rowan.edu/education_facpub/6.

Al Otaiba, S., & Fuchs, D. (2002). Characteristics of children who are unresponsive to early literacy intervention: A review of the literature. *Remedial and Special Education, 23*(5), 300–316.

American Psychiatric Association. (2022). *Diagnostic and statistical manual of mental disorders* (5th ed., text rev.). American Psychiatric Association Publishing.

Arciuli, J., & Bailey, B. (2019). Efficacy of ABRACADABRA literacy instruction in a school setting for children with autism spectrum disorders. *Research in Developmental Disabilities, 85,* 104–115.

Armbruster, B. B., Lehr, F., & Osborn, J. (2003). Put reading first: The research building blocks for teaching children to read kindergarten through grade 3. (2nd ed.). Jessup, MD: National Institute for Literacy.

Åsberg, J., & Dahlgren-Sandberg, A. (2010). Discourse comprehension intervention for high-functioning students with autism spectrum disorders: preliminary findings from a school-based study. *Journal of Research in Special Educational Needs, 10*(2), 91–98.

Atkinson, L., Slade, L., Powell, D., & Levy, J. P. (2017). Theory of mind in emerging reading comprehension: a longitudinal study of early indirect and direct effects. *Journal of Experimental Child Psychology, 164,* 225–238.

Bae, Y.S. (2013). Word problem solving of students with autistic spectrum disorders and students with typical development. [Unpublished doctoral dissertation]. Columbia University.

Bailey, B., Arciuli, J., & Stancliffe, R. J. (2017). Effects of ABRACADABRA instruction on spelling in children with autism spectrum disorder. *Scientific Studies of Reading, 21*(2), 146–164.

Banda, D. R., and Therrien, W. J. (2008). A teacher's guide to meta-analysis. *Teaching Exceptional Children, 41*(2), 66–71.

Baron-Cohen, S., Leslie, A. M., & Frith, U. (1985). Does the autistic child have a 'theory of mind?' *Cognition, 21,* 37–46.

Baron-Cohen, S., Tager-Flusberg, H., & Cohen, D. J., eds. (1993). *Understanding Other Minds: Perspectives From Autism.* Oxford: Oxford University Press.

Bean, A., Perez, B., Dynia, J. & Kaderavek, J. (2020). Book-reading engagement in children with autism and language impairment: Associations with emergent-literacy skills. *Journal of Autism and Developmental Disorders, 50,* 1018-1030.

Beck, J. S. (2016). Concept Identification and Formation in Adolescents Diagnosed with Autism Spectrum Disorder. *Theses and Dissertations*. 6366. https://scholarsarchive.byu.edu/etd/6366

Beckerson, M., Paisley, C., Murdaugh, D., Holm, H., Lemelman, A., Spencer, A., O'Kelley, S., & Kana, R. (2024). Reading comprehension improvement in autism. *Frontiers in Psychiatry, 15*, 1-14.

Bell, N. (2007). *Visualizing and Verbalizing: For Language Comprehension and Thinking.* Paso Robles, CA: Nancibell, Inc.

Bethune, K. S., & Wood, C. L. (2013). Effects of wh-question graphic organizers on reading comprehension skills of students with autism spectrum disorders. *Education and Training in Autism and Developmental Disabilities, 48*(2), 236–244.

Biemiller, A. (2001). Teaching vocabulary: Early, direct, and sequential. *American Educator, (25)*, 24–28, 47.

Biemiller, A. (2007). The influence of vocabulary on reading acquisition. In *Encyclopedia of Language and Literacy Development*. London, ON: Canadian Language and Literacy Research Network.

Borenstein, M., Hedges, L. V., Higgins, J. P. T., & Rothstein, H. R. (2009). *Introduction to Meta-analysis.* John Wiley & Sons.

Brock, J., Norbury, C. F., Einav, S., & Nation, K. (2008). Do individuals with autism process words in context? Evidence from language-mediated eye-movements. *Cognition, 108*(3), 896–904.

Brown, H.D. & Lee, H. (2025). *Principles of Language Learning and Teaching: A Course in Second Language Acquisition, Seventh Edition.* New York: Routledge.

Brown, H., Oram-Cardy, J., & Johnson, A. (2013). A meta-analysis of the reading comprehension skills of individuals on the autism spectrum. *Journal of Autism and Developmental Disorders, 43*(4), 932–955.

Buron, K. D., & Wolfberg, P., eds. (2008, 2014). *Learners on the Autism Spectrum: Preparing Highly Qualified Educators.* Shawnee Mission, KS: Autism Asperger Publishing Co.

Cain, K. (2003). Text comprehension and its relation to coherence and cohesion in children's fictional narratives. *British Journal of Developmental Psychology, 21*, 331–335.

Calhoon J. A. (2001). Factors affecting the reading of rimes in words and nonwords in beginning readers with cognitive disabilities and typically developing readers: Explorations in similarity and difference in word recognition cue use. *Journal of Autism and Developmental Disorders, 31*(5), 491–504.

Campbell, M. A. (2010). Effects of Pronoun Identification Instruction on Text Comprehension for Children With Autism. Psy.D. diss., Fairleigh Dickinson University. *ProQuest Dissertations & Theses A&I.*

Carnahan, C., & Williamson, P., eds. (2012). *Quality Literacy Instruction for Students With Autism Spectrum Disorders.* Shawnee Mission, KS: AAPC Textbooks.

Carnahan, C. R., Williamson, P. S., & Christman, J. (2011). Linking cognition and literacy in students with autism spectrum disorder. *Teaching Exceptional Children, 43*, 54–62.

Carnahan, C. R., & Williamson, P. S. (2013). Does compare-contrast text structure help students with autism spectrum disorder comprehend science text? *Exceptional Children, 79*(3), 347–366.

Carnahan, C. R., Williamson, P., Birri, N., Swoboda, C., & Snyder, K. K. (2015). Increasing comprehension of expository science text for students with autism spectrum disorder. *Focus on Autism and Other Developmental Disabilities, 31*(3), 208–220.

Carpenter, M., Pennington, B. F., & Rogers, S. J. (2002). Interrelations among social-cognitive skills in young children with autism. *Journal of Autism and Developmental Disorders, 32*(2), 91–106.

CAST. (2014). *Transforming Education Through Universal Design for Learning.* http://www.cast.org/.

Centers for Disease Control and Prevention (CDC). (2025). *Data and statistics on autism spectrum disorder.* https://www.cdc.gov/autism/data-research/index.html.

Centers for Disease Control and Prevention (CDC). (2008). *Frequently asked questions-prevalence.* http://www.cdc.gov/ncbddd/autism/faq_prevalence.htm#howmanyinUS

Centers for Disease Control and Prevention (CDC). (2023). *Spotlight on a new pattern in racial and ethnic differences emerges in autism spectrum disorder (ASD) identification among 8-year-old children.* https://www.cdc.gov/ncbddd/autism/addm-community-report/spotlight-on-racial-ethnic-differences.html.

Chang, Y-C, Menzies, H.M., & Osipova, A. (2020). Reading comprehension instruction for students with autism spectrum disorder. *The Reading Teacher, (74)*3, 255-264.

Chen, L., Abrams, D.A., Rosenberg-Lee, M., Iuculano, T., Wakeman, H.N., Prathap, S., Chen, T., & Menon, V. (2019). Quantitative analysis of heterogeneity in academic achievement of children with autism. *Clinical Psychological Science, 7*(2), 362-380.

Chiang, H., & Lin, Y. (2007). Reading comprehension instruction for students with autism spectrum disorders: A review of the literature. *Focus on Autism and Other Developmental Disabilities, 22*(4), 259–268.

Childcare.gov. (2025) *Supporting children's learning through play.* https://childcare.gov/consumer-education/support-my-childs-health-development/supporting-childrens-learning-through-play#:~:text=Play%20encourages%20children's%20brain%20development,effect%2C%20and%20build%20memory%20skills.

Children's Hospital of Philadelphia. (2017). *Brain scan may predict if infants will be diagnosed with autism.* https://www.chop.edu/news/brain-scan-may-predict-if-infants-will-be-diagnosed-autism.

Clemens, N. H., & Fuchs, D. (2021). Commercially developed tests of reading comprehension: Gold standard or fool's gold? *Reading Research Quarterly, 57*(2), 385–397.

Colasent, R., & Griffith, P. L. (1998). Autism and literacy: Looking into the classroom with rabbit stories. *Reading Teacher, 51*, 414–420.

Cronin, K. A. (2014). The relationship among oral language, decoding skills, and reading comprehension in children with autism. *Exceptionality, 22*(3), 141–157.

Cutting, L. E., & Scarborough, H. S. (2006). Prediction of reading comprehension: Relative contributions of word recognition, language proficiency, and other cognitive skills can depend on how comprehension is measured. *Scientific Studies of Reading, 10*(3), 277–299.

Dapretto, M., Davies, M. S., Pfeifer, J. H., Scott, A. A., Sigman, M., Bookheimer, S. Y. & Iacoboni, M. (2006). Understanding emotions in others: Mirror neuron dysfunction in children with autism spectrum disorder. *Nature Neuroscience, 9*, 28–30.

Davidson, M. M., Kaushanskaya, M., & Ellis Weismer, S. (2018). Reading comprehension in children with and without ASD: The role of word reading, oral language, and working memory. *Journal of Autism and Developmental Disorders, 48*(10), 3524–3541.

Dennis, M., Lockyer, L., & Lazenby, A. L. (2000). How high-functioning children with autism understand real and deceptive emotion. *Autism, 4*(4), 370–381.

Diamond, L., & Gutlohn, L. (2006). *Teaching vocabulary*. http://www.readingrockets.org/article/9943.

Douglas, E. (2005). *Reading comprehension and English language learners*. http://www.learnnc.org/lp/editions/ell-readcomp0708/724?style=print.

Doyle, B. T., & Iland, E. D. (2004). *Autism Spectrum Disorders From A to Z: Diagnosis, Assessment and More*. Arlington, TX: Future Horizons Publishers.

Drill, R. B., & Bellini, S. (2022). Combining readers theater, story mapping, and video self-modeling interventions to improve narrative reading comprehension in children with autism spectrum disorder. *Journal of Autism and Developmental Disorders, 52*(1), 1–15.

Duke, N. K., Ward, A. E., and Pearson, P. D. (2021). The science of reading comprehension instruction. *The Reading Teacher, 74*(6), 663–672.

Dyson, L. (2015). The literacy competence of children with autism spectrum syndrome: A systematic review of three decades of research. *The International Journal of Literacies, 21*(3-4), 1-16.

Ehren, B. J. (2005). Looking for evidence-based practice in reading comprehension instruction. *Topics in Language Disorders, 25*(4), 310–312.

Ehren, B. J., & Nelson, N. W. (2005). The responsiveness to intervention approach and language impairment. *Topics in Language Disorders, 25*(2), 120–131.

El Zein, F., Gevarter, C., Bryant, B., Son, S. H., Bryant, D., Kim, M., & Solis, M. (2016). A comparison between iPad-assisted and teacher-directed reading instruction for students with autism spectrum disorder (ASD). *Journal of Developmental and Physical Disabilities, 28*, 195–215.

El Zein, F., Solis, M., Vaughn, S., & McCulley, L. (2014). Reading comprehension interventions for students with autism spectrum disorders: a synthesis of research. *Journal of Autism and Developmental Disorders, 44*, 1303–1322.

Emerich, D. M., Creaghead, N. A., Grether, S. M., Murray, D., & Grasha, C. (2003). The comprehension of humorous materials by adolescents with high-functioning autism and Asperger's syndrome. *Journal of Autism and Developmental Disorders, 33*(1), 253–257.

Engel, K.S. (2018). Reading comprehension instruction for young students with high functioning autism: Forming contextual connections. City University of New York, *CUNY Academic Works*. https://academicworks.cuny.edu/gc_etds/2774.

Engelmann, S., Hanner, S., & Johnson, G. (1989). *Corrective Reading*. Eugene, OR: Science Research Associates.

Escalona, A., Field, T., Nadel, J., & Lundy, B. (2002). Brief report: Imitation effects on children with autism. *Journal of Autism and Developmental Disorders, 32*(2), 141–144.

Every Student Succeeds Act, 20 U.S.C. § 6301 (2021).

Fasih, P., Izadpanah, S., & Shahnavaz, A. (2018). The effect of mnemonic vocabulary instruction on reading comprehension of students. *International Journal of Applied Linguistics, 7*(3), 49-60.

Faitaki, F., Hessel, A.K. & Murphy, V.A. (2022). Vocabulary and grammar development in young learners of English as an additional language, in M. Schwartz (Ed.). *International Handbook of Early Language Education.* Springer International Handbooks of Education (428-444). Springer: Cham.

Fernandes, F. D. M., de La Higuera Amato, C. A., Cardoso, C., Navas, A. L. G. P., & Molini-Avejonas, D. R. (2016). Reading in autism spectrum disorders: A literature review. *Folia Phoniatrica et Logopaedica, 67*(4), 169–177.

Finnegan, E., & Mazin, A. L. (2016). Strategies for increasing reading comprehension skills in students with autism spectrum disorder: A review of the literature. *Education and Treatment of Children, 39*, 187–219.

Flores, M. M., & Ganz, J. B. (2007). Effectiveness of direct instruction for teaching statement inference, use of facts, and analogies to students with developmental disabilities and reading delays. *Focus on Autism and Other Developmental Disabilities, 22*, 244–251.

Flores, M., & Ganz, J. B. (2009). Effects of direct instruction on the reading comprehension of students with autism and developmental disabilities. *Education and Training in Developmental Disabilities, 44*(1), 39–53.

Floyd, S., Jeppsen, C., & Goldberg, A.E. (2020). Brief report: Children on the autism spectrum are challenged by complex word meanings. *Journal of Autism and Developmental Disorders, (51)*7, 2543-2549.

Fotheringham, J. B. (1991). Autism: Its primary psychological and neurological deficit. *Canadian Journal of Psychiatry, 36*(9), 686–692.

Frith, U., ed. (1991). *Autism and Asperger Syndrome.* Cambridge, United Kingdom: Cambridge University Press.

Frith, U. (2004). Emanuel Miller lecture: Confusions and controversies about Asperger syndrome. *Journal of Child Psychology and Psychiatry, 45*(4), 672–686.

Gately, S. E. (2008). Facilitating reading comprehension for students on the autism spectrum. *Teaching Exceptional Children, 40*(3), 40–45.

Gillam, R. B., & Pearson, N. A. (2004). *Test of Narrative Language.* Austin, TX: Pro-Ed.

Gillam, R.B. & Pearson, N.A. (2017). *Test of Narrative Language.* Western Psychological Services (WPS).

Gillett, A. (2010). *Using English for academic purposes: A guide for students in higher education.* http://www.uefap.com/vocab/build/building.htm.

Glut, D. F. (1980). *Star Wars: The Empire Strikes Back.* New York: Ballantine Books.

Gough, P. B., and Tunmer, W. E. (1986). Decoding, reading, and reading disability. *Remedial and Special Education, 7*(1), 6–10.

Grigorenko, E. L., Klin, A., Pauls, D. L., Senft, R., Hooper, C., & Volkmar, F. (2002). A descriptive study of hyperlexia in a clinically referred sample of children with developmental delays. *Journal of Autism and Developmental Disorders, 32*(1), 3–12.

Grigorenko, E. L., Klin, A., & Volkmar, F. (2003). Annotation: Hyperlexia: Disability or superability? *Journal of Child Psychology and Psychiatry, 44*(8), 1079–1091.

Griswold, D. E., Barnhill, G. P., Myles, B. S., Hagiwara, T., & Simpson, R. L. (2002). Asperger syndrome and academic achievement. *Focus on Autism and Other Developmental Disabilities, 17*(2), 94–102.

Guli, L. A., Wilkinson, A. D., and Semrud-Clikeman, M. (2008). *Social Competence Intervention Program: A Drama-Based Intervention for Youth on the Autism Spectrum.* Champaign, IL: Research Press.

Haigh, S. M., Walsh, J. A., Mazefsky, C. A., Minshew, N. J., & Eack, S. M. (2018). Processing speed is impaired in adults with autism spectrum disorder and relates to social communication abilities. *Journal of Autism and Developmental Disorders, 48*(8), 2653–2662.

Hamilton, L. & Hayiou-Thomas, M. (2022). The foundations of literacy. In M. J. Snowling and C. Hume (Eds.), *The science of reading: A Handbook,* (2nd ed., pp. 125-147). Wiley-Blackwell.

Hao, Y., Banker, S., Schafer, M., Zhang, E., Barkley, S., Trayvick, J., Peters, A., Thinakaran, A., McLaughlin, C., Gu, X., Foss-Feig, J., & Schiller, D. (2025). A unique neural and behavioral profile of social anxiety in autism. *Research Square,* rs.3.rs-6514342.

Happé, F. (1993). Communicative competence and theory of mind in autism: A test of relevance theory. *Cognition, 48,* 101–119.

Happé, F. (1994). An advanced test of theory of mind: Understanding of story characters' thoughts and feelings by able autistic, mentally handicapped, and normal children and adults. *Journal of Autism and Developmental Disorders, 24,* 101–119.

Happé, F. (1997). Central coherence and theory of mind in autism: Reading homographs in context. *British Journal of Developmental Psychology, 15,* 1–12.

Happé, F., & Frith, U. (1996). The neuropsychology of autism. *Brain, 119,* 1377–1400.

Happé, F., & Frith, U. (2006). The weak coherence account: Detail-focused cognitive style in autism spectrum disorders. *Journal of Autism and Developmental Disorders, 36,* 5–25.

Harris, G. J., Chabris, C. F., Clark, J., Urban, T., Aharon, I., Steele, S., McGrath, L., Condouris, K., & Tager-Flusberg, H. (2006). Brain activation during semantic processing in autism spectrum disorders via functional magnetic resonance imaging. *Brain and Cognition, 61,* 54–68.

Henderson, L.M., Clarke, P., & Snowling, M. (2014). Reading comprehension impairments in autism spectrum disorder. *L'Annee Psychologique, 114*(4), 779-797.

Hobson, R. P. (1993). Understanding persons: The role of affect. In S. Baron-Cohen, H. Tager-Flusberg, and D. Cohen, eds., *Understanding other minds: Perspectives from autism,* pp. 204–227. New York: Oxford University Press.

Holman, D. (2004). *Reading profiles of children with autism and hyperlexia: Toward an explanation of reading comprehension deficits* [Unpublished doctoral dissertation]. University of Southern California, Los Angeles.

Hou, W., Liang, S. & Li, J. (2025). The effects of dialogic reading interaction and engagement in young autistic children: A randomized, controlled preliminary study. *Journal of Autism and Developmental Disorders*. Advance online publication retrieved from https://doi.org/10.1007/s10803-025-06886-w.

Howorth, S., Lopata, C., Thomeer, M., & Rodgers, J. (2016). Effects of the TWA strategy on expository reading comprehension of students with autism. *British Journal of Special Education, 43*(1), 39–59.

Hoy, J. A., Hatton, C., & Hare, D. (2004). Weak central coherence: A cross-domain phenomenon specific to autism? *Autism, 8*(3), 267–281.

Huemer, S. V., & Mann, V. (2010). A comprehensive profile of decoding and comprehension in autism spectrum disorders. *Journal of Autism and Developmental Disorders*, 40(4), 485–493.

Intermountain Therapy Animals. (2025). *"What is R.E.A.D.?"* https://therapyanimals.org/read/.

Jacobs, D. W., & Richdale, A. L. (2013). Predicting literacy in children with a high-functioning autism spectrum disorder. *Research in Developmental Disabilities, 34*(8), 2379–2390.

James, I. (2003). Singular scientists. *Journal of the Royal Society of Medicine, 96*, 36–39.

Johnson, L., & Lamb, A. (2007). *Critical and creative thinking: Bloom's taxonomy.* http://eduscapes.com/tap/topic69.htm.

Jones, C. R. G., Happé, F., Golden, H., Marsden, A. J. S., Tregay, J., Simonoff, E., Pickles, A., Baird, G., & Charman, T. (2009). Reading and arithmetic in adolescents with autism spectrum disorders: Peaks and dips in attainment. *Neuropsychology, 23*(6), 718–728.

Just, M. A., Cherkassky, V. L., Keller, T. A., Kana, R. K., & Minshew, N. J. (2007). Functional and anatomical cortical underconnectivity in autism: Evidence from an FMRI study of an executive function task and corpus callosum morphometry. *Cerebral Cortex, 17*(4), 951–961.

Just, M., Cherkassky, V. L., Keller, T. A., & Minshew, N. (2004). Cortical activation and synchronization during sentence comprehension in high-functioning autism: Evidence of underconnectivity. *Brain, 127*, 1811–1821.

Just, M. A., Keller, T. A., Malave, V. L., Kana, R. K., & Varma, S. (2012). Autism as a neural systems disorder: A theory of frontal-posterior underconnectivity. *Neuroscience and Biobehavioral Reviews, 36*(4), 1292–1313.

Kaderavek, J. N., and Rabidoux, P. (2004). Interactive to independent literacy: A model for designing literacy goals for children with atypical communication. *Reading & Writing Quarterly, 20*, 237–260.

Kanner, L. (1943). Autistic disturbances of affective contact. *Nervous Child, 2*, 217–250. https://autismtruths.org/pdf/Autistic%20Disturbances%20of%20Affective%20Contact%20-%20Leo%20Kanner.pdf.

Khowaja, K., & Salim, S. S. (2013). A systematic review of strategies and computer-based intervention (CBI) for reading comprehension of children with autism. *Research in Autism Spectrum Disorders, 7*, 1111–1121.

Kim, S.H.S., Bal, V.H., & Lord, C. (2018). Longitudinal follow-up of academic achievement in children with autism from age 2 to 18. *Journal of Child Psychology and Psychiatry, 59*(3), 258-267

Kim, S.Y., Rispoli, M., Lory, C., Gregori, E., & Brodhead, M. T. (2018). The effects of a shared reading intervention on narrative story comprehension and task engagement of students with autism spectrum disorder. *Journal of Autism and Developmental Disorders*, *48*(10), 3608–3622.

Kinnard, E., Stewart, C., & Tchanturia. K. (2018). Investigating alexithymia in autism: A systematic review and meta-analysis. *European Psychiatry, 55*, 80-89.

Kluth, P., & Chandler-Olcott, K. (2008). *A Land We Can Share.* Baltimore: Paul H. Brookes Publishing.

Knight, V. F., Wood, C. L., Spooner, F., Browder, D. M., & O'Brien, C. P. (2014). An exploratory study using science e-texts with students with autism spectrum disorder. *Focus on Autism and Other Developmental Disabilities, 30*(2), 1–14.

Keough, K.L. (2024). "How Pretend Play Helps Children Build Skills." https://childmind.org/blog/how-pretend-play-helps-children-build-skills/#:~:text=Pretend%20play%20also%20provides%20opportunities,et%20al.%2C%202024).

Korhonen, Veera. (2024). "Number of 3 to 21 Year Olds With Autism Served Under the Individuals With Disabilities Education Act (IDEA) in the United States From 2000/01 to 2022/23.*"* https://www.statista.com/statistics/236348/number-of-disabled-youth-with-autism-in-the-us/.

Leach, J. M., Scarborough, H. S., & Rescoria, L. (2003). Late-emerging reading disabilities. *Journal of Educational Psychology, 95*(2), 211–225.

Lehr, F., Osborn, J., & Hiebert, E. H. (2004). *A Focus on Vocabulary: Research-Based Practices in Early Reading Series.* https://www.researchgate.net/publication/378070810_A_Focus_on_Vocabulary_Research-Based_Practices_in_Early_Reading_Series.

Leslie, L., & Caldwell, J. S. (2010). *Qualitative Reading Inventory–5.* Boston: Allyn & Bacon.

Levine, M. (2002). *Educational Care: A System for Understanding and Helping Children with Learning Differences at Home and at School.* 2nd ed. Cambridge, MA: Educators Publishing Service.

Lenz, B. K., & Hughes, C. A. (1990). A word identification strategy for adolescents with learning disabilities. *Journal of Learning Disabilities, 23*(3), 149–158, 163.

Lindamood-Bell Learning Processes. (2009). *2008 Learning Center Results.*

Litman, A., Sauerwald, N., Green Snyder, L., Foss-Feig et. al. (2025). Decomposition of phenotypic heterogeneity in autism reveals underlying genetic programs. *Nature Genetics, 57, 1611-1619.*

Lopata, C., Thomeer, M.L., Rodgers, J.D., Donnelly, J.P., McDonald, C.A., Volker, M.A., Smith, T.H., & Wang, H. (2019). Cluster randomized trial of a school intervention for children with autism spectrum disorder. *Journal of Clinical Child & Adolescent Psychology, (48)*6, 922-933.

Loveland, K., McEvoy, R., Tunali, B., & Kelley, M. L. (1990). Narrative storytelling in autism and Down's syndrome. [sic]. *British Journal of Developmental Psychology, 8*(1), 9–23.

Lucas, R., & Norbury, C. F. (2014). Levels of text comprehension in children with autism spectrum disorders (ASD): The influence of language phenotype. *Journal of Autism and Developmental Disorders, 44*(11), 2756–2768.

Macdonald, D., Luk, G., & Quintin, E. M. (2022). Early reading comprehension intervention for preschoolers with autism spectrum disorder and hyperlexia. *Journal of Autism and Developmental Disorders, 52*(4), 1652–1672.

Mason, L. H. (2013). Teaching students who struggle with learning to think before, while, and after reading: Effects of self-regulated strategy development instruction. *Reading & Writing Quarterly: Overcoming Learning Difficulties, 29*(2), 124–144.

Marzano, R. J. (2009). "Teaching Word Parts to Enhance Student Understanding." www.visualthesaurus.com/cm/booknook/1838.

Mayes, S.D., & Calhoun, S.L. (2008). WISC-IV and WIAT-II Profiles in children with high-functioning autism. *Journal of Autism and Developmental Disorders, 38,* 428–439.

McClain, M. B., Haverkamp, C. R., Benallie, K. J., Schwartz, S. E., & Simonsmeier, V. (2021). How effective are reading comprehension interventions for children with ASD?" A meta-analysis of single-case design studies. *School Psychology, 36*(2): 107–121.

McIntyre, N. S., Solari, E. J., Grimm, R. P., Lerro, L. E., Gonzales, J. E., & Mundy, P. C. (2017). A comprehensive examination of reading heterogeneity in students with high-functioning autism: Distinct reading profiles and their relation to autism symptom severity. *Journal of Autism and Developmental Disorders, 47*(4), 1086–1101.

Mention, B., Pourre, F., & Andanson, J. (2024). Humor in autism spectrum disorders: A systematic review. *L'Encephale, 50*(2), 200–210.

Miller, L. E., Burke, J. D., Troyb, E., Knoch, K., Herlihy, L. E., & Fein, D. A. (2017). Preschool predictors of school-age academic achievement in autism spectrum disorder. *The Clinical Neuropsychologist, 31*(2), 382-403.

Minshew, N.J. & Goldstein, G. (1998). Autism as a disorder of complex information processing. *Mental Retardation and Developmental Disabilities Research Reviews, 4,* 129-136.

Minshew, N. J., Goldstein, G., & Siegel, D. J. (1995). Speech and language in high-functioning autistic individuals. *Neuropathology, 9*(2), 255–261.

Minshew, S., & Williams, D. L. (2008). "Brain–Behavior Connections in Autism." In K. D. Buron and P. Wolfberg, eds., *Learners on the Autism Spectrum: Preparing Highly Qualified Educators.* Shawnee Mission, KS: Autism Asperger Publishing Co.

Murdaugh, D. L., Maximo, J. O., Cordes, C. E., O'Kelley, S. E., & Kana, R. K. (2017). From word reading to multisentence comprehension: Improvements in brain activity in children with autism after reading intervention. *NeuroImage: Clinical, 16,* 303-312.

Murphy, M.J. (2024). "Connection-Based Learning: Fostering Relationships for Student Success." https://www.k12digest.com/connection-based-learning-fostering-relationships-for-student

success/#:~:text=When%20students%20practice%20empathy%2C%20active%20listening%2C%20 and,stage%20for%20improved%20academic%20and%20social%20outcomes.

Museum of Science, Boston. (1998). *Oceans Alive.*

Myles, B. S., Hilgenfeld, T. D., Barnhill, G. P., Griswold, D. E., Hagiwara, T., & Simpson, R. L. (2002). Analysis of reading skills in individuals with Asperger syndrome. *Focus on Autism and Other Developmental Disabilities, 17*(1), 44–48.

Nation, K., Clarke, P., Wright, B., & Williams, C. (2006). Patterns of reading ability in children with autism spectrum disorder. *Journal of Autism and Developmental Disorders, 36*(7), 911–919.

Nation, K., & Norbury, C. F. (2005). Why reading comprehension fails: Insights from developmental disorders. *Topics in Language Disorders, 25*, 21–33.

National Early Literacy Panel. (2008). *Developing Early Literacy: Report of the National Early Literacy Panel.* Washington, DC: National Institute for Literacy.

National Institute for Literacy. (2009). *Glossary.*

National Institute of Child Health and Human Development (NICHD). (2000). *Report of the National Reading Panel: Teaching Children to Read—An Evidence-Based Assessment of the Scientific Research Literature on Reading and Its Implications for Reading Instruction.* http://www.nichd.nih.gov/ publications/pubs/nrp/smallbook.

National Research Council. (2001). *Educating Children With Autism.* Washington, DC: National Academy Press.

National Technical Assistance Center on Transition Center (2015). *Evidence-Based Practices Quality Indicators.* http://www.transitionta.org/.

Newman, T. M., Macomber, D., Naples, A. J., Babitz, T., Volkmar, F., & Grigorenko, E. (2007). Hyperlexia in children with autism spectrum disorders. *Journal of Autism and Developmental Disorders, 37*, 760–774.

Nicolosi, M., & Dillenburger, K. (2024). The effect of phonics skills intervention on early reading comprehension in an adolescent with autism: A longitudinal study. *Behavioral Interventions, 39*(3), 1-15.

No Child Left Behind Act of 2001. 20 U.S.C. § 6301 et seq. (2008).

Norbury, C. F. (2004). Factors supporting idiom comprehension in children with communication disorders. *Journal of Speech, Language, and Hearing Research, 47*(5), 1179–1194.

Norbury, C. F., & Bishop, D. V. M. (2002). Inferential processing and story recall in children with communication problems: A comparison of specific language impairment, pragmatic language impairment, and high-functioning autism. *International Journal of Language & Communication Disorders, 37*, 227–251.

Norbury, C. F., Brock, J., Cragg, L., Einav, S., Griffiths, H., & Nation, K. (2009). "Eye-movement patterns are associated with communicative competence in autistic spectrum disorders." *Journal of Child Psychology and Psychiatry, 50*, 834–842.

O'Connor, N., & Hermelin, B. (1994). Two autistic savant readers. *Journal of Autism and Developmental Disorders, 24*(4), 501–515.

O'Connor, I. M., & Klein, P. D. (2004). Exploration of strategies for facilitating the reading comprehension of high-functioning students with autism spectrum disorders. *Journal of Autism and Developmental Disabilities, 34*(2), 115–127.

Ogle, D. M. (1986). K-W-L: A teaching model that develops active reading of expository text. *Reading Teacher, 39*, 564–570.

Ohnemus, E., ed. (2002). *No Child Left Behind: A Desktop Reference.* https://eric.ed.gov/?id=ED471334.

Ostrolenk, A., Forgeot d'Arc, B., Jelenic, P., Samson, F., & Mottron, L. (2017). Hyperlexia: Systematic review, neurocognitive modeling, and outcome. *Neuroscience and Biobehavioral Reviews, 79*, 134-149.

Palincsar, A. S., & Brown, A. L. (1984). Reciprocal teaching of comprehension-fostering and comprehension-monitoring activities. *Cognition and Instruction, 1*(2), 117–175.

Pears, K.C., Fisher, P.A., Kim, H.K., Bruce, J., Healey, C.V., & Yoerger, K. (2013). Immediate effects of a school readiness intervention for children in foster care. *Early Education and Development, 24*(6), 771–791.

Peter, M. (2009). "Drama: Narrative pedagogy and socially challenged children." *British Journal of Special Education, 36*(1), 13–17.

Pittet I., Kojovic N., Franchini M. & Schaer M. (2022). Trajectories of imitation skills in preschoolers with autism spectrum disorders. *Journal of Neurodevelopmental Disorders, 14*(2), 1-13.

Prescott, J. O. (2003). "The Power of Reader's Theater." *Scholastic Instructor.* http://teacher.scholastic.com/products/instructor/readerstheater.htm.

Randi, J., Newman, T., & Grigorenko, E. L. (2010). Teaching children with autism to read for meaning: Challenges and possibilities." *Journal of Autism and Developmental Disorders, 40*, 890–902.

Reutebuch, C. K., El Zein, F., Kim, M. K., Weinberg, A. N., & Vaughn, S. (2015). Investigating a reading comprehension intervention for high school students with autism spectrum disorder: A pilot study. *Research in Autism Spectrum Disorders, 9*, 96–111.

Ricketts, J., Jones, C. R., Happé, F., & Charman, T. (2013). Reading comprehension in autism spectrum disorders: The role of oral language and social functioning. *Journal of Autism and Developmental Disorders, 43*(4), 807–816.

Roberts, E. (2013). Autism and reading comprehension: Bridging theory, research and practice. [Unpublished doctoral dissertation]. Institute of Education, University of London.

Root, J. R., Stevenson, B. S., Davis, L. L., Geddes-Hall, J., & Test, D. W. (2017). Establishing computer-assisted instruction to teach academics to students with autism as an evidence-based practice. *Journal of Autism and Developmental Disorders, 47*, 275–284.

Roth, M. (2007, January 24). "Understanding of Autism Grows as Pittsburgh Researchers Track Brain Action." *Pittsburgh Post-Gazette.* www.ccbi.cmu.edu.

Roux, C., Dion, E., Barrette, A., Dupéré, V., & Fuchs, D. (2015). Efficacy of an intervention to enhance reading comprehension of students with high-functioning autism spectrum disorder. *Remedial and Special Education, 36*, 131–142.

Sadoski, M., & Paivio, A. (2007). Toward a unified theory of reading. *Scientific Studies of Reading, 11*, 337–356.

Saldaña, D., & Frith, U. (2007). Do readers with autism make bridging inferences from world knowledge? *Journal of Experimental Child Psychology, 96*(4), 310–319.

Salvia, J., & Ysseldyke, J. E. (2004). *Assessment in Inclusive and Special Education.* 9th ed. Boston: Houghton Mifflin.

Salvia, J., Ysseldyke, J. E., & Witmer, S. (2017). *Assessment in Special and Inclusive Education.* 13th ed. Boston: Cengage Learning.

San Diego Unified School District. (1996). *Semantic Feature Analysis.*

Sanchez, M. (2003). Text Organization Structures. https://www.slideshare.net/slideshow/text-organization-structures-introduction/36661681.

Scruggs, T. E., & Mastropieri, M. A. (2000). The effectiveness of mnemonic instruction for students with learning and behavior problems: An update and research synthesis. *Journal of Behavioral Education, 10*(2/3), 163–173.

Shanahan, T. (2006). *The National Reading Panel Report: Practical Advice for Teachers.* Naperville, IL: Learning Point Associates.

Shanahan, T. (2017). "Can I Still Rely on the National Reading Panel Report?" https://www.readingrockets.org/blogs/shanahan-on-literacy/can-i-still-rely-national-reading-panel-report.

Singh, B.D., Moore, D.W., Furlonger, B.E., Anderson, A., Fall, R. & Howorth, S. (2020). Reading comprehension and autism spectrum disorder: A systematic review of interventions involving single-case experimental designs. *Journal of Autism and Developmental Disorders*, 8(1), 3-21.

Slavin R. E. (1995). Best evidence synthesis: An intelligent alternative to meta-analysis." *Journal of Clinical Epidemiology*, 48(1), 9–18.

Snow, C. E. (2002). *Reading for Understanding: Toward a Research and Development Program in Reading Comprehension.* Santa Monica, CA: RAND.

Solis, M., El Zein, F., Vaughn, S., McCulley, L. V., 7 Falcomata, T. S. (2014). Reading comprehension interventions for students with autism spectrum disorders: An alternating treatments comparison. *Focus on Autism and Other Developmental Disabilities, 29*(4), 227-240.

Solis, M., El Zein, F., Vaughn, S., McCulley, L. V., & Falcomata, T. S. (2016). Reading comprehension interventions for students with autism spectrum disorders. *Focus on Autism and Other Developmental Disabilities, 31*(4), 284–299.

Sorenson Duncan, T., Karkada, S. M., Deacon, H., 7 Smith, I. M. (2021). Building meaning: Meta-analysis of component skills supporting reading comprehension in children with autism spectrum disorder. *Autism Research, 14*(5), 840–858.

Spector, J. (1992). Predicting progress in beginning reading: Dynamic assessment of phonemic awareness. *Journal of Educational Psychology, 84*(3), 353–363.

Spooner, F., Ahlgrim-Delzell, L., Kemp-Inman, A., & Wood, L. A. (2014). Using an iPad® with systematic instruction to teach shared stories for elementary-aged students with autism. *Research and Practice for Persons with Severe Disabilities, 39*(1), 30-46.

Spooner, F., Kemp-Inman, A., Ahlgrim-Delzell, L., Wood, L., & Davis, L. (2015). Generalization of literacy skills through portable technology for students with severe disabilities. *Research and Practice for Persons with Severe Disabilities, 40 (1), 52-70.*

Stanovich, K. E. (1986). Matthew effects in reading: Some consequences of individual differences in the acquisition of literacy. *Reading Research Quarterly, 21*, 360–407.

Stringfield, S. G., Luscre, D., & Gast, D. (2011). Effects of a story map on Accelerated Reader post-reading test scores in students with high-functioning autism. *Focus on Autism and Other Developmental Disabilities, 26*, 218–229.

Strong, C. J., Mayer, M., & Mayer, M. (1998). *The Strong Narrative Assessment Procedure.* Eau Claire, WI: Thinking Publications.

Syriopoulou-Delli, C. K., & Gkiolnta, E. (2020). Review of assistive technology in the training of children with autism spectrum disorders. *International Journal of Developmental Disabilities*, *68*(2), 73–85.

Tager-Flusberg, H. (1985). The conceptual basis for referential word meaning in children with autism. *Child Development*, *56*(5), 1167–1178.

Tárraga-Mínguez, R., Gómez-Marí, I., & Sanz-Cervera, P. (2020). Interventions for improving reading comprehension in children with ASD: A systematic review. *Behavioral Sciences, 11*(1), 3.

Texas Reading Initiative. (2002). "Promoting Vocabulary Development: Components of Effective Vocabulary Instruction." Online revised edition.

The Teacher Toolkit (n.d.). "Frayer Model." https://www.theteachertoolkit.com/index.php/tool/frayer-model

Thorne, J. C., & Coggins, T. E. (2007). Exploring the utility of narrative analysis in diagnostic decision making: Picture-bound reference, elaboration, and fetal alcohol spectrum disorders. *Journal of Speech, Language, and Hearing Research, 50*(2), 459–474.

Thurstone, T. (2003). *Reading for Understanding: A Complete Program.* Columbus, OH: SRA McGraw-Hill.

Torgesen, J. (n.d.). *Florida's Reading First Assessment Plan: An Explanation and Guide.*

Torgesen, J. (2004). "Preventing Early Reading Failure." https://www.keystoliteracy.com.

Travers, J. C., Higgins, K., Pierce, T., Boone, R., Miller, S., & Tandy, R. (2011). Emergent literacy skills of preschool students with autism: A comparison of teacher-led and computer-assisted instruction. *Education and Training in Autism and Developmental Disabilities, 46*, 326–338.

Treichel, N., Dukes, D., Barisnikov, K., & Samson, A. (2021). How cognitive, social, and emotional profiles impact humor appreciation: Sense of humor in autism spectrum disorder and Williams syndrome. *Humor- International Journal of Humor Research,(35)*1, 1-21.

Truch, S. (2004). "Stimulating Basic Recall in Hyperlexic Students Using the Visualizing/Verbalizing Program." https://www.readingfoundation.com

Turkeltaub, P. E., Flowers, D. L., Verbalis, A., Miranda, M., Gareau, L., & Eden, G. F. (2004). The neural basis of hyperlexic reading: An fMRI case study. *Neuron, 41*, 11–25.

Turner, H., Remington, A. & Hill, V. (2017). Developing an intervention to improve reading comprehension for children and young people with autism spectrum disorders. *Educational and Child Psychology, 34*(2), 13-26.

University of Illinois at Urbana-Champaign. (2009, February 12). "All Work and No Play Makes for Troubling Trend in Early Education." https://news.illinois.edu/all-work-and-no-play-makes-for-troubling-trend-in-early-education/.

University of Illinois at Urbana-Champaign. (1998, September 8). "Kids Who Don't Get Along with Others Also Less Likely to Learn." *ScienceDaily*. https://www.sciencedaily.com/releases/1998/09/980908073710.htm.

University of Victoria, Counselling Services, Learning Skills Program. (n.d.). "Bloom's Taxonomy." http://www.coun.uvic.ca/learn/program/hndouts/bloom.html.

Urrea, A. L., Fernández-Torres, V., Rodriguez-Ortiz, I. R., & Saldaña, D. (2024). The use of technology-assisted intervention in vocabulary learning for children with autism spectrum disorder: A systematic review. *Frontiers in Psychology, 15*, 1-16.

Vandercook, T., & Montie, J. (2010). *Together We Make a Difference: An Inclusive Service Learning Curriculum for Elementary Learners with and Without Disabilities*. Minneapolis, MN: The National Inclusion Project.

Vaughn, S., & Fletcher, J. M. (2012). Response to intervention with secondary school students with reading difficulties. *Journal of Learning Disabilities, 45*(3), 244–256.

Vernon, D. S., Schumaker J. B., & Deshler D. D. (1993, 1996). *The SCORE Skills: Social Skills for Cooperative Groups*. Edge Enterprises, Inc.

Vogindroukas, I., Stankova, M., Chelas, E.N., & Proedrou, A. (2022). Language and speech characteristics in autism. *Neuropsychiatric Disease and Treatment, (18)*, 2367-2377.

Vogindroukas, I., Papgeorgiou, V., & Vostanis, P. (2003). Pattern of semantic errors in autism: A brief research report. *Autism, 7*(2), 195–200.

Vukelich, C., Enz, B., Roskos, K.A. & Christie, J. (2020). *Helping Young Children Learn Language and Literacy: Birth Through Kindergarten 5th Edition*. Pearson.

Wahlberg, T. J. (2001a). *Text Comprehension in Individuals With Autism: The Ability to Comprehend Written Text in High-Functioning Individuals With Autism*. Doctoral diss., Northern Illinois University, DeKalb, IL.

Wahlberg, T. J. (2001b). "Cognitive Theories and Symptomology of Autism." In T. J. Wahlberg, F. Obiakor, S. Burkhardt, and A. Rotatori, eds., *Autistic Spectrum Disorders: Educational and Clinical Interventions*, 3–17. New York: Elsevier Science.

Wahlberg, T. J. (2001c). "The Control Theory of Autism." In T. J. Wahlberg, F. Obiakor, S. Burkhardt, and A. Rotatori, eds., *Autistic Spectrum Disorders: Educational and Clinical Interventions*, 19–35. New York: Elsevier Science.

Wahlberg, T. J., & Magliano, J. P. (2004). The ability of high-functioning individuals with autism to comprehend written discourse. *Discourse Processes, 38*(1), 119–144.

Wei, X., Blackorby, J., & Schiller, E. (2011). Growth in reading achievement in a national sample of students with disabilities ages 7 to 17. *Exceptional Children, 78* (1), 89–106.

Wei, X., Christiano, E. R., Yu, J. W., Wagner, M., & Spiker, D. (2014). Reading and math achievement profiles and longitudinal growth trajectories of children with an autism spectrum disorder. *Autism, 19*(2), 200-210.

Whalon, K., Al Otaiba, S., & Delano, M. E. (2009). Evidence-based reading instruction for individuals with autism spectrum disorders. *Focus on Autism and Other Developmental Disabilities, 24*, 3–16.

Whalon, K., & Hanline, M. F. (2008). Effects of a reciprocal questioning intervention on the question generation and responding of children with autism spectrum disorder. *Education and Training in Developmental Disabilities, 43*, 367–387.

Whalen, K. & Hart, J.E. (2011). Adapting an evidence-based reading comprehension strategy for learners with autism spectrum disorder. *Intervention in School and Clinic, 46*(4), 195-203.

Whalon, K., Martinez, J., Shannon, D.K., Butcher, C., & Hanline, M.F. (2015). The impact of reading to engage children with autism in language and learning (RECALL). *Topics in Early Childhood Special Education, 35*(2), 1-14.

Whalen, K., Moss, D., Ilan, A. B., Vaupel, M., Fielding, P., Macdonald, K., et al. (2010). Efficacy of TeachTown Basics computer-assisted intervention for the intensive comprehensive autism program in the Los Angeles Unified School District. *Autism: The International Journal of Research and Practice, 14*, 179–197.

White, T. G., Power, M. A., and White, S. (1989). Morphological analysis: Implications for teaching and understanding vocabulary growth. *Reading Research Quarterly, 24*, 283–304.

White, T. G., Sowell, J., & Yanagihara, A. (1989). Teaching elementary students to use word-part clues. *The Reading Teacher, 42*, 302–308.

Willems, K., Loveall, S.J., Goodrich, J.M. & Lang, D. (2025). Correlation between emergent literacy skills and reading abilities in young autistic children: A meta-analysis. *Language, Speech and Hearing Services in Schools, 56*, 847-863.

Williams, C., Wright, B., Callaghan, G., & Coughlan, B. (2002). Do children with autism learn to read more readily by computer-assisted instruction or traditional book methods? A pilot study. *Autism, 6*(1), 71–91.

Williams, D. L., Goldstein, G., & Minshew, N. J. (2006a). "Neuropsychologic functioning in children with autism: Further evidence for disordered complex information-processing." *Child Neuropsychology, 12*(4–5), 279–298.

Williams, D. L., Goldstein, G., & Minshew, N. J. (2006b). The profile of memory function in children with autism. *Neuropsychology, 20*(1), 21–29.

Williams, D., Minshew, N., & Goldstein, G. (2015). Further understanding of complex information processing in verbal adolescents and adults with autism spectrum disorders. *Autism, 19*, 859–867.

Williamson, P., Carnahan, C. R., Birri, N., & Swoboda, C. (2015). Improving comprehension of narrative using character event maps for high school students with autism spectrum disorder. *The Journal of Special Education, 49*(10), 28–38.

Williamson, P., Carnahan, C. R., & Jacobs, J. A. (2012). Reading comprehension profiles of high-functioning students on the autism spectrum: A grounded theory. *Exceptional Children, 78*, 449–469.

Wilson, L. O. (2016). "Anderson and Krathwohl: Bloom's Taxonomy Revised." https://www.quincycollege.edu/wp-content/uploads/Anderson-and-Krathwohl_Revised-Blooms-Taxonomy.pdf.

Wolfberg, P. J., & Schuler, A. L. (1993). Integrated play groups: A model for promoting the social and cognitive dimensions of play in children with autism. *Journal of Autism and Developmental Disorders, 23*(3), 467–489.

Yopp, H. K. (1988). The validity and reliability of phonemic awareness tests. *Reading Research Quarterly, 23*(2), 159–177.

APPENDIX A

Comparing Expectations of Grade Four and the Emergence of Comprehension Issues

Researchers Leach, Scarborough, and Rescoria studied the grade levels at which students with reading problems are typically identified in school (2003). Autism was not the focus of the study, but the results are relevant.

- Students with a decoding issue or dyslexia were usually identified by third grade.
- This makes sense due to the focus on decoding for students in grades one through three.

Elementary-age readers with a significant comprehension-only reading deficit were typically late-identified (fourth or fifth grade) or not identified at all.

- The test scores for the research revealed significant comprehension problems.
- The researchers theorize that when it comes to students with comprehension issues, significant deficits are present from a younger age, yet they don't interfere with the students' progress in the primary grades (grades one through three).
- By fourth and fifth grade those same lexical, syntactic, oral language, conceptual, inferential, reasoning, and organizational issues *do* impact learning.

This situation is consistent with the experiences of students with autism and comprehension issues, which are well-documented by researchers in our field.

What is it about fourth grade that causes students to suddenly struggle?

- Fourth grade is a scholastic turning point that can be harder for all students.
- It can be especially difficult for a reader with undiagnosed comprehension issues.

Figure A1 expands on information from Chapter 5. It summarizes the expectations commonly seen from fourth grade and up, and explains several reasons why a student with hyperlexia could have trouble meeting those expectations.

- Some of this information has been gleaned from literature, including the many articles and texts used to prepare this book.
- Other original thoughts result from personal experience and my advocacy work.
- Understanding how a particular student is affected by the challenges described here can open a conversation between parents and teachers and provide a way to pinpoint specific concerns.

Figure A1

Expectations from Fourth Grade and Up
The Mismatch with Hyperlexia
Learn to Read vs. Read to Learn

The first three years of school (K–2) focus heavily on teaching all students how to read.
- It is *assumed* that most students have the basics of reading mastered by fourth grade and that those who decode well understand what they read.
- From fourth grade on, students need to understand and learn a substantial amount of academic content and new vocabulary by reading textbooks and independently reading chapter books in literature.

If a child comes to school already knowing how to read well, s/he will probably get along fine at least through third grade, because phonics, decoding, fluency, and understanding facts are the focus.
- The assumption that good decoding (word recognition) translates to good comprehension is a distinct disadvantage for readers with hyperlexia.
- Limited comprehension can cause the child to start to fall behind.
- If the student with autism doesn't understand at least 90% of the grade-level content while reading, the material is at his or her frustration level. This can cause gaps in learning concepts and ideas.
- The student may struggle to understand narratives, or stories. They may also have difficulty with expository material, such as textbooks in social studies and science, especially those outside their area of knowledge or interest.
- Some of the first signs that the student is not understanding include difficulty in retelling, sequencing, summarizing, predicting, and answering *why* and *how* questions.

Reading Better, Reading More

Good readers expand understanding and vocabulary through exposure and practice.
- Good readers often "take off" in reading around fourth grade and enjoy reading a variety of materials.
- The California Department of Education estimates that in addition to their regular school reading, by grade four, students read one half million words annually, including "a good representation of grade-level-appropriate narrative and expository text (e.g., classic and contemporary literature, magazines, newspapers, online information)."
- Through their leisure reading, students learn unusual and rare words they do not learn from conversation.
- The amount of time spent reading significantly contributes to word knowledge (Lehr and colleagues 2004).

When students with hyperlexia understand less and become frustrated, they may lose their interest and motivation to read.
- This further limits exposure to novel ideas and vocabulary (the Matthew effect). As a result, they may begin to fall behind their peers who continue to grow in skills and exposure.
- Students on the spectrum tend to read in their area of interest, deepening their vocabulary in a specific area (they become specialists). This may limit exposure to a wide array of different words and ideas (limiting general knowledge).
- When a child who started out as a strong and enthusiastic reader suddenly loses interest in reading, everyone needs to ask WHY and find the reason.
- It's important to NOT blame children for their reading problems by assuming they are not paying attention or not trying. Children WANT to succeed!
- The child may read the same book over and over. Even if a lot of time is spent doing this, little growth in general vocabulary results.
- Other red flags at this stage include that students only choose easy or familiar material, things they read when younger, or material related to their favorite interest.

Mismatch Between Skill Sets and Task Demands

Students from fourth grade onward begin to use and apply the information they acquire through reading.

- Academic tasks such as writing paragraphs and longer themes are based on adequate comprehension.
- Reading chapter books in literature requires higher-level thinking and executive function (planning) skills. Students may be required to move back and forth from a physical text book to paper or screens, or from one screen to another during writing activities.
- Homework often includes using a textbook to understand material and find answers.
- Independent projects are added to the curriculum, such as building models and writing basic research reports.

For students with hyperlexia, the frustration level can apply not only to reading but to other academic tasks that depend on comprehension.

- Students can struggle to follow along with instruction and keep pace with work demands.
- Work production related to reading, such as writing assignments, book reports, and homework, can become frustrating tasks.
- Mathematics includes more language and reading based activities such as word problems. Word problems are also called story problems because they involve reading a narrative.
- Organizational tasks that are language and comprehension based, such as following instructions and managing projects, can also become very difficult.
- The cumulative pileup of demands and increased frustration can cause formerly successful students to shut down, give up, or require a greater level of support to get things done.

Complexity

Material in fourth grade becomes complex and moves from concrete to abstract. Content may go beyond the student's personal experiences and require imagination, perspective taking, and relating the unknown to the known.

- Students who relied on good memory in the earlier grades may begin to struggle when academic demands require more sophisticated cognitive processes such as abstraction, inference, synthesis, and logic.
- While other students expand comprehension, the ability to infer and grasp abstract concepts, and other higher-level thinking skills, the gap in understanding for the student with autism is likely to widen from fourth grade on unless the issue is identified and addressed effectively.

Developmental Timelines

Language and thinking develop according to predictable timelines.
- Traditionally, age seven is called "the age of reason," an idea that emphasizes continuous growth in thinking and expressing thoughts.
- Complex, higher-order skills such as logic and reasoning develop over time and synchronize with higher-level language skills.
- Most fourth graders are developing these skills as expected.

A student with a developmental disability like autism is less likely to have developed higher-order thinking and language skills to the level expected on the timeline expected.
- As a result, there can be a mismatch between the demands of grade-level tasks and the student's ability to meet them.
- This delay can affect listening comprehension, reading comprehension, writing, problem-solving, mathematics, social studies, and other academic tasks.

Peers Catch Up

By third or fourth grade, "everyone is a reader."
- Most classmates who learned to decode at the typical pace often understand what they read without a struggle.
- Their reading fluency supports their simultaneous comprehension, as expected.

The noticeable decoding ability in kindergarten and primary grades seen in readers with hyperlexia is no longer a strength.
- By fourth grade, decoding is an expected skill.
- The "average reader" who understands text in fourth grade has a tremendous advantage over someone who can decode but does not understand.
- However, this distinction may not yet be obvious.

Homework

Homework in elementary school is supposed to be independent practice, a review of familiar material that students can complete on their own in a short period of time. Elementary school homework generally should take about 20 minutes per assignment.

One of the first signs that a student does not understand what s/he reads is a homework struggle.
- Parents often need to actively help the student to get it done.
- This can include getting involved in the content material and re-explaining concepts.
- Then, the student goes back to school with the work done and a complete understanding of the material.
- They may even ace their tests.

In effect, this process masks the fact that the student did not understand the material that was taught in class. S/he does not come home able to do the work independently.
- The lengthy re-teaching that is often required on a daily basis becomes a part of the family routine. Lengthy homework time often replaces other activities that families would like to do, including with other children in the family.
- If this situation is not explained to the teacher, the teacher assumes that the work was completed in the expected way in the expected amount of time.
- Thus, the teacher may have no idea of the struggle or the amount of time involved at home in re-teaching.

Demand for Independence

Preparation for the demands of junior high/middle school begins around fourth grade. Students are encouraged to be as independent and responsible as possible.

Many learning tasks that were done in groups and explained in primary grades are assigned as independent, individual class work.
- For many reasons, students with autism can be overwhelmed by these demands and feel unable to cope.
- This can produce a state of anxiety that interferes with understanding and learning.

Reading Affects Math

Word problems add the complexity of language to problem solving.

Many students with hyperlexia do very well with mathematics through third grade.
- Math facts, including multiplication tables, may be learned with ease due to strong rote memory.
- Early math concepts may be well developed.
- Students with autism may excel in math in the early grades, but begin to slow down around fourth grade.

Students with hyperlexia may miss the relevant information or focus on the wrong details in word problems.
- The student may be able to do a problem if it is presented using numbers, but struggle to "translate" the written words into mathematical calculations.
- As math concepts become more complex, difficulties with problem-solving and higher-level thinking skills can also cause a decline in math performance.

Changes in Instruction/Setting

The pace of instruction often increases in fourth grade, due to the amount of material that is reviewed and new material that is presented.
- Upper grades in many districts have larger class sizes.
- Some schools have classroom rotations by subject, where each teacher teaches a specific subject to all children in the grade level.

Teachers may rely on whole-group instruction and independent work, leaving less time for individual support or small-group work in the classroom.
- A high student-teacher ratio can affect the teacher's opportunity to identify and focus on individual needs, through no fault of the teacher.
- For schools with rotation classes, some teachers may be less familiar with the learning needs of particular students.

Need to Respond to Instruction

A lecture format for group lesson presentation is often used starting in fourth grade. Typical students often respond well to whole-group instructional methods.

If the student with autism and hyperlexia spontaneously learned to read, s/he may have managed material in the primary grades without having to depend on being taught.

- Instead of responding to instructional methods, the good decoder may have depended on intact skill sets and good memory for facts.
- A student with autism may have gotten into the habit of tuning out the teacher who is talking about familiar things s/he already knows and can do.

When the material, skill, or demands are new and the student must focus on learning from the teacher, the struggle to benefit from instruction can begin.

- Attention, executive function, information-processing problems, and auditory processing issues often seen in autism can make it more difficult to learn.
- The link between poor comprehension of written material seen in hyperlexia and poor comprehension of oral language must be taken into account when lecture methods are used from fourth grade on.

Sometimes, students who work with an instructional assistant get in the habit of waiting for clarification of instruction from the adult, rather than tuning in to the teacher. It is important to be aware that this may be the case for a particular student and take steps to change this habit.

Social Aspects of Group Work

The ability to work in groups or teams and cooperate with others is highly valued at school.

- Fourth grade is often the start of focused group work, including peer tutoring, group projects, and cooperative learning.
- The teacher may rely on student group work to reinforce key concepts.

When a student has social and communication difficulties, s/he may not have the same level of success or benefit from group work.

- Difficulty in understanding may not be obvious to adults, especially if the student is not disruptive. This may be especially true for girls on the spectrum who tend to try and fit in with their classmates rather than acting out.
- In addition, some students with autism may feel anxious or uncomfortable in group interactions, which can also depress learning.
- Adults may be less aware of the level of contribution and understanding of an individual student when they work in a group.

APPENDIX B

Assessing Young Readers and Common Core Standards

This appendix supplements the research and information presented in Chapter 5, "Masking and Unmasking: Identification and Assessment of Comprehension Issues."

- Part 1 of the appendix discusses ways to assess the comprehension of young readers with autism, prior to fourth grade.
- Part 2 provides additional examples of Common Core Standards for Informational Text, Vocabulary and Speaking and Listening

Part 1
Attend to Young Readers: Be Vigilant from the Start

It's never too early to identify a student's reading difficulties. If a young reader is known to have hyperlexia or has autism and is a good decoder, recognizing many words in print, parents and professionals can consider the child at-risk for comprehension issues from the start of their reading career, and certainly from the start of school.

- The National Early Literacy Panel report urges teachers to emphasize comprehension in the early grades, rather than waiting until students have mastered the basics of reading (2008).
- Listening *and* reading comprehension skills should be supported as early as kindergarten to help early readers gain meaning from text.

The advantages of early intervention in children with a developmental disability such as autism are well supported (National Research Council 2001).

- Similarly, intervening proactively to build comprehension skills (and related language and vocabulary skills) from the start may help prevent or limit the gap in understanding (MacDonald and colleagues 2022, National Early Literacy Panel 2008).

- With this in mind, adults can be alert to potential difficulties in reading comprehension, vigilant in probing for understanding, and proactive in addressing any comprehension gaps as soon as they are recognized.

Signs of Comprehension Problems in K–3

The early learning difficulties of young readers with hyperlexia are relevant to problems that appear later. Recognizing this connection can be helpful when looking back and reviewing the educational history of an older reader who is having difficulty.

Students with autism who are good decoders are often considered "shining stars" in kindergarten and the primary grades.

- Their scores on quantitative measures like the number of sight words recognized, number of words read per minute, standardized test scores, and report cards are often excellent.
- Because the emphasis up to grade three is on *learning to read*, it is unlikely that anyone would have concerns about someone who **appears to read very well.**

According to Torgesen (n.d.), three specific areas of difficulty are the most reliable early indicators that young children will experience difficulty reading for meaning:

1. Kindergartners' difficulty with phonemic awareness or letter-sound fluency.
2. Early difficulties acquiring grade-level oral language skills.
3. First through third graders' difficulty in fluently translating text into spoken language (talking about what they read).

Torgesen explains that children with strengths in these key precursor skills are substantially more likely to become competent readers who can derive meaning from text. If a child is known to have autism and/or was a precocious, self-taught reader, it is important to assess and support the skills shown in Figure B1.

Figure B.1 Three Key Precursor Skills for Reading Comprehension

Phonemic awareness or letter-sound fluency (not just sight-word reading).
Grade-level oral language skills (including vocabulary and oral language for different purposes, such as social interaction and conversation).
Fluent translation of text into spoken language, also known as *retelling* or *expanding* thoughts.

Upon closer examination, young readers with hyperlexia **may exhibit** one or more of Torgesen's three indicators in grades one or two. For other students, difficulties in any of these areas might be noticed after third grade. Let's explore each of them.

Phonemic Awareness or Letter-Sound Fluency

The definition of phonemic awareness is "the ability to hear, identify, and manipulate the individual sounds—phonemes—in spoken words" (Armbruster and colleagues 2003, p. 4). It might be surprising to learn that some good decoders with autism struggle with tasks of phonemic awareness. Due to verbal fluency reading individual words, weakness in these areas might not be suspected.

Remember that readers with hyperlexia do not base word identification on sounding out words. Instead, they learn words as chunks or wholes (Grigorenko et al. 2003). There are two views of this phenomenon:

 a. Whole words are memorized, or
 b. Word recognition is based on visual recognition of patterns that the letters make, but not by combining letter sounds

The second theory is supported by anecdotes of children with hyperlexia who are great at word games with missing letters, like *Wheel of Fortune* and Hangman, from an early age. The ability to quickly decipher incomplete words has also been documented in research (Newman et al. 2007).

With dependence on either of those mechanisms for word recognition, phonemic awareness or letter-sound fluency may be **weaker than expected**, or be **inconsistent** (Newman et al. 2007). As a result, when it comes to breaking sounds apart, putting them back together, or manipulating them, some readers with hyperlexia will struggle.

This may explain a surprising finding sometimes seen in a record review of upper-grade readers with comprehension issues, as in my own experience with many advocacy clients:

- They had documented weakness in phonemic awareness or **letter-sound fluency** as kindergarteners or in the early grades.
- This was not considered an area of concern because word reading (decoding) was intact.

This weakness can continue to affect these readers in upper grades.
- They will have difficulty identifying and sounding out long, unfamiliar, and technical words that appear in grade-level reading material.
- This is especially relevant as academic content and textbooks become more difficult.

Measuring Phonemic Awareness
Teachers are very familiar with testing phonemic awareness. Testing or screening for phonics and sounding out words is done routinely when students are learning to decode. Three ways of measuring include the decoding of nonsense words, producing invented spellings, and manipulating phonemes (sounds). Figure B.2 provides a brief explanation of these common phoneme tasks.

Figure B.2

Measuring Phonemic Awareness
Seven levels of skills are involved in phonemic awareness. It's important to be sure the young reader with autism, like any young reader, is able to manipulate sounds in all of these ways.
"Simple" phonemic skills include **rhyming; identifying sounds at the beginning, end, or middle of a word; segmenting** (breaking apart the sounds heard in a word); and **blending** (saying a word after hearing the individual sounds) (Spector 1992).

More complex or "compound" phonemic manipulation skills include **deletion**, **substitution**, and **switching** of phonemes (Yopp 1988).
• Deletion includes asking the child to leave a sound off a word, for example, to say "hat" without the 'h' [sound].
• Substitution is a task where the person is asked to replace one sound for another. A vowel or consonant can be substituted, as in this example:
    Say "can."
    Replace the 'c'[sound] with a 'p' [sound] "pan."
    Replace the 'a' [sound] with the 'i' [sound] "pin."

Switching of phonemes involves asking the person to change the order of the sounds heard in a single word, such as saying the last sound in a word first. An example is pig, asking the person to say the 'p' [sound] at the end of the word, which would be "ig- p," reminiscent of the "pig Latin" game of childhood.
Invented Spelling is when children create their own spellings for words to express themselves in writing. Invented spelling is a sign of a child's phonemic awareness as they write "words" the way they hear them. An example is writing the name "Emily" as "m-l-e."
Decoding of Nonsense Words is the ability to "sound out" made-up words by using knowledge of letter-sound relationships. An example of a nonsense word is "frax"; it has no meaning. The reader combines the sounds that the letters represent to decode nonsense words, just as they do to sound out real words.

Activities involving the manipulation of phonemes, decoding of nonsense words, or invented spellings can identify difficulties for some autistic readers, that can be addressed.

Other children with hyperlexia score well on these types of measures.

- If a reader with signs of comprehension problems is "cleared" of a phonemic awareness problem, that's good news.
- Attention can be paid to other aspects of comprehension.

Oral Language and Vocabulary

Problems with oral language and a limited vocabulary are predictors of poor comprehension, even for someone with good decoding skills (Lucas & Norbury 2014). Of the three red flags for early readers, **problems with vocabulary and oral language are likely to affect readers with hyperlexia.**

The National Institute for Literacy defines *vocabulary* as the words that a person must know to communicate effectively (2009).

- *Oral vocabulary* refers to words used in speaking, or words recognized when listening.
- Children have an easier time making sense of words in print that are already part of their oral vocabulary.

Reading vocabulary refers to "the kind of words that students must know to read increasingly demanding text with comprehension" (Lehr, Osborn, & Hiebert, 2004). Readers need to know the meaning of most of the words they read to understand what they are reading.

- Vocabulary knowledge is a strong predictor of reading success.
- The main reason for problems understanding text is an **inadequate vocabulary** (Biemiller 2001, 2007).

Vocabulary is expanded when readers are able to identify words *and* know what the words mean. It is estimated that most readers acquire the majority of their vocabulary by reading. Vocabulary size impacts a person for their entire life (Biemiller 2007).

Insight into the mechanics of hyperlexia can help parents and professionals understand vocabulary and word meaning issues.

- Readers with hyperlexia tend to identify words without understanding what they mean.
- For this reason, hyperlexia is sometimes called *word calling*.
- As a result, readers with hyperlexia do not add new words (or as many new words) to their personal vocabulary through reading. They don't categorize and store new word meanings in memory to use later.

The Matthew effect, mentioned in Chapter 1, says, "The rich get richer, and the poor get poorer" (Stanovich 1986). The Matthew effect applies to vocabulary acquisition.

- Those with good vocabularies understand more of what they read.
- They read more and expand their vocabulary further.

Vocabulary expert Biemiller notes that "words and meanings *not* encountered *cannot be learned*" (2007, p. 3).

- Those with weaker vocabularies read less and, therefore, continue to lose ground.
- They cannot keep pace with lessons, they fall behind their classmates, and they are less prepared for the material in the upper grades and beyond.
- As a result, they read less, they understand less of what they read, and the Matthew effect continues.

The Matthew effect in vocabulary is a central, often unrecognized, component of the profile of readers with autism, who may lose their passion for reading and thereby reduce opportunities to grow their vocabulary. When vocabulary is limited, more words in the text will be unfamiliar.

- Unfamiliar words reduce understanding and increase frustration in reading.
- Vocabulary-challenged children have to learn vocabulary at above-average rates to catch up with their peers (Biemiller 2001).
- This means that they require more assistance and explicit instruction to increase their vocabulary.

Identifying the Issue

Adults in a hyperlexic child's life should be **alert** to potential vocabulary difficulties, **sensitive** to the signs of the problem, **selective** in assessing understanding of word meaning, **proactive** in addressing any gaps, and **collaborative** to support vocabulary, language, academic, and comprehension skill development.

Readers with autism might not fit the typical profile of a vocabulary-challenged student, such as being an English language learner, or factors related to their socioeconomic status, etc. (Faitaki, Hessel & Murphy 2022).

- Students with autism should be considered at-risk, or vocabulary challenged, due to their developmental differences in communication, socialization, behavior, information processing, and higher-level thinking skills.
- If a student with hyperlexia is also an English language learner and/or affected by factors related to socioeconomic status, adults need to be **even more vigilant** about the risk of vocabulary deficits, and the potential need for intervention.

How can a parent or teacher know if an at-risk child with autism is experiencing difficulties with oral language and vocabulary growth? This is a difficult question because vocabulary weakness is often masked.

- Many very verbal students with hyperlexia are "subject experts," with a specialized vocabulary that makes them sound like little professors. Even from a very young age, these students may do very well speaking or writing on topics of great interest to them.
- Good decoders with autism often have strengths in vocabulary when vocabulary is defined as **"object naming"** or "labeling." Their receptive vocabulary ("understanding") may be considered strong if they can point to a picture when given a word.

Receptive and expressive vocabulary scores of readers with hyperlexia are often in the average range, yet comprehension is compromised when they read text.

- Verbal competence may mask the lack of understanding of common words.
- For these reasons, readers with hyperlexia often progress through school for many years without raising concerns about their oral vocabulary.

Retelling: Translating Text into Spoken Language

The ability to fluently translate text into spoken language can be one of the most obvious signs of a comprehension issue in a young reader with hyperlexia. It usually continues to be a problem for older students.

- **Retelling, sequencing, answering inferential questions,** and **expanding on answers** are four ways to demonstrate fluent translation of ideas from text into spoken language.
- Probing these four skills can be very revealing when a problem exists.

Looking closely at a young student's ability to perform these four tasks in school and at home is a simple method of screening. It can be especially revealing to informally compare the quality of the responses to other children in the same class who have similarly developed verbal skills.

- Probing for understanding is a chance to go beyond factual or superficial understanding.
- Even if the young student can give a correct answer, when probed, s/he may have difficulty explaining why it is correct, or *how* s/he knows it is true.

When a problem is suspected in translating text into spoken language, a reading specialist, language specialist, resource specialist, or educational therapist should be consulted.

Opportunities to Observe and Probe

Biemiller's suggestions to pay attention to phonemic awareness, vocabulary, and retelling skills are a good starting point for focusing on the skill development of children with autism in kindergarten and the primary grades.

- Informal observations are an excellent way to gather information about the skills children are expected to have and the skills they can demonstrate.
- In particular, observing story time at school can be very telling.

For example, the ability to **predict** is a known problem in the development of children with autism because of problems understanding cause and effect.

- **Asking children to predict, an activity common in storybook reading, is not the same as teaching them to predict.**
- The fact is that most children spontaneously know how to predict and are just practicing a skill from their repertoire during story time.

It's important to observe the **quality** of the response and the **success** children with autism have when asked to predict. Many will try to predict, but their responses may be consistently off the mark.

- When the child tries to answer a prediction question, s/he may give a "bizarre" answer that has little or nothing to do with the story or plot.
- The child may "borrow" and repeat something from one of their favorite books or movies that is not relevant to the story being read.
- Some children on the spectrum wait silently when asked to predict because they don't have an answer.
- **This may go unnoticed, even when a particular child has NO answer 100% of the time.**
- Once they are noticed, problems with prediction and other story time activities can reveal issues or concerns about comprehension skills and be addressed.

Informal observations during other interactive, language-based classroom activities can also help to identify concerns about young readers. If a difficulty is suspected, it can be confirmed by giving the student an opportunity to demonstrate a particular skill.

- It's a good idea to have different observers view the same activity on several occasions.
- This will help determine if there's a pattern of difficulty across observers and across time.
- Careful attention to **consistent difficulties** of a reader with hyperlexia can indicate emerging challenges.

Informal Observation Checklists

The following two checklists, Figure B.3 and Figure B.4, can help when observing and collecting information about comprehension during daily reading at school and at home. The ideas come from decades of personal and professional experience as an observer of story time. You can use these formats for observation, or create your own.

- If difficulties are seen or concerns arise, they can be addressed with the classroom teacher or the special education team at school.
- The school team, which by definition always includes the parents, can discuss whether the child needs to be evaluated further and/or how specific needs should be individually addressed.

Figure B.3

A Checklist for Story Time at School

Observe the child during story time on several occasions. Use the list below to check off any behaviors you see.

- You may add notes about your observations, for example, if the child did not seem to be paying attention to the story, or how many times s/he disengaged during the time you were watching.
- Also note is how many times the teacher asked the group a question (a cue for a choral or group response), and of those, how many times the child responded.

Check off situations you observe, and note how many times they occurred:

❑ Inconsistent attention or failure to keep pace with the teacher.

❑ When questioned, the child could not explain the meaning of a word in the story, even after it was explained to the class.

❑ The child did not volunteer to answer when the teacher asked questions.

❑ The child did not consistently "answer together" or participate in group choral responses about a story.
  - ○ Did it appear that s/he did not grasp the meaning needed to reply (when the other children could)?
  - ○ Did it appear that the child was not keeping pace with the interaction?
  - ○ Did the child have a delay and answer after the class had moved on?

❑ The child answered concrete questions.

❑ (How many were answered? Of those, how many were correct?)

❑ The child answered inferential/abstract questions, such as, "Why did the girl...?" or, "Why do you think...?"

❑ (How many were answered? Of those, how many were correct?)

❑ The child answered prediction questions.

❑ (How many were answered? Of those, how many were correct?)

❑ Was the child noticeably more active or restless than the other children?

❑ Was the child noticeably quieter or more withdrawn than the other children?

❑ Did the child maintain the sitting posture on the floor or in a chair like the other children?

❑ Did the child respond to a request or direct question?

❑ If so, how? If not, what happened next?

❑ Did the child do anything noticeably different than the other children, or anything unexpected?

Figure B.4

A Checklist for Story Time at Home

Your family may have a special reading routine, particularly if your young child is fascinated with letters and numbers or has hyperlexia.

- The next time it is time to read, think about the questions below and answer any that you can.
- During reading, you may wish to *probe* (such as asking what a word means) or try something different to see how the child responds.
- One option is to have one parent or caregiver read with the child and another adult use the checklist to guide the observation.

❑ Does the child insist on reading the same stories every day? In the same order?

❑ Would you describe the child's role in story time as active or passive?

❑ Would you describe the child's role in story time as interactive or aloof?

❑ Does it depend on whether the book is about a preferred topic?

❑ Does the child answer your concrete questions?

❑ (How many were asked? How many were answered? Of those, how many were correct?)

❑ Does the child answer your inferential/abstract questions, such as, "Why did the girl...?" or, "Why do you think...?"

❑ (How many were asked? How many were answered? Of those, how many were correct?)

❑ Does the child answer your prediction questions?

❑ (How many were asked? How many were answered? Of those, how many were correct?)

❑ Can the child retell the story, with appropriate amounts of key information (or does s/he have to tell *everything*?)

❑ Can your child explain what a word in the story means?

❑ Does your child follow your lead when you want to change up the way you interact with the book or choose an unfamiliar story?

Part 2
Examples of Common Core Standards for Informational Text, Vocabulary, and Speaking and Listening
Kindergarten and Grade 4

Chapter 5 discussed using the Common Core Standards or your state standards to do an informal review of the skills that a learner of any age has not mastered.

- The skills learned in the early grades are built upon in each subsequent year of school.
- A **knowledge gap** can develop when a students has not mastered an earlier standard that is being expanded upon in a later grade.
- Identifying any standards that are not met is the first step in addressing them.

This section provides a few examples of English Language Arts Standards that contribute to reading comprehension. Comparing the expectations for Kindergarten and 4th grade shows the importance of identifying any foundational skills that are missing. Please refer to the information provided by your school district or State Department of Education for more information about the standards.

Common Core Standards for English Language Arts

Kindergarten Standards for Informational Text

Key Ideas and Details

1. With prompting and support, ask and answer questions about key details in a text.
2. With prompting and support, identify the main topic and retell key details of the text.
3. With prompting and support, describe the connection between two individuals, events, ideas or pieces of information in a text.

Craft and Structure

4. With prompting and support ask and answer questions about unknown words in a text.
5. Identify the front cover, back cover, and title page of a book.
6. Name the author and illustrator of a text, and define the role of each in presenting the ideas or information in a text

Integration of Knowledge and Ideas

7. With prompting and support, describe the relationship between illustrations and the text in which they appear (e.g., what person, place, thing, or idea in the text an illustration depicts).
8. With prompting and support, identify the reasons an author gives to support points in a text.
9. With prompting and support, identify basic similarities in and differences between two texts on the same topic (e.g., in illustrations, descriptions, or procedures).

Range of Reading and Level of Text Complexity

10. Actively engage in group reading activities with purpose and understanding.

Common Core Standards for English Language Arts

Grade 4 Standards for Informational Text

Key Ideas and Details

1. Refer to details and examples in a text when explaining what the text says explicitly and when drawing inferences from the text.
2. Determine the main idea of a text and explain how it is supported by key details; summarize the text.
3. Explain events, procedures, ideas, or concepts in a historical, scientific, or technical text including what happened and why, based on specific information in the text.

Craft and Structure

4. Determine the meaning of general academic and domain-specific words or phrases in a text relevant to *a grade 4 topic or subject area.*
5. Describe the overall structure (e.g., chronology, comparison, cause/effect, problem/solution) of events, ideas, concepts, or information in a text or part of a text.
6. Compare and contrast a firsthand and secondhand account of the same event or topic; describe the differences in focus and the information provided.

Integration of Knowledge and Ideas

7. Interpret information presented visually, orally, or quantitatively (e.g., in charts, graphs, diagrams, timelines, animations, or interactive elements on Web pages) and explain how the information contributes to an understanding of the text in which it appears.
8. Explain how an author uses reasons and evidence to support particular points in a text.
9. Integrate information from two texts on the same topic in order to write or speak about the subject knowledgeably.

Range of Reading and Level of Text Complexity

10. By the end of the year, read and comprehend informational texts, including history/social studies, science, and technical texts, in the grades 4-5 text complexity band proficiently, with scaffolding as needed at the high end of the range.

Speaking and Listening

1. Participate in collaborative conversations with diverse partners about *kindergarten topics and texts* with peers and adults in small and larger groups.
    a. Follow agreed upon rules for discussions, listening to others and taking turns speaking about the topics and texts under discussion.
    b. Continue a conversation through multiple exchanges.
2. Confirm understanding of a text read aloud or information presented orally or through other media by asking and answering questions about key details and requesting clarification if something is not understood.
3. Ask and answer questions in order to seek help, get information, or clarify something that is not understood.

Presentation of Knowledge and Ideas

4. Describe familiar people, places, things and events and, with prompting and support, provide additional detail.
5. Add drawings or other visual displays to descriptions as desired to provide additional detail.
6. Speak audibly and express thoughts feelings and ideas clearly.

Vocabulary Acquisition and Use

7. Determine or clarify the meaning of unknown and multiple-meaning words and phrases based on *kindergarten reading and content*.
    a. Identify new meanings for familiar words and apply them accurately (e.g., knowing *duck* is a bird and learning the verb *to duck*).
8. Use the most frequently occurring inflections and affixes (e.g., -ed, -s, re-, un- pre-, -ful, -less) as a clue to the meaning of an unknown word.
    With guidance and support from adults explore world relationships and nuances in word meanings.
    a. Sort common objects into categories such as shapes or foods to gain a sense of the concepts the categories represent.
    b. Demonstrate understanding of frequently occurring verbs and adjectives by relating them to their opposites (antonyms).
    c. Identify real life connections between words and their use such as noting places at school that are colorful when reading about color words.
    d. Distinguish shades of meaning among verbs describing the same general action such as walk, march, strut and prance by acting out the meanings.
9. Use words and phrases acquired through conversations or from reading and being read to, and respond to texts.

Common Core English Language Arts Standards

Grade 4

Speaking and Listening

1. Engage effectively in a range of collaborative discussions one-on-one, in groups, and teacher-led with diverse partners on grade 4 topics and texts, building on others' ideas and expressing their own clearly.
    a. Come to discussions prepared, having read or studied required material. Explicitly draw on that preparation and other information known about the topic to explore ideas under discussion.
    b. Follow agreed upon rules for discussions and carry out assigned roles.
    c. Pose and respond to specific questions to clarify or follow up on information, and make comments that contribute to the discussion and link to the remarks of others.
    d. Review the key ideas expressed and explain their own ideas and understanding in light of the discussion.
2. Paraphrase portions of a text read aloud, or information presented in diverse media and formats, including visually, quantitatively, and orally.
3. Identify the reasons and evidence a speaker provides to support particular points.

Presentation of Knowledge and Ideas

4. Report on a topic or text, tell a story, or recount an experience in an organized manner, using appropriate facts and relevant, descriptive details to support main ideas or themes; speak clearly at an understandable pace.
5. Add audio recordings and visual displays to presentations when appropriate to enhance the development of main ideas or themes.
6. Differentiate between contexts that call for using formal English to present ideas, and situations where informal discourse is appropriate as in small group discussion. Use formal English when appropriate to task and situation. See grade four language standards for specific expectations.

Vocabulary Acquisition and Use

7. Determine or clarify the meaning of unknown and multiple meaning words and phrases based on *grade 4 reading and content*, choosing flexibly from a range of strategies.
    a. Use context (e.g., definitions, examples, or restatements in text) as a clue to the meaning of a word or phrase.
    b. Use common, grade-appropriate Greek and Latin affixes and roots as clues to the meaning of a word (e.g., *telegraph, photograph, autograph*).
    c. Consult reference materials (e.g., dictionaries, glossaries, thesauruses), both print and digital, to find the pronunciation and determine or clarify the precise meaning of key words and phrases.

Common Core English Language Arts Standards

8. Demonstrate understanding of figurative language, word relationships, and nuances in word meanings.
   a. Explain the meaning of simple similes and metaphors (e.g., *as pretty as a picture*) in context.
   b. Recognize and explain the meaning of common idioms, adages, and proverbs.
   c. Demonstrate understanding of words by relating them to their opposites (antonyms) and to words with similar but not identical meanings (synonyms).
9. Acquire and use accurately grade-appropriate general academic and domain-specific words and phrases, including those that signal precise actions, emotions, or states of being (e.g., *quizzed, whined, stammered*) and that are basic to a particular topic (e.g., *wildlife, conservation*, and *endangered* when discussing animal preservation).

APPENDIX C

Standardized Assessments That May Help Reveal a Comprehension Issue

The discussion about assessments in Chapter 5 made it clear that standardized tests are not necessarily the gold standard for detecting reading comprehension problems in individuals with hyperlexia.

- Some researchers were surprised that despite known comprehension issues, their study subjects tested in the average range on some standardized measures (Griswold and colleagues 2002; Holman 2004; Myles and colleagues 2002; Newman and colleagues 2007).
- This difficulty is also confirmed in the everyday experience of parents and educators.

To help with this situation, I've created tables that describe various evaluations to consider, depending on the needs of the individual and the professionals conducting the testing. The tables and the discussion that follows them are provided to assist in choosing and using reliable options in an informed, discerning way.

The assessment measures are divided into three categories: Reading Comprehension, Word Reading, and Language-Based Measures.

- Reading comprehension and word reading skills should both be measured to determine if a student has an **internal discrepancy**. This means that the student's reading comprehension is comparatively lower than their own word reading scores, fitting the profile of hyperlexia.
- The results can also be used to determine whether the student has an **external discrepancy**, meaning that their reading comprehension is lower than that of peers of their age or grade.

○ This type of score can indicate that a student who was previously on par with peers is experiencing new difficulties.

○ An external discrepancy can also indicate an academic decline due to comprehension issues.

Language-Based Measures are provided to follow the lead of researchers who are analyzing the link between oral language and reading comprehension in autistic students (Jacobs & Richdale 2013; Norbury 2004; Ricketts and colleagues 2013).

- Within each category, the assessments are arranged in alphabetical order.
- Assessments are individually administered unless otherwise noted.

This information is not an endorsement of particular products or companies. The tables are also not exhaustive. Other assessments are available. My goal is to help narrow down the options and zero in on tests with demonstrated, accurate results.

The tests and subtests listed were identified in three ways:

- They're mentioned in the literature about reading and autism as evaluation tools that were used to accurately identify reading difficulties (Sorenson Duncan, Karkada, Deacon & Smith 2021). In these cases, a few recent studies that used a particular measure are noted.
- They were recommended by language specialists with extensive experience with this population, one who is also an educational therapist and one who is also the parent of a child on the spectrum (Schnee & Legler, personal communication, Jan. 2010). The language-based assessments are matched to known areas of difficulty identified in autism, such as language processing, vocabulary, etc.
- In a private review of client records and/or in my advocacy work with hundreds of families, they were the "breakthrough tests" that revealed comprehension issues for specific individuals.

C.1 Reading Comprehension Measures

The following 11 measures are often used by educational professionals and researchers.

---

1. **Detroit Test of Learning Aptitude (DTLA-4, DTLA-5)**
   Hammill 1998

This test of specific cognitive abilities can be used for children from age 6 to 17 years, 11 months.
- o   The DTLA-5 doesn't have a specific subtest dedicated to reading comprehension. Instead, it assesses reading comprehension indirectly by measuring the underlying cognitive skills needed for successful reading comprehension.
- o   These include verbal reasoning, vocabulary, and knowledge acquisition.
- o   Relevant subtests include Word Opposites, Design Sequences, Sentence Imitation, Reversed Letters, Story Construction, Design Reproduction, Basic Information, Symbolic Relations, Word Sequences, and Story Sequences.
- o   The Story Construction subtest can be analyzed to see if the person is able to create a cohesive and coherent story with relevant ideas and details from reading.

---

2. **Gray Oral Reading Test (GORT-4, GORT-5)**
   Wiederholt & Bryant 2012

The GORT evaluates oral reading fluency and comprehension in individuals from age 6 to 23 years, 11 months. The test subject reads 16 developmentally sequenced passages aloud from Form A or Form B.
- o   Each passage is progressively more difficult. After each passage, the tester orally asks five open-ended comprehension questions. The reader does not have access to the passage to respond.
- o   Question types range from recall of details to those requiring higher-order processing, such as synthesis of the main idea, understanding of causal relations, or predicting.

Used by Maximo, Murdaugh, O'Kelley, & Kana 2017; McIntyre & colleagues 2017; and Ozsayin 2017

326

3. **KTEA-III Kaufman Test of Educational Achievement, Third Edition**
Kaufman & Kaufman 1998

The Comprehensive Form of this test of academic achievement can be used to assess reading skills, oral language, and writing skills for individuals from age 4 years, 6 months through age 25. Subtests include Reading Comprehension, Reading Vocabulary, and Listening Comprehension. New normative data was collected in the US in 2011–2013.

4. **Neale Analysis of Reading Ability (NARA, NARA-II, NARA-III)**
Neale 1999

The test of oral reading measures the accuracy, comprehension, and rate of reading for students ages 6 to 19 years. It also includes an assessment of silent reading. The assessment results provide detailed diagnostic information and a method to check whether specific skills have been acquired.

Used by Arciuli, Stevens, Trembath, & Simpson 2013; Bailey, Arciuli, & Stancliffe 2017; Henderson et al. 2014; Jacobs & Richdale, 2013; Kim, Bal, & Lord 2018; Lucas & Norbury 2014; Nation et al. 2006; Norbury & Nation 2011; and Roberts 2013

5. **Norris Educational Achievement Test (NEAT)**
Switzer & Gruber 1992

This diagnostic achievement measure offers measures of oral reading and comprehension, and written language for individuals ages 4 years to 17 years, 11 months.
o   The assessment is designed to be sensitive to vocabulary, word meaning, and the relationships between words, phrases, and sentences.
o   "Prototypical essays" for the Written Language Test provide clear-cut, objective scoring guides for multiple grade levels, so the student's writing sample can be compared to grade-level peers. Criteria include the number of words and complete sentences used, organization of writing, and logical exposition.

6. **Peabody Individual Achievement Test PIAT-Revised, Normative Update**
   Markwardt 1998

With PIAT-R/NU, only items within a student's range of difficulty are administered.
- The Reading Recognition subtest includes 100 items to measure recognition of printed letters and ability to read words aloud.
- The Reading Comprehension subtest includes 82 test items (sentences). The student reads each sentence silently and then chooses an answer from an array of four pictures that best illustrates the meaning of the sentence.
- The General Information subtest measures reasoning and factual knowledge in the content areas of science, history, humanities, and social studies. Questions are read aloud, and the child responds orally.

Used by Leach, Scarborough & Rescoria 2003

7. **Test of Reading Comprehension, Fourth Edition (TORC-4)**
   Brown, Wiederholt & Hammill 2008

This test of silent reading comprehension can be used for students ages 7 years to 17 years, 11 months.
- The TORC-3 includes General Reading Comprehension and a Reading Comprehension Quotient.
- Diagnostic Supplements measure subject matter vocabulary in mathematics, social studies, and science.
- Subtests include Relational Vocabulary, Sentence Sequencing, Sentence Completion, Paragraph Construction, Text Comprehension, and Contextual Fluency.

8. **Weschler Individual Achievement Test (WIAT-II)**
Weschler 2001

The WIAT-II can be used to measure the academic skills and problem-solving abilities of children from pre-school to grade 12. Results can be used to guide intervention and IEP plans.
- The Word Reading test assesses phonological awareness and decoding skills through tasks such as naming letters, manipulating sounds in words, and reading words from lists.
- The Reading Comprehension test assesses reading comprehension skills taught in the classroom. Tasks include matching words to pictures, reading sentences aloud, and responding orally to oral questions about reading passages.
- Oral Language tests include Listening Comprehension, which measures the ability to listen for details. Students select from an array of multiple-choice pictures to match a spoken word.
- The Oral Expression test assesses the student's general use of oral language. Tasks include repeating sentences and generating lists. Test subjects are also asked to describe scenes and activities in pictures.
- The test also measures silent reading speed.

Used by Chen and colleagues 2019; Mayes & Calhoun 2008; and Miller and colleagues 2017

9. **Wide Range Achievement Test (WRAT-3, WRAT-4, WRAT-5)**

As the name says, this test can be used to assess a wide range of fundamental academic skills in reading, spelling, and math.
- The subtest for Word Reading is not timed. Students identify letters and words.
- The Reading Comprehension Subtest measures understanding at the sentence level to determine if the words in the sentence are understood, as well as the meaning of the whole sentence.
- This test can be administered individually or in small groups.

Used by Bae 2013

10. **Weschler Objective Reading Dimensions (WORD)**
Rust, Golombok, & Trickey 1993

This assessment for children aged 6 to 16 is specifically designed to assess reading skills. It is based on the Wechsler Individual Achievement Test (WIAT) (Psychological Corporation 1991) The WORD is normed on British children. Subtests include Basic Reading, Reading Comprehension, and Spelling.

This test has now been superseded by the WIAT-II. The WORD is included here as a reference in case this test appears in a student's educational record and because In 2007, this assessment was used to reveal the significant comprehension issues of sixteen teenage subjects with autism and hyperlexia in a study by Saldana and Frith.

Those interested in the WORD may wish to follow up with the WIAT-II.

Used by Jones et al. 2009; Ricketts et al. 2013; and Saldaña & Frith 2007

11. **Wide Range Assessment of Memory and Learning (WRAML2, WRAML3)**
Sheslow & Adams 1990, 2003

The WRAML measures immediate (short-term) memory, delayed memory, and working memory in visual, auditory, and learning domains. It can also be used to identify verbal, visual, and global memory deficits for individuals for age 5-90.

The Verbal Memory Index Score is calculated from three subtests:
o   In the Number/Letter sequence memory task, the participant hears a random mix of numbers and letters and repeats them.
o   In the Sentence Memory task, the participant repeats progressively longer meaningful sentences.
o   Story Recall asks the reader to recall details about two orally presented short stories.

Of note, the 2006 article by Williams, Goldstein, and Minshew compared WRAML scores for 38 children with autism ages 8-16 years old and 38 matched controls.
o   Results showed that the memory profile of the autistic children was significantly different from that of the control group.
o   Noticeable difficulties were seen in memory for **complex** visual information and **complex** verbal information, supporting the theory of autism as a disorder of complex information processing.

Used by Beckerson and colleagues 2024; McIntyre and colleagues 2017; and Williams, Goldstein & Minshew 2006

C.2 Word Reading Tests

Some researchers used Tests of Word Reading from assessments that have already been described.

- These include the GORT-5, NARA-III, WIAT-II, WRAT 3 or 4, and WORD.
- In addition, several researchers used an evaluation described here, the Test of Word Reading Efficiency, TOWRE or TOWRE-2.

Test of Word Reading Efficiency, TOWRE or TOWRE-2
Torgesen et al. 1999, 2012

This quick test measures the speed and accuracy of word reading. It only takes five to ten minutes to administer and can be used for individuals aged 6 to 24 years, 11 months.

○ **The Sight Word Efficiency (SWE)** subtest assesses how many real words the participant can read in 45 seconds.

○ **The Phonemic Decoding Efficiency (PDE)** subtest assesses how many non-words the participant can read in 45 seconds.

Used by Lucas & Norbury 2015; Norbury & Nation 2011; McIntyre and colleagues. 2017

C.3 Language Tests

The following seven assessments are primarily administered by speech-language pathologists (SLPs). They may also be administered by psychologists, educational diagnosticians, and educational therapists.

> 1. **Comprehensive Assessment of Spoken Language (CASL)**
>   Carrow-Woolfolk 1999

This assessment for ages 3 to 21 measures expressive language across four structural categories:

- o **Lexical/semantic:** Knowledge and use of word meanings and word combinations, such as phrases and sentences.
- o **Syntactic:** Knowledge and use of grammar.
- o **Supralinguistic:** Understanding language that goes beyond the literal or surface meaning of words and sentences (inference, idioms, etc.).
- o **Pragmatic language:** Knowledge and use of the social language, rules, and conventions that govern how to use language in different contexts.

Fourteen subtests can be used alone or in combination to assess specific language skills. Examples include core tests in Nonliteral Language, Meaning from Context, Inference, and Ambiguous Sentences. These tests can help measure comprehension of abstract and higher-level language, such as nonliteral language, ambiguous sentences, indirect requests, sarcasm, idioms, and figurative language.

The Supralinguistic Index Score represents understanding of complex language and meaning gained from context and inference.

> Used by Lopata et al. 2019 and Knight, Wood, Spooner, Browder & O'Brien 2014

2. Clinical Evaluation of Language Fundamentals–4th or 5th Edition
Semel, Wiig, & Secord 2003

This assessment evaluates both receptive and expressive language skills and can be used for individuals ages 5 to 21. The CELF is often used by SLPs to diagnose language disorders.

Subtests can be used or combined to measure specific areas, including:
- Receptive language: Understanding language and following directions.
- Expressive language: Using language to communicate thoughts and ideas, including sentence structure and vocabulary.
- Pragmatics: Social language skills, such as turn-taking in conversations and interpreting body language.
- Semantics: Vocabulary, word meaning, and word relationships
- Morphology: Word structure.
- Syntax: Sentence structure.

The **Formulated Sentences** subtest can indicate problems in syntax and semantics (the relationships between words, phrases, and sentences).
Note: This was the most surprising and revealing subtest for Tom at age 13. Ten printed words are randomly arranged in a box. The participant needs to organize the words into a sentence.
- The Recalling Sentences subtest gets longer and more complex and is sensitive to language impairment and auditory processing.
- Subtests such as Phonological Awareness, Rapid Automatic Naming, Number Repetition, Familiar Sequences, Word Associations, and Working Memory composite can help identify skill deficits.
- The Pragmatics Profile and the Observational Rating Scale explore social interactions and classroom language performance.

Used by Cronin 2014; Engel 2018; Lucas & Norbury 2015; McIntyre and colleagues 2017; Ricketts and colleagues 2013; and Roberts 2013

3. Illinois Test of Psycholinguistic Ability-3rd Edition ITPA-3
Hammill, Mather & Roberts 2001

This test of spoken and written linguistic processes focuses on language performance for individuals from age 5 through 12 years, 11 months.
- Twelve subtests include Sentence Sequencing, Spoken Analogies, Spoken Vocabulary and Written Vocabulary.
- In the Morphological Closure subtest (small, smaller, _____) students provide missing information in response to a prompt.
- The subtests of Sound Deletion and Sound Spelling measure phonemic skills and auditory-based skills.

4. **Test for Auditory Comprehension of Language-3rd Edition (TACL-3)**
   Carrow &Woolfolk 1999

This test for children ages 3 through 9 years, 1 month measures receptive listening vocabulary, grammar, and syntax. It takes about 15 to 25 minutes to administer. Three categories of language can be assessed:
- Category 1, Vocabulary, assesses the auditory comprehension of nouns, verbs, adjectives, and adverbs, and words representing basic concepts.
- Category 2, Grammatical Morphemes assesses auditory comprehension of function words and inflection.
- Category 3, Elaborated Phrases and Sentences, measures understanding of word relations and elaborated phrase and sentence constructions.
- Test items include questions, negative sentences, active and passive voice, direct and indirect object, embedded sentences, and compound sentences.

5. **Test of Auditory Processing Skills (TAPS-3)**
   Martin & Brownell 2005

This test for children ages 4 through 18 years is designed to be used as one test in a battery.
- It measures "what a person does with what is heard."
- Subtests include Word Discrimination, Word Memory, Sentence Memory, Numbers Forward, and Numbers Reversed.
- New subtests include Phonological Segmentation, Phonological Blending, Auditory Comprehension, and Auditory Reasoning.
- It can be useful to evaluate auditory comprehension, discrimination of sounds, and auditory closure.
- The test may also be useful in testing for difficulty with phonemic awareness or letter-sound fluency.
- These are very important areas to assess for readers with hyperlexia!

Used by McIntyre and colleagues 2017

6. **Test of Language Competence-Expanded Edition (TLC-E)**
Wiig & Secord 1989

The TLC evaluates higher-level language abilities, also called *metalinguistics*.

Level 1 is for children ages 5 to 9 years. Level 2 is for children ages 10 to 18 years.
- Subtests include Ambiguous Sentences, Listening Comprehension, Making Inferences, Oral Expression, Recreating Speech Acts, Figurative Language, and a supplemental memory subtest.
- The Figurative Language test and Making Inferences subtests may be sensitive to readers with hyperlexia. The Figurative Language subtest was mentioned in Norbury 2004.

Used by Norbury 2004

7. **Test of Problem Solving 2-Adolescent (TOPS 2-Adolescent)**
Bowers, Huisingh & LoGiudice 2007

This test of pragmatic (social) language and critical thinking skills is for children ages 12 to 17. It takes about 40 minutes to administer.
- Subtests include Making Inferences, Determining Solutions, Problem Solving, Interpreting Perspectives, and Transferring Insights
- The test taps into critical thinking skills that can affect reading comprehension, such as inference, problem solving, perspective taking, and insight.

Match or Mismatch? Important Considerations When Choosing Standardized Tests

A main concern when using standardized testing is the design of the test. Specifically, it's important to know or define what a particular test or evaluation actually measures.

- Standardized tests are designed to measure specific **constructs**, such as intelligence, comprehension, decoding skills, and so on, depending on the particular focus of the assessment instrument.
- Test designers use specific definitions of these types of constructs. The definition affects the design of the test (Salvia, Ysseldyke & Witmer, 2017).

When it comes to reading comprehension, it's key to determine if there is a good match between what a particular test or subtest is designed to measure and what *you* are trying to measure.

- The test designers' definition of *comprehension* described in the test manual and the manner in which their test is designed to measure it may be very surprising!
- To choose appropriate assessment materials, it is important to read the relevant portion of the test manual.
- To be sure a test is a good match, clarify the definitions of comprehension that the test designers are using and what a particular test or subtest is intended to measure.

The relevant questions to answer when using a reading comprehension test or subtest from any other assessment are as follows:

1. What is the definition of comprehension?
2. How is comprehension measured?
3. Can the test or subtest reveal the suspected areas of deficit?

Consider, as an example, the Woodcock-Johnson Psychoeducational Battery III Tests of Achievement (also called the WJ-III-ACH). This highly-regarded evaluation instrument is commonly used in schools and remedial clinics.

- Regarding the test design and standardization, Salvia, Ysseldyke and Witmer report that the norms, reliability, and validity appear adequate (2017).
- This means that the test is expected to accurately measure the constructs as they are defined for the assessment.

Figure C.1 quotes how reading comprehension is described in the test manual. I was quite surprised to read this when I was learning to conduct the assessment during my master's program in special education.

- I've added headers to help you follow the discussion.
- As you read it, consider if this is how you would define reading comprehension, and if you agree with the test authors' view of the construct.
- This is an example of how to take advantage of the descriptions in a test manual to decide whether the test as described measures what you would like to measure, or not.

Figure C.1

WJ-III-ACH Test 9 Reading Comprehension Subtest: Test Manual Definitions

Comprehension or word recognition?

"An independent measure requires reasonable expectation that subjects have prior familiarity with the words used in the passages and have knowledge of any concepts that are prerequisite for processing the passage contents. If these conditions are not met the so-called passage comprehension is confounded with word recognition skills and knowledge."

In other words, in order to be valid, the test must ensure that the participants' performance is based on their ability to understand the text presented, rather than rely on what the person already knows about the subject.

Comprehension or information processing?

"Some tests of reading comprehension are actually tests of information processing that happen to use reading as the medium of communication. Asking a subject to study a passage and then answer questions about the content, such as to state the author's purpose or to predict what may happen next, does not tap into skills specific to reading. It taps language processing and cognitive skills."

I would ask, "Don't we want to tap into language processing and cognitive skills because reading is a language-based, active thinking process?" The ability to predict story events or understand the author's purpose are two key elements of comprehension. If you want to measure those things, the authors are stating that this test is not designed to do so.

Comprehension or language processing?

"However scores from [language processing] tests do not measure the essence of reading comprehension, but instead reflect performance on a confounded language processing task with indeterminate diagnostic results. A program of remedial instruction planned for a subject may be ineffective if it is assumed that the problem is the subject's reading skill when the problem is actually a symptom of a broader language processing skill." (pp.80–81).

Individuals with autism often experience multiple developmental challenges to understand and use oral and written language. Specific difficulties include vocabulary, grammar, categorizing, and organizing thoughts. Language skills are critical for reading comprehension. It's important to know that these test authors are clearly saying that their test does NOT measure underlying language skills. Those who choose the test should not expect the results to reveal language-related issues. Therefore, if you wish to measure language skills and build any missing skills, choose a test that is designed for that purpose.

Another important point about the reading comprehension subtest of the evaluation of the WJ-III-ACH is that it uses a modified cloze design.

- The person being evaluated reads a sentence or short passage and fills in a blank with a word or phrase from the choices provided.
- According to the test manual, this is intended to measure "how well a subject understands written discourse as it is read" (p. 80).

The test authors have very specific reasoning behind this procedure as a measure of comprehension.

- They explain that using the modified cloze format, the reader will "dynamically apply a variety of vocabulary and comprehension skills in the process of arriving at the point where the missing word can be supplied in a passage" (p.80).
- The design of this test is based on the authors' specific definition of what reading comprehension *is* and *is not*.

Reading the authors' definition of comprehension, and integrating this information with the knowledge that students with autism and comprehension issues may perform in the average range in this subtest (Holman 2004; Myles and colleagues 2002; Newman and colleagues 2007) convinces me that it may actually be more effective to measure broader language skills to get to the bottom of the comprehension issue in autism! In fact, many researchers are coming to this conclusion, including Jacobs and Richdale (2013), Lucas and Norbury (2007), and Sorenson Duncan and colleagues (2021).

The research also helps confirm the idea that to choose appropriate assessment materials it is *important* to read the relevant portion of the test manual.

- Clarify what a particular test or subtest is intended to measure, the definitions of comprehension, and the manner in which it is measured (fill in the blank, multiple choice, etc.)
- This will help decide if there is a good match between what a particular test or sub-test is designed to measure and what you are trying to measure.

Who Is Norm?

Diagnostic reading assessments and screening tools need to be "valid, reliable, and based on scientifically based reading research" (NCLB 2001, Part B Sec. 1208(7)(C)(i)).

- To make the test valid and reliable, the test questions are tested on a "normative sample," a group of individuals used to establish the typical or average performance on a test or measure.
- This sample of people is carefully selected by test designers to represent the larger population for whom the test is intended.
- Many test designers use the United States Census to match the percentage of the population of different races, so the test is appropriate for people of different races.
- Test designers may consider socio-economic variables in the selection of the group.

Do standardized tests include people with autism in the normative sample?

That is a good question to ask. The answer is that some do, and some don't. The information is found in the test manual. If only people *without* autism participated in the testing that was used to define average, above average, or below-average performance, are the results valid when someone with autism takes the test?

Assessment experts Salvia, Ysseldyke and Witmer caution that when a test is used with a group that was not included in the normative sample, the accuracy of the results may be affected (2017).

- Comparing the scores and performance of people with autism to a "sample group" of individuals who do not have it is not considered optimal practice.
- Therefore, it is very important, before selecting a standardized test, to look at the test manual to see if the normative sample included persons with disabilities, and, if stated, people with autism.
- If people with autism are not included, parents and educational professionals should discuss whether the results should be interpreted with caution.

APPENDIX D

Materials for Teaching Comprehension Strategies

This appendix supplements Chapters 6, 7 and 8 that discuss evidence-based and promising practices to improve reading comprehension.

- Part 1 of this appendix provides information and materials for using primer passages and an informative title to improve reading comprehension.
- Part 2 provides information for teaching students to use graphic organizers and text structure to improve comprehension.
- Part 3 provides information and materials to teach anaphoric cueing, connotation, and homographs.

Part 1
How To Support Reading Comprehension Using Primer Passages and An Informative Title

Readers with autism are disadvantaged when they don't have the right amount of relevant background knowledge. Using primer passages can help.

- Primer passages are a **structured**, **controlled** way to provide relevant information.
- The **simplified format** improves understanding of a more complex passage
- This helps students **notice and remember important main ideas**, which is the purpose of reading.
- Important vocabulary words can be highlighted and explained in the primer passage to improve understanding.

Building on the research by Wahlberg and Magliano (2004) described in Chapter 6, this section describes the steps to use primer passages to pre-teach factual concepts and stimulate relevant prior knowledge.

- Figure D.1 breaks down the process into clear steps.
- As a demonstration, Figure D.2 presents my sample passage about oceans, along with five facts to pre-teach before reading.

Figure D.1

	Steps for Using a Primer Passage, Informative Title, and Image
1	Before reading, point out the title of the passage. In the example below, it is *Looking at the Seas*.
2	Connect the title to the illustration. Ask students to make observations about the image.
3	Review the five facts. Ask students which facts they **already knew**, and which ideas are **new**.
4	Ask students to relate each fact to the picture, one fact at a time.
5	Read the passage together.
6	Check for understanding of the main points (recall and comprehension) by asking questions based on the facts, such as, "Why is Earth called the water planet?"
7	After reading, check whether students understand why the passage has the title it does.
8	Reinforce this and any other *connections* between the title, the facts, the illustration, and the text.

Figure D.2

Basic Facts about Oceans
(extracted from the passage, "Looking at the Seas")

1. Our Earth is a water planet. 71% of its surface is water. This is why Earth is called the "water planet."
2. There are four main oceans, the Atlantic, Pacific, Indian, and Arctic.
3. Some people think there is a fifth ocean around Antarctica.
4. All oceans and seas are connected, and the same water travels through them all.
5. A long time ago, all the land on our planet might have been grouped closely together.

Looking at the Seas

If you look down at our planet from outer space, most of what you see is water; 71% of the planet's surface is covered by ocean, and it is because of this that the Earth is sometimes called "the water planet." Only about three-tenths of our globe is covered with land.

The ocean wraps the globe and is divided into four major regions: the Atlantic Ocean, the Pacific Ocean, the Indian Ocean and the Arctic Ocean. Some scientists consider the waters around Antarctica to be a separate, fifth ocean as well. These oceans, although distinct in some ways, are all interconnected; the same water is circulated throughout them all.

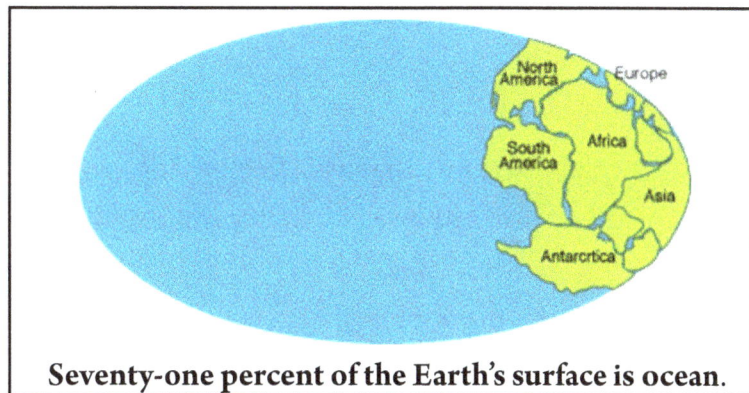

Seventy-one percent of the Earth's surface is ocean.

If all the continents were crammed into one corner of the Earth, the vast extent of the world ocean could easily be seen. In reality, of course, the continents are not bunched together as shown in the figure, but instead are spread out over the entire Earth's surface. Most oceanographers, however, believe that a long time ago in the Earth's geological history, all the continents were once grouped closely together in much the same manner.

From "Oceans Alive" at http://www.mos.org/oceans/planet/index.html. Used with permission, courtesy of the Museum of Science, Boston.

To enrich the activity, you might ask one or two inferential questions that come to mind. Consider asking students what questions they have about the material, or questions and comments that come to their minds, to finish the activity.

Create Your Own Primer Passages

There are a variety of ways to develop primer passages. They can be created by teachers, other educational specialists, parents, or students.

- For **narratives**, provide relevant facts that are central to the plot, setting, characters, conflict, emotional content, or historical context of a story.
- For **expository text**, provide and discuss key ideas that you want the reader to learn from the material. Include explanations or use a favorite subject to make comparisons that clarify abstract concepts or complex relationships.

During reading, understanding of the **main idea** is reinforced.

- The reader gets a sense of what information is most important and what ideas or details are less important. After using a primer passage, the information can be used to complete a graphic organizer.

Using Primer Passages in the Classroom

It's often said that the teaching methods that are effective for learners with autism can benefit every learner. The use of primer passages, an informative title, and relational cues is a good example of this.

- You may have many students in your classroom who have limited world knowledge due to limited experiences (such as never having seen an ocean).
- Primer passages with informative titles are ideal for English learners. Many instructional programs for ELs **include ready-made primer passages**.

A primer passage can be used as a class-wide pre-reading activity, in a small group, with pairs of students, or in individual remediation sessions. Douglas (2005) suggests a way to use primer passages as a class activity:

1. The teacher prepares and presents a short passage on a transparency, whiteboard, or smartboard.

2. The teacher and students read the material together.
3. Students identify key words, and the teacher circles or underlines them. The group works together to clarify the meaning of the words.
4. Finally, the group writes a one or two-sentence summary of the passage that includes the key words.

This technique can be practiced with a class for several passages of text. After that, students can try the technique on their own, in pairs, or in small groups.

- Students can also create summaries after reading, to be used as primer passages by English language learners, next year's students, or others who need them.
- Preparing summaries **for others** reinforces the student's understanding of the main ideas in the material.
- The option of creating primer passages for others (such as classmates who are English learners) or as a service-learning experience can also contribute to improved self-esteem, working as part of a group, motivation, and other known benefits of service learning (Vandercook & Montie 2010).
- The activity can also pique the students' interest and comfort level with the material and motivate them to read.

Part 2
This section includes ideas for teaching students to use graphic organizers and improve comprehension by understanding text structure.

Teaching Students to Use Graphic Organizers

Regardless of the format or purpose of the graphic organizer that's selected, it's a good idea to demonstrate how to complete it using familiar materials of high interest, such as a favorite book or topic. This engages the learner and makes the activity very motivating.

- When using preferred material, the person is only learning one new thing at a time (the skill of using the graphic organizer), rather than trying to understand unfamiliar content material *and* learn *and* apply a new skill at the same time.
- For example, if the student loves books about *Star Wars*, use a paragraph from a **Star Wars** book to fill in a main idea and supporting details in a graphic organizer.
- Once the student demonstrates understanding of how to use the visual tool, you can apply the process to academic content.

Steps for teaching how to use a graphic organizer can be followed each time a new type of graphic organizer is introduced, as shown in Figure D.3.

Example of Teaching Using Special Interests
From *Star Wars: The Empire Strikes Back* by Donald F. Glut

Main Idea	Supporting Detail
The Ugnaughts were afraid.	They grunted and shivered.

Figure D.3

	General Steps for Teaching the Use of Graphic Organizers
1	Preselect the type of graphic organizer you want to present, matched to the type of curricular material you are using and the purpose you have in mind. An example is choosing a graphic organizer to prepare to write a book report.
2	Start by explaining what graphic organizers are, what they are used for, and why it helps or benefits the student to use one.
3	Model/demonstrate how to use a particular organizer (on a board, overhead, or on a computer) while students fill out individual copies.
4	Conduct guided practice, in which students are supported to fill in their forms until they are able to do so independently.
5	If the student has difficulty writing, consider providing pieces of paper with an array of word choices (a word bank) that the student can place onto the organizer. Providing word options makes the activity about the ideas, not the process of handwriting. The use of a computer with PowerPoint slides as mentioned above, or other tech tools can also reduce handwriting demands.

More on Teaching Text Structure or Text Organization

Information about text structure was presented in the original version of *Drawing a Blank* in the category of visual tools. Teaching text structure was a promising option because of the many ways that it's a good fit for the cognitive profile of readers with hyperlexia.

- Now, single-case studies are verifying the effectiveness of text structure for readers with autism as a stand-alone strategy or as part of an intervention package, making the topic relevant here.
- This section provides additional information and tips for teaching.

Start with Familiar Examples

Newspapers, magazine articles, scripts, instructional manuals, novels, and textbooks are examples of printed material designed to present information.

- Each of these types of materials has a somewhat different purpose: to share current news, to inform, to entertain, or to teach.
- The way the material is organized (the format) is designed with the purpose and the reader in mind.
- For this reason, certain types of material have a **predictable style of organization, called the text structure.**

For example, most textbooks are divided into chapters that begin by describing what will be learned, and end with a summary of what was discussed.

- The text structure of printed material helps the reader follow along with the author's thoughts *and* organize their own thinking while reading.
- Understanding the organization of text also helps readers locate information before, during, or after reading.

Text Features Draw the Eye (but not literally!)

One way that text is organized is through the use of *text features*.

- For example, the familiar format of a newspaper includes a large **headline** at the top of the front page, drawing attention to the most important story.
- Newspapers are full of other **visual cues** like photographs and headings that suggest what information will appear. This organizes the material and guides the reader.
- A large newspaper is divided into **sections** that focus on certain topics, like sports, entertainment, and so on. Each category has its place or space.

People often take advantage of this spatial organization to read the paper in a particular order, depending on their interests. The familiar, predictable format of a newspaper helps readers understand and enjoy the material.

Internal Structures of Text

In addition to the visual or spatial organization of materials (text features), there are **internal structures** of text organization.

- Authors intentionally use particular structures and patterns and help readers notice and connect important ideas.
- Readers can learn the common patterns of text structure for *expository* (informational) and *narrative* text (fiction and non-fiction stories).
- Understanding and recognizing text organization and structure can help any reader understand and learn new information.
- Figure D.4 . summarizes common features of narrative and expository text.

Figure D.4

Predictable Text Structures of Narratives and Expository Text

Text structures have a predictable presentation of information.
- Understanding the structure can help the reader know what to expect and where to find information.
- For example, in a compare-and-contrast sequence, the author discusses the similarities and differences between two things.

Narrative text structures include formats that tell a story. Examples include letters, poems, plays, diaries, or other stories about personal experiences. Narratives can be fiction or non-fiction.
- Elements of narrative text structure include the main idea, the author's purpose, and the point of view (who the storyteller is).
- Central text structure elements within a story include the sequence of events (what happened), the plot (including conflict/resolution), and the characters.
- Remember that narratives may be more difficult for readers with autism than expository text. This is due to the potentially complex social-emotional context of stories, which is often inferred rather than stated.
- Readers may require additional support for understanding and analyzing narratives through text structure and graphic organizers.

Expository text frequently includes particular structures to organize the content material. Common text structures in texts and instructional material include compare and contrast, cause and effect, processes, and chronological sequences.

Specific **signal words** are directly related to particular structures.
- For example, signals in a compare-and-contrast structure include the words *in common, similarly, different from, in contrast,* and *both.*
- Students can be taught to recognize cause and effect by looking for words such as *because, reasons for, as a result,* and *therefore.*

Text structures can be translated into a matching graphic organizer to capture key information.

An example is a Venn Diagram that matches well with compare-and-contrast text structure, or a story map to sequence events in a story.

Teaching text structure and recording ideas from the text using a graphic organizer makes the information manageable, concrete, and visual.

Perceiving Patterns and Signals

Various types of text structure help the reader perceive **patterns**. In addition to internal structures that are similar from one text to another, other consistencies can help with understanding.

Headings in text are an example of a text feature called a **cue**. *Cues* are signals from the author that help the reader know what to expect.

- A heading can cue the reader that the author is changing topics.
- This prepares the reader for the material that is to come and allows the reader to activate prior knowledge to relate to the text (Duke, Ward & Pearson, 2021).
- Recognizing particular signal words or word cues can help with tasks known to be difficult for readers with autism.

Within paragraphs, other visual cues are used, such as putting words in **bold** or *italics* for emphasis. An author may clarify the meaning of a highlighted word by adding an example, a definition, or a synonym. Other higher-level processes that may be supported by looking for concrete cues in text include:

- Distinguishing supporting details from the main idea (with cues such as *for example* or *for instance*).
- Recognizing the author's point of view (with cues such as *in my opinion* or *I think*).

Writers also use **sequence markers** (like the words *first, next,* and *finally*) to help the reader know where s/he is between the start and end of the material and prepare for a transition when the end of the material is coming. Finally, the author may use a summary to repeat key ideas and signal the end of a section (UCI 2007).

Advantages of Text Structure Instruction for Readers with Hyperlexia

The National Reading Panel recommends teaching about text structure and showing typically developing students how to use it (NICHD 2000). Text structure instruction has clear support in single-case studies for readers with autism. Figure D.5 presents ten reasons why this strategy is a good fit for autistic readers.

Figure D.5

Benefits of Teaching Text Structure to Readers with Autism
1. Text structures are concrete and predictable.
2. Visual cues in text structure relate well to visual-spatial strengths in autism.
3. Many individuals with autism are highly skilled at perceiving patterns. Once they understand text structures, they will be able to spot them and take advantage of them to manage reading demands.

4. Headings create a **visual framework** that highlights main ideas and supports memory. This structure also helps with writing and retelling.
   O The reader can be taught to preview headings as part of a reading routine to get a sense of the material before starting to read.
   O Headings within text can serve the same purpose as a title of a text to stimulate relevant prior knowledge and clarify the meaning of the text under the heading.

5. Previewing the various text structures used in a text *before* reading gives the reader a sense of the order in which the material will be presented and the length of the text.
6. Information gained from previewing text structure may help the reader know the purpose for reading and recognize a personal benefit or relevance of reading the material, which may help with interest or motivation to read.

7. Determining the order and flow of the material by identifying headings is a good way to create an outline before reading.
   O Headings can be used while reading to note the main ideas under each heading.
   O In addition, notes can be written on matched graphic organizers to capture and summarize information.

8. Text features, such as words in **bold** or *italics*, can be targeted for learning vocabulary before reading.
9. Knowing how to use text structures to read more efficiently can help readers with autism deal with the workload and demands of upper-elementary grades, junior high, and high school, which have a greater focus on expository text.
10. Using text structures for narratives or stories can provide a framework for improving the understanding of story elements and plot, as well as provide clues to the meaning of character actions, interactions, and dialogue.

Tailoring Teaching

Teaching text structures includes teaching the general concept of text structures (as in the introduction to this section) and teaching students to recognize specific text structures and their purposes. Explicit instruction in small groups is ideal, according to the research in Chapter 7. There is no one-size-fits-all formula for how to teach because the approach depends on the focus, needs, and reading level of the student(s) you're working with.

To tailor teaching to a reader with autism, it's a good idea to use examples and practice materials in the student's area of high interest as a way to engage interest and start with something familiar.

- For example, if the student loves books about the planets, find sample material about the planets to use to illustrate the concept of text structure in general or a specific type of text structure.
- After presenting the lesson, provide text from a favorite topic or book for guided and independent practice.
- Figure D.6 presents general steps for teaching any text structure.

Figure D.6

Teaching Text Structure
1. Preselect the text structure element you want to present, related to expository or narrative content.
2. Use a graphic organizer or primer passage to stimulate relevant prior knowledge about text structures the student is already familiar with and uses.
3. Explain the particular type of text structure, what it is used for, and why it helps the student to use it. Provide examples.
4. Select a short sample text matched to the independent reading level of the student. Identify the text structure element in context, explain what it is, and make the connections with text to demonstrate its usefulness.
5. Provide materials and opportunities for guided practice until the student can demonstrate mastery using the text structure independently.
6. Follow up with opportunities for the student to generalize the skill to different content areas or a variety of reading material in whole group reading or independent reading.

Part 3
This section includes a sample lessons, worksheets, and other materials for teaching anaphoric cuing, connotation, and homographs.

I associate an owl with anaphoric cuing because asking the questions Who? Whose? and Whom? are central to the activity and sounds like an owl hooting. The owl icon serves as a visual (and auditory) reminder that when a sentence contains a pronoun, the reader needs to stop and ask questions before continuing. Figure D.7 is a bookmark that you might like to copy and provide to students as a reminder when they learn this technique.

Figure D.7

Who? Whose? Whom? Bookmark

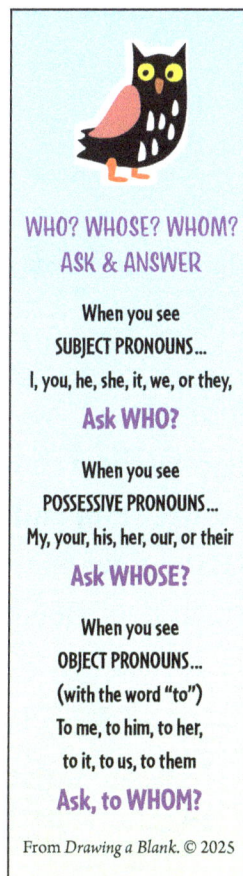

WHO? WHOSE? WHOM?
ASK & ANSWER

When you see
SUBJECT PRONOUNS...
I, you, he, she, it, we, or they,
Ask WHO?

When you see
POSSESSIVE PRONOUNS...
My, your, his, her, our, or their
Ask WHOSE?

When you see
OBJECT PRONOUNS...
(with the word "to")
To me, to him, to her,
to it, to us, to them
Ask, to WHOM?

From *Drawing a Blank.* © 2025

Bookmark adapted with permission from Sara M. Finegan at **www.readerswithautism.com**, **www.thedemandingclassroom.com**.

Drawing a Blank

Who? Whose? Whom? Anaphoric Cuing Activity For Personal or Subject Pronouns

This sample lesson plan includes worksheets you can use or adapt for the needs and reading levels of your students. The sample lesson is written for classroom instruction but can be adapted for use with small groups or individuals.

Preparation and Prerequisites

- Before teaching, review personal or subject pronouns (I, you, he, she, it, we, they).
- Make copies of the worksheets included here as Figure D.8 and D.9 (or create your own).
- Prepare several paragraphs from curricular material or grade-level reading passages for guided practice of this skill. (See examples below).
- **Anaphoric cuing** is not a user-friendly term! Decide on what to call this strategy and some cue words to use to remind students to use it. Ideas include **"Ask Who"** or **"Stop and Link."**

Adaptations

This lesson can be adapted to teach anaphoric cuing of possessive pronouns (mine, yours, his, hers, ours, theirs, whose) and object pronouns used with the word *to* (it, me, you, him, her, us, them).

Steps for Explicitly Teaching the Strategy

This lesson plan uses a script that you can follow closely or loosely.

1. **Tell why anaphoric cueing is important and how it helps.**

   When we read, we need to know what all the words mean. Sometimes we're not sure what a word means. When that happens, we need to stop and figure out what it means. This helps us understand better when we are reading.

2. **Explain precisely what it is.**

   We're going to learn how to link pronouns in a sentence to the person or thing they match.

356

3. **Relate it to something the student already knows or does.**

   Write this sentence on the board or overhead: "She won the race."

   Lead a discussion, as follows:

   When you read the sentence, "She won the race," What is the first thing you think? You ask yourself, "Who?" Underline the pronoun she. The pronoun *she* does not tell us enough. We want to know who "she" is, but the answer isn't there.

   Write a second sentence *above* the first sentence: "Sara trained hard for two weeks."

   Ask the following question:

   Now can you tell me who won the race?

   Circle the word *Sara*. Draw an arrow to link *she* and *Sara*.

   Then say the following:

   Pronouns represent a person on thing in a sentence. When you see a pronoun, **stop** and ask, **"Who?"** Next, connect the pronoun to a person or thing. Look in the sentences nearby for the answer.

4. **Demonstrate/model the skill.**

   Demonstrate the skill using the example on the worksheet provided, *Figure D.9*. Model and "think aloud," narrating how you stop when you see the pronoun in the second sentence.

   Say the following:

   Most of us ask questions when things are not clear. It's very helpful to do the same thing when we're reading. That way we understand better.

   Let's read these two sentences together: "John went to the store. He bought some bread."

   Who bought some bread? [Call on a student.] John is the correct answer, John bought the bread.

   Circle *John* in the first sentence. Underline he in the second sentence. Draw an arrow to connect the word *he* back to the word *John*.

   The word *he* in the second sentence means John from the first sentence. *He* is a pronoun. The pronoun stands for a person, John.

A pronoun is like a **stop sign**. When you see a pronoun, stop and ask, "Who?" Then make the link between the pronoun and the person. You can find the answer in a sentence nearby.

5. **Conduct guided practice.**

   Work together to do a few more items on the worksheet. Have the students finish independently and then discuss the answers.

6. **Check for understanding.**

   Provide sample material from class material so that students can apply the strategy. Ask them to preview the material and underline all pronouns before reading, and then circle the referent subjects and draw the connecting arrows while reading.

   Here's an example of a useful practice passage from *Star Wars: The Empire Strikes Back* by Donald F. Glut:

   > "The Wookiee grabbed the metal leg and inspected it closely. As he growled angrily at the huddled Ugnaughts, they shivered and grunted like a pack of frightened pigs."

7. **Conduct independent practice.**

   Have the students apply the strategy to more text. Photocopy pages of text that students can write on. Have students preview and mark all the subject pronouns before reading. They can use pencil or a highlighter. They can then use a pencil to circle the referent person or thing and link it to the pronoun with an arrow.

8. **Support generalization.**

   Prompt and monitor use of the strategy during reading instruction. Check in during free reading time to encourage students to use the technique and reinforce the benefit to the reader.

   You may use or adapt the two worksheets that follow to support anaphoric cuing.

Figure D.8

Subject Pronoun Review

Some pronouns take the place of a person's name as the subject of a sentence.
Examples are *I, you, he, she, we,* and *they*.
These pronouns are called *personal pronouns* or *subject pronouns*.

Directions: Read each pair of sentences. Fill in the blank with the correct personal pronoun.

1. James loves dogs. _____ likes cats too.
2. Rosa likes to babysit. _____ is babysitting on Saturday.
3. Sam and Flora are going to the movies. _____ want to see the new movie in 3D.
4. My younger sister and I have matching sweaters. _____ like many of the same things.
5. Jane's father is a firefighter. _____ drives the hook-and-ladder truck.

Think Flexibly: Exceptions to the Rules

Sometimes a subject pronoun does not refer to a person.

- The subject pronoun *it* can refer to an object or some other thing.
- When writing about animals, use *he* for a male and *she* for a female animal.
- A surprising example is that the subject pronoun *she* is used to refer to a large ship.

Think flexibly to fill in the blanks below.

1. My dog Sophie just had six puppies. _____ seems to be enjoying her litter.
2. James said, "The weather is cold now that winter is here. I think _____ is colder every day."
3. The ship builders cheered when the new cruise ship launched, saying, "May _____ sail for many years."

Figure D.9

Subject Pronouns: Make the Connection

Ask, "Who?" when you see a personal or subject pronoun.

Some pronouns take the place of a person's name as the subject of a sentence.

Examples are *I, you, he, she, it, we,* and *they.*

These pronouns can also be used in questions.

Directions:

Underline the personal pronoun in each pair of sentences below.

When you look at the pronoun, ask, "Who?"

Then draw an arrow to the name or word that shows who the pronoun refers to. Circle it.

When you have the answer, fill in the blank. Follow the example.

Example: John went to the store. He bought some bread.

He = John

1. My mother and I are baking a birthday cake. We want to surprise Grandma.

   We = _____

2. Tom went into the kitchen. He asked his mother, "What's for dinner? I'm hungry!"

   He = _____

3. Geraldo and Scott have been friends for a long time. They are on the same baseball team.

   They = _____

4. The teacher saw that Emily did not bring a lunch and asked, "Do you have money to buy lunch?"

   You = _____

5. Mrs. Carter is the librarian. She knows where to find any book in the library.

   She = _____

Technology Option

You may also want to have students practice anaphoric cueing using a computer word processing app.

1. Select a short text that contains people's names, and referent pronouns (e.g. Sarah/ she).
2. Provide the text for students to copy and paste or type into a word-processing document. Students should copy and paste the complete paragraph three times.
3. Ask students to use the word processing highlight feature to highlight all subject pronouns in the first text.
4. They should use the "Find and Replace" feature to substitute the actual names for the pronouns in the second text.
5. Finally, they re-read the third (unmarked original) text to show how making the connection between pronouns and names (or other referents) improves understanding.

Teaching Connotation: "What to Say?"

"What to Say?" is an original word choice exercise in which the parent or professional creates a scenario, creates fill-in-the-blank sentences, and offers synonym options. Refer to the What to Say? worksheet below, Figure D.10.

*   With support, the learner evaluates the connotation of the synonym options and chooses a word to fill in the blank.
*   The scenario in a What to Say? activity spells out the subtle thoughts and feelings of the people in the story to help the learner understand *when* and *why* to use different word options.

Feel free to adapt this activity for whole group or individual instruction and to the age, interests, and other needs of your learners. The scenarios used to teach should be simple, personal, and relatable. Students or clients can also make their own scenarios, worksheets, or comic strips based on the model.

Figure D.10

What to Say?

Grandma loves to cook. Whenever her grandson Jaime comes over, she makes his favorite food, macaroni and cheese. Sometimes the recipe turns out great, but sometimes it is not as good. Grandma always asks, "How was your macaroni and cheese, Jaime?"

Sometimes when it does not taste really good, Jaime is not sure what to say. He does not want to hurt Grandma's feelings, so he wants to say something *positive*. Let's help him out!

Here are four synonyms that mean something tastes good:

delicious   **tasty**   **scrumptious**   **yummy**

Each word for "tastes good" is a little different. There is some hidden meaning in each word. Think about a food you love. Use each of the words above once to fill in the blank with the words that mean "tastes good" to show *how* good something tastes.

1. A little bit good   _____
2. Pretty good   _____
3. Really good   _____
4. The best ever   _____

Putting words in order from "a little" to "the most" is called *ranking*. Ranking synonyms can help you match the right word to the right situation.

What Can Jaime Say?

You will see a hint about what Jamie is really thinking. Use the ranking above to pick the word that fits best with what Jamie is thinking. Fill in the blank.

    A. Jamie is thinking, "This macaroni and cheese tastes a little bit good." He says, "Thanks, Grandma, this is _____."

    B. Jamie is thinking, "This is the best macaroni and cheese I ever ate." He says, "Thanks, Grandma, this is _____."

    C. Jamie is thinking, "This macaroni and cheese tastes OK." He says, "Thanks, Grandma, this is _____."

    D. Jamie is really enjoying the macaroni and cheese. It is good enough to have seconds. He says, "Thanks, Grandma, this is _____."

This activity can also be carried out using a comic strip format. Comic strips include drawing *thought bubbles,* showing an unspoken idea that stays in someone's head, and *speech bubbles* to show what someone actually says. This method helps contrast the fact that someone may think one thing and say another (for good reason).

Teaching Homographs

Chapter 8 explains what homographs are and the rationale for teaching them to students with autism. For this lesson, I have created a special homograph list that only includes words that meet all three of these criteria:

1. Spelled the same.
2. Pronounced differently.
3. Have two different meanings.

As you look at each word listed in Figure D.11, remember to pronounce it in two different ways (aloud or in your head). These words may be targeted for explicit teaching based on the current reading level, level of performance, and needs of a particular student.

Many of the homographs on the list are close to the fourth-grade reading level (where readers with hyperlexia are often stuck).

- I chose words that a fourth grader is likely have in his or her vocabulary with a single meaning attached as a basis to build a second meaning and pronunciation. An example is *desert* a noun meaning "a dry place" and *desert*, a verb meaning "to abandon."
- Feel free to add on to the list with other words that meet these criteria or meet your needs.

Figure D.11 Emily's List of Homographs

Address	Does	Perfect	Resume
Bow	Dove	Permit	Separate
Close	Excuse	Present	Sewer
Combine	House	Process	Sow
Conduct	Lead	Produce	Tear
Conflict	Live	Project	Use
Contest	Minute	Read	Wind
Convert	Number	Rebel	Wound
Desert	Object	Record	

Note: This is an original list created for this book. Because there is a limited number of homographs, the likelihood that this list includes words found in other lists a coincidence.

For the purposes of this homograph strategy, I omitted words that are pronounced the **same** but have different meanings, like *state* (geography) and *state* (make a statement). Multiple-meaning words are sometimes referred to as *homographs*, even though their pronunciation does not change. Additional vocabulary development is likely to be needed for words with multiple meanings.

- My logic is that first focusing on the words that **change pronunciation based on meaning** will make the idea of homographs obvious.
- Once the homograph strategy is learned, you will be able to hear the difference! A foundation in this area can support learning the more subtle or "quiet" type of homograph.

The homograph lesson below follows an eight-step lesson plan. The model is written at about a fourth-grade instructional level.

- One step consists of explaining *why* the student should learn the concept and how it will help him or her.

- In the introduction to the lesson, you may wish to carefully link the new concepts to the known (stimulating appropriate prior knowledge) or show how the information is relevant to the learner.

The lesson plan uses a script that you can follow closely or loosely. The steps of the lesson plan can be carried out over the course of more than one class period or intervention session.

- Feel free to change the format or content for your students' needs. The material can be adapted to the instructional level or other needs of students.
- The lesson is written for small or whole group instruction; it can be modified for working with one person.

Three prerequisite skills are needed to participate in the homograph lesson. The student must be able to:

- Recognize and decode words and sentences.
- Know the parts of speech, such as noun, verb, adjective, and adverb.
- Understand and recognize homonyms.
- Understand the syllabication and accentuation of multi-syllable words.

For simplicity, I used <u>underlining</u> as a way to indicate accentuation or emphasis in multiple-syllable words. If the student or client has experience or knowledge of diacritical marks and "dictionary pronunciation," these elements can be added to the lesson.

Homograph Lesson

1. **Introduce the Lesson.**

   Today we're going to learn about special words called *homographs*. Learning about homographs helps you understand words when you read. Let's try it.

   I'm going to spell a word, and I want you to write it down. Write it down but don't say anything. Ready? D-E-S-E-R-T. Again, that's D-E-S-E-R-T. (As you call out the instruction, write the word twice on a whiteboard, overhead, or piece of paper.)

   When I count to three, I want everyone to read the word out loud to me, together. One. Two. Three. [Jumbled response from the group]. It seems to me I am hearing two different things. I am hearing "*des*-ert" and I am hearing "de-*zert*." [As you speak, underline the first syllable of the first word. Underline the second syllable of the second word.]

   Can this be right? Can a word be spelled one way and pronounced two different ways? [Call on a student.] How did you pronounce the word? *Des*-ert. Can you tell us what that means? So you're saying desert, like a dry place, like the Sahara Desert. Raise your hand if you also pronounced it *des*-ert.

   Who pronounced it a different way? [Call on a student]. How did you say it? What does it mean when we say "de-*zert*?" You're saying desert, like go away or leave, like desert the ship. It looks like the way we say a word like D-E-S-E-R-T changes what it means!

   Let's try another one. Write it down, but don't say anything. Ready? R-E-C-O-R-D. [Write the word twice on a whiteboard, overhead, or piece of paper.] When I count to three, I want everyone to read the word out loud to me, together. One. Two. Three. [Response from the group].

I'm hearing two different things. I am hearing "*rec*-ord" and I am hearing "re-*cord*." [As you speak, underline the first syllable of the first word. Underline the second syllable of the second word.] Can this be right? Another word spelled one way and pronounced two different ways?

[Call on a participant]. How did you pronounce the word? "*Rec*-ord." Can you tell us what that means? OK, so you are thinking of *rec*-ord as a top score, like the world record in swimming. That makes *record* a noun. You put the accent on the first syllable to show this meaning.

Who pronounced it a different way? [Call on a person.] What does "re-*cord*" mean? [Participant replies.] OK, you are saying "re-*cord*" is something you do, like record a song. Raise your hand if you also pronounced it "re-*cord*." When you accent the second part of this word, it is a verb, something you do.

Wow! Did anyone notice that depending on how we say this word, it can be a noun *or* a verb? Is this also true for D-E-S-E-R-T?

2. **Explain Precisely What a Homograph Is.**
   There is a special name for words that we write the same but say differently, like D-E-S-E-R-T and R-E-C-O-R-D. These words are called *homographs*. *Homo* means "same" and *graph* means "write." Homographs are words that are written the same.

   The interesting thing about homographs is that there is <u>one</u> way to write the word but <u>two</u> *different ways* to say it.
   The spelling of the word stays the same. The meaning of the word *changes* depending on how we say it!

3. **Tell why It Is Important/How It Helps to Recognize Homographs.**

   When you see a word that you can say in two ways, how do you know the right way to pronounce it? [Accept responses.] In our examples, it was fine to say the words either way and for them to have either meaning, because they were just words by themselves. But when we read a sentence, how we pronounce homographs matters because *only one way makes sense.*

   We need to have a way to figure out how to pronounce a homograph correctly so we can understand the right meaning for the sentence.

4. **Relate It to Something the Student Already Knows or Does.**

   Remember when we learned about homo*nyms*? Homonyms are words that *sound* the same but are spelled differently, like pear p-e-a-r, and pair, p-a-i-r. Homographs are spelled the same but *sound different.* [Add emphasis/explanation so the connection sinks in, or pick a different concept to relate to.] Homographs have different meanings, depending on how we say them. We have to pay attention to how the word *sounds* when we say it to understand the meaning.

5. **Model/Demonstrate the Skill.**

   Here's an example: [Show the written example.]
   Amy will buy a special birthday *present* for her mom.
   Pay attention to the underlined word, but **don't say anything yet!**

   I need a volunteer to look at the underlined word and read the sentence out loud. [Have volunteer read aloud.] Very good. Where did you put the accent when you read the underlined word? *Pres*-ent. That is correct.

   Raise your hand if you also thought the word should be pronounced *pres*-ent. In this sentence, what does *present* mean? How did you know which way to say it? (Accept several responses.)

You've noticed many things. There are clues in the sentence to let us know what pronunciation of the word we need to use.

These are called *context clues* or *context cues*. Paying attention to the clues or cues helps us figure out the correct meaning of the word.

In our example, "Amy will buy a special birthday *present* for her mom," the verb *buy* gives us a signal that a word that follows will be a "thing." A present or a gift is a thing.

The verb *buy* is our clue that we need to say the word that follows as a noun, with the accent on the first syllable. When we see a context clue like *buy* we can pick the right way to say the word, so it makes sense in the sentence.

The word *birthday* is another clue. It is an adjective that tells us that a noun is coming. So we pick the pronunciation for *present* that makes it a noun.

6. **Check for understanding.**

I need another volunteer to try this sentence. [Show the example]:

Kevin will *present* his oral report on Tuesday.

Where did you put the accent when you read the underlined word? "Pre-*zent*" is correct.

Raise your hand if you also thought the word should be pronounced "pre-zent."

In this sentence, what does *present* mean? How did you know which way to pronounce it? [Accept several responses.]

The clue in this sentence is the word *will*. When we see the helping verb *will*, we think about some kind of action. The word *will* is our clue that we need to say the word *present* as a verb, with the accent on the second syllable.

An important instructor comment particularly directed to learners with autism:
When you're reading out loud and you make a mistake, it is OK to correct it. In fact, it's a good idea. I'm going to show you what I mean: "Kevin will '*pre*-sent' his

report 'pre-_zent_' his report on Tuesday." I just corrected my mistake. This is called self-correcting. Once I saw the word _report_, I knew that saying "pres-ent" like a gift did not make sense. I needed to pick "pre-_zent_" as a verb.

When you are reading out loud, or even reading to yourself, and you realize you made a mistake, correct it. Go back, reread, and pick the right way to say the word so it makes sense. Self-correcting helps you get the right meaning when you read. If you make a mistake, that's fine, and it's a good idea to fix it.

7. **Conduct guided practice with the student.**

Now you'll have a chance to practice looking for clues to read homographs using your worksheet. [You can use, adapt, or expand the worksheet shown in Figure D.12.]

Figure D.12

Reading Homographs

Spelled the Same – Pronounced Differently – Different Meanings

Glossary

Conduct con <u>duct</u> [kuhn-DUKT]	a verb that means "behave, perform, carry out, or guide"
Conduct <u>con</u> duct [KON-dukt]	a noun that means "behavior"
Present pre <u>sent</u> [pruh-ZENT]	a verb that means "to give"
Present <u>pre</u> sent [PREZ-uhnt]	a noun that means "gift" or "time" (now)
Produce pro <u>duce</u> [pro-DUCE]	a verb that means "create, make, or manufacture"
Produce <u>pro</u> duce [PRO-duce]	a noun that means "farm or garden products"
Wound [wownd]	a verb that means "to turn a handle to make a clock mechanism work"
Wound [woond]	a noun that means "an injury"

Directions

Read each sentence. Decide if the underlined word is a noun or verb.
Fill in the blank with N for "noun" or V for "verb."
Circle words in the sentence that gave you a clue.
If there is more than one syllable, underline the syllable that is accented.

Example	Noun or verb?	
Jim (waited to) present his gift to Sam.	V	pre **sent**
Sam was (excited) to (open) her present.	N	**pre** sent

	Noun or verb?	
That is no way to conduct yourself!	_____	con duct
Jane won an award for good conduct.	_____	con duct
Tyler bought carrots in the produce department.	_____	pro duce
Spielberg is going to produce a new movie.	_____	pro duce
The nurse treated Jay's wound.	_____	
Grandpa wound his watch yesterday.	_____	

Diacritical pronunciation from Encarta Dictionary: English (North America) online
Definitions from synonym/thesaurus feature of Microsoft Word

8. **Conduct Independent Practice: Apply the Strategy to Meaningful Text.**

Select text from curricular material or grade-level literature that contains homographs to practice. Provide the example and have the student read aloud.

As s/he reads, ask the person to explain what they're thinking while reading, or "think aloud." Listen for and reinforce comments on the use of context clues, self-correction, deciding if the sentence makes sense, and so on.

Generalization and Other Applications

Here are some ideas to support independent use and generalization.

1. Do a small-group or paired activity in which the student writes two homograph sentences and exchanges with another student or group to read aloud.

2. Conduct a follow-up activity using a page of text that contains homographs. Have the student mark *noun* or *verb*, underline the emphasized syllable, and circle the context clues.

3. Assign homework or an outside activity in which the student writes his or her own homograph paragraph and takes turns reading it aloud with someone else.

4. For practice and reinforcement in a classroom setting, post a list of the homographs the class has been exposed to. Encourage and reward students for adding to the list. Individual students can also create personal lists.

5. Create games or ask students to create homograph games.

6. Expand on the idea of "spelled the same" to explore multiple-meaning words that are spelled and pronounced the same but have more than one meaning (such as *row, saw, nail*, etc.).

7. A free game of fifty of these types of homographs is available at http://www.ezschool.com/Games/Homographs.html. This type of activity can also provide inspiration for your own activities.

APPENDIX E

Teaching Word Parts

As discussed in Chapter 8 my son, Tom, reported that learning the meaning of prefixes, suffixes, and root words was *the* vocabulary breakthrough for him. He made use of it whenever possible to understand word meaning in context while reading. The chapter also discusses the many advantages of teaching word parts to autistic students.

- Learning word parts is like applying a mathematical formula to reading. Adding up the meaning of the parts helps readers discover the meaning of a whole word. This may be both fascinating and reinforcing for some individuals.
- The charts and lists provided in this Appendix are concrete and visual. They may be appealing to individuals who like lists or are good at memorizing.
- Four of the charts include space for the learner to add in their personal examples, to reinforce meaning by connecting to vocabulary words that they already know and understand. They can choose words from their area of interest or expertise, increasing interest and engagement.

The 20 Most Frequent Prefixes in Printed School English

Rank	Prefix	Percent of All Prefixed Words
1	un-	26%
2	re-	14%
3	in-, im-, il-ir- (not)	11%
4	dis-	7%
5	en-, em-	4%
6	non-	4%
7	in-, im- (in)	3%
8	over-	3%
9	mis-	3%
10	sub-	3%
11	pre-	3%
12	inter-	3%
13	fore-	3%
14	de-	2%
15	trans-	2%
16	super-	1%
17	semi-	1%
18	anti-	1%
19	mid-	1%
20	under- (too little)	1%
	All others	3%

Other Important Prefixes

PREFIX	MEANING	EXAMPLE	PERSONAL EXAMPLES
ab-	away from	absent	
ad-	to, toward	advise, advance	
anti- contra-	opposed to	anticrime contradict	
auto-	self	autonomy	
bene-	good	benevolent	
com- con-	together	combine converge	
de-	from, away	decline	
dis-	negation, opposite	disadvantage	
en-	in, into	engage	
ex-	out of	exchange	
inter-	between	interstate	
mono-	one	monopoly	
multi-	many	multicolor	
non- un-	not	nonsense unprepared	
pre-	before	preregister	
re-	back, again	return	

	The 20 Most Frequent Suffixes in Printed School English	
Rank	**Suffix**	**Percent of All Suffixed Words**
1	-s, -es	31%
2	-ed	20%
3	-ing	14%
4	-ly	7%
5	-er, -or (agent)	4%
6	-ion, -tion, -ation, -ition	4%
7	-able, -ible	2%
8	-al, -ial	1%
9	-y	1%
10	-ness	1%
11	-ity, -ty	1%
12	-ment	1%
13	-ic	1%
14	-ous, -eous, -ious	1%
15	-en	1%
16	-er (comparative)	1%
17	-ive, -ative, -tive	1%
18	-ful	1%
19	-less	1%
20	-est	1%
	All others	7%

Other Important Suffixes

SUFFIX	MEANING	EXAMPLE	PERSONAL EXAMPLES
-able	capable of	manageable	
-al	relating to	rational	
-ation	process of	maturation	
-ative	nature	formative	
-ence	condition	confidence	
-ful	full of	beautiful	
-ic	pertaining to	prolific	
-ism	practice	socialism	
-ist	one who does	scientist	
-less	without	homeless	
-ology	study of	biology	
-ous	having, full of	wondrous	

Important Root Words			
ROOT	**MEANING**	**EXAMPLE**	**PERSONAL EXAMPLES**
act	do, move	active	
close	close, end	foreclose	
dict	to speak	contradiction	
grad	to step	graduation	
man	hand	manual	
phon	sound	microphone	
port	carry	portage	
quest	ask	question	
script	write	description	
temp	mix, time	temporary	
volve	to roll	revolve	

| \multicolumn{5}{c}{**Common Greek and Latin Roots**} | | | | |
ROOT	MEANING	ORIGIN	EXAMPLES	PERSONAL EXAMPLES
aud	hear	Latin	audiophile, auditorium, audition	
astro	star	Greek	astrology, astronaut, asteroid	
bio	life	Greek	biography, biology	
dict	speak, tell	Latin	dictate, predict, dictator	
geo	earth	Greek	geology, geography	
meter	measure	Greek	thermometer, barometer	
min	little, small	Latin	minimum, minimal	
mit, mis	send	Latin	mission, transmit, remit, missile	
ped	foot	Latin	pedestrian, pedal, pedestal	
phon	sound	Greek	phonograph, microphone, phoneme	
port	carry	Latin	transport, portable, import	
scrib, script	write	Latin	scribble, manuscript, inscription	

Common Greek and Latin Roots				
spect	see	Latin	inspect, spectator, respect	
struct	build, form	Latin	construction, destruction, instruct	

The material in this appendix was adapted from T.G White, J. Sowell, and A. Yanagihara, (1989). Teaching elementary students to use word-part clues. *The Reading Teacher*, 42, 302-308.

APPENDIX F

The Visualizing and Verbalizing® (V/V®) Program

Whenever I think of the skill of visualizing, I automatically think of the Visualizing and Verbalizing® (V/V®) program. Visualizing and Verbalizing® is a commercial program from Lindamood Bell. It uses a structured approach to enhance visualization and comprehension skills (Bell, 2007).

Specialized online or in-person training is needed to use the V/V® program. Information is available at the Lindamood Bell website, https://lindamoodbell.com/.
- I participated in training on V/V® with program creator Nancy Bell and her team to better understand the program.
- I'm in no way an expert, but wish to share basic information and some recent research that may be of interest to readers.

The first part of this section presents an outline of how the intervention is carried out.
- This is followed by information from Lindamood Bell's annual data reports, focusing on comprehension gains for students with an autism diagnosis and for students with a diagnosis of hyperlexia.
- The third part of this section summarizes a 2024 study that was the first to specifically measure changes in reading comprehension in students with ASD and hyperlexia who received intensive remediation using the V/V system (Beckerson and colleagues).
- The section concludes with an overview of potential pros and cons of V/V for students with autism and/or hyperlexia.

How is the V/V Program Carried Out?

Here's a simple description of how Visualizing and Verbalizing® (V/V®) intervention is carried out, describing what the educator, therapist or clinician does, and what the student is asked to do. I will use the term *clinician* to reference a professional delivering the intervention in a Lindamood Bell clinic, or any trained interventionist.

- In V/V,® the clinician shows a picture to the student. The clinician provides a framework for description by introducing "structure words." The student learns to describe the pictures thoroughly to include features like shape, size, and color. As the student progresses, structure words are expanded to include features such as movement, mood, background, and sound.

- After becoming proficient at describing pictures, the student learns to visualize familiar objects. They describe them using structure words. The student advances to visualize and describe nouns and fantasy images.

- The next stage includes listening to a single sentence verbalized by the clinician, and visualizing it. Generalization is supported by asking the student to describe the image of a target noun in various simple sentences and contexts.

- This is followed by creating images for an entire paragraph. The clinician asks guiding questions for each sentence related to the main concept of the paragraph, and the student creates a visualization. After reading the paragraph, the student provides an "image summary" by verbally describing the image created for each sentence. Finally, the student summarizes the paragraph by verbally paraphrasing.

- The next stage in the intervention includes HOTS, higher order thinking skills. The student follows the same process of sentence-by-sentence imagery. The clinician guides visualization by asking inferential and main idea questions. This requires the student to engage in critical thinking and draw conclusions about the text.

- The intervention continues to whole-page images.

Data Reports

Lindamood Bell publishes data annually based on the pre- and post-testing of the students in their centers.

- One of the earliest Lindamood Bell reports in 2009 showed that the gains in comprehension made specifically by students with autism and with hyperlexia using V/V® (Lindamood-Bell Learning Processes, 2009) were lower than those made by students with other diagnoses.

- Lindamood Bell's 2024 data summary reported on the progress of 1,085 students with ASD who received Comprehension Instruction Only at any time between January, 2008 and December, 2023.
  - Students were of an average age of 12. They received 132.5 hours of instruction on average.
  - The report stated that "On average, students with a prior ASD diagnosis who received Visualizing and Verbalizing instruction achieved significant improvements in comprehension."
  - They made large (statistically significant) standard score changes in the categories of Word Opposites and Written Language Comprehension.
  - Medium gains were made in Vocabulary.
- Lindamood Bell's 2024 data summary reported on the progress of 103 students with a diagnosis of "hyperlexia." who received Comprehension Instruction Only any time between January, 2008 and December, 2023.
  - The students were of an average age of 12.4. They received an average of 120.9 hours of instruction..
  - The report stated that "On average, students with a prior Hyperlexia diagnosis who received Visualizing and Verbalizing instruction achieved significant improvements in comprehension."
  - They made a large (statistically significant) standard score change in the category of Written Language Comprehension.
  - Medium gains were made in Vocabulary and Word Opposites, bringing these students into the "average range" on these measures.

New Independent Research

A 2024 study by Beckerson and colleagues was the first research to specifically measure changes in reading comprehension in students with ASD who were involved in intensive remediation using the V/V system.

- The thirty-nine students with autism who participated had an average age around 10. The "control group" of 26 non-autistic students did not have poor comprehension skills and did not receive V/V intervention. They were included in the study to compare their baseline comprehension skills to those of autistic students prior to intervention.

- Twenty-two study participants in Cohort A received 200 hours of face-to-face instruction, 5 days a week, in 4-hour sessions, for 10 weeks at a Lindamood Bell Center, in a one-on-one, distraction-free environment.
- Cohort B, the waitlisted group, received the same remediation program after Cohort A completed theirs.
- The Gray Oral Reading Test-4 (GORT-4) comprehension scores significantly differed from baseline to post-intervention for Cohort A (showing improvement), but not for Cohort B. In other words, the results were **positive and significant** for the cohort who received the intervention.
- Beckerson and colleagues suggest that the "V/V intervention may help improve reading comprehension for autistic children with the discrepant poor comprehender reading profile" (p.10). They also suggest that strategies to improve verbal memory may have an indirect but positive effect on reading comprehension in hyperlexic autistic children.
- The study authors "suggest that results be interpreted with a degree of caution" because the study was limited by a relatively small sample size.

Pros and Cons to Consider

Visualizing is a critical skill for reading comprehension, retelling and writing. It may be one of the most difficult skills to teach neurodivergent learners. There are pros and cons to using a commercial program such as V&V for readers with autism and/or hyperlexia.

Pros include potential progress to be made.
- The positive results from Beckerson's 2024 study are encouraging, especially because the GORT-4, which was used to measure progress before and after the intervention, includes a wide range of comprehension skills. Remember, however, that the gains were achieved after 200 hours of intensive one-to-one instruction!
- Lindamood Bell openly shares data based on the pre and post-testing of the students in their centers on their website. The information is organized by categories that include diagnosis and targeted skills. This provides an opportunity to analyze

the information and make an informed decision about the program "fit" for a particular learner.

Cons or drawbacks may include:
- The cost of the program and the number of hours required for the intervention.
- The time commitment of travel to a Lindamood Bell center (if there is one in your community). Some school reading specialists are trained in the V/V program. An in-school option might mitigate transportation factors.

Conclusion

Regarding the Center data, it is encouraging to hear that students achieved a statistically significant standard score change in the category of Written Language Comprehension. The gains were achieved after an average of 120 hours of intensive instruction. This may cause one to ask, "Are there other effective ways to achieve the same results with a similar or lesser amount of instruction?"

As with every decision to be made, teams need to gather enough information to consider the potential benefits and drawbacks of the intervention. They can then determine whether a particular option is appropriate for a particular individual.

www.ingramcontent.com/pod-product-compliance
Lightning Source LLC
Chambersburg PA
CBHW080415030426
42335CB00020B/2460